Fit to Fly

A Pilot's Guide
to Health and Safety

Fit to Fly
A Pilot's Guide
to Health and Safety

Richard O. Reinhart, MD

TAB TAB BOOKS Inc.
Blue Ridge Summit, PA

FIRST EDITION
FIRST PRINTING

© 1993 by **TAB Books**.
TAB Books is a division of McGraw-Hill, Inc.

Library of Congress Cataloging-in-Publication Data

ISBN 0-8306-2070-2 Hard
ISBN 0-8306-2059-1 Paper

TAB Books offers software for sale. For information and a catalog, please contact TAB Software Department, Blue Ridge Summit, PA 17294-0850.

Acquisitions Editor: Jeff Worsinger
Editorial Team: Tracey L. May, Editor
                Susan D. Wahlman, Supervising Editor
                Joanne Slike, Executive Editor
Production Team: Katherine G. Brown, Director
                Lisa Mellott, Typesetter
                Olive Harmon, Typesetter
                Tina Sourbier, Typesetter
                Susan Handsford, Typesetter
                Toya Warner, Layout
                Nancy Mickley, Proofreader
Design Team: Jaclyn J. Boone, Designer
                Brian Allison, Associate Designer
Cover: Holberg Design, York, Pa.   TAB1

Contents

Introduction   **viii**

The human factors of safe flight   x
Are you incapacitated?   xi

1   Your challenges in flight   **1**

Atmospheric ingredients   1
The physics of gases   4
How the atmosphere affects you   8
How you are constructed   9

2   Flying above 5,000 feet AGL   **22**

Essential oxygen   23
Poisons in the air   34
Cabin decompression   36
Ear blocks and other problems   36
The bends   40

3   Disorientation in flight   **46**

Types of disorientation   47
Visual illusions in flight   60
Coping with disorientation   62
Flicker vertigo   63
The airsick pilot   63

4   Flying in heat and cold extremes   **65**

Basics of heat exchange   66
Temperature control in the body   68
Flying when hot   70
Flying when cold   73
Dehydration   77
Radiation   77

5 Self-imposed medical problems 79

Playing doctor   79
Caffeine   88
Miscellaneous abuses   91
Alcohol and other drugs   93

6 Vision 104

Light and lenses   105
Getting to 20/20   109
Night vision   111
Seeing in the sunlight   114
Factors affecting visual acuity   116
Visual illusions   116

7 Hearing 118

Anatomy and physiology of the ear   118
Surrounded by sound   120
Perception of sound   123
Measurement of hearing   124
Noise and hearing loss   124
Other types of hearing loss   128
Hearing conservation   129

8 Sleep, jet lag, and fatigue 131

Sleep   132
Circadian rhythms   137
Fatigue   141

9 Stress management, CRM, and the safe pilot 148

Stress   148
CRM   150
What is CRM?   152
What's learned in CRM?   153
CRM training program   154

10 Inflight medical emergencies   **156**

First aid   157
Transporting ill passengers   159
Basic survival techniques   160

11 Pilot health maintenance   **162**

Nutrition and diet   163
Keeping in shape   166
Flight physicals   166

12 Protecting your FAA medical certificate   **174**

Who's who?   175
What's what?   177
Typical certification scenario   179
Ideal certification scenario   180
Grounded   182
Getting your medical back   184

Appendix
The ideal pilot's medical evaluation   **185**
Index   **189**

Introduction

"Oh, I have slipped the surly bonds of earth and danced the skies on laughter silvered wings; sunward I've climbed and joined the tumbling mirth of sun split clouds and done a hundred things you have not dreamed of . . ."

It sounds magical, but ask any pilot to describe in three words how to fly an airplane, and the response will probably be: needle, ball, airspeed. These are the fundamentals of flying. As your hours build, each flight becomes a new training experience. Hours of dual/solo practice make you proficient, and learning commercial maneuvers, instrument flight, and the ultimate ATP rating round out the complete pilot, ready for anything that's thrown your way. Yet the more you "dance" around the skies, the more you realize that while flying might rely on a few basics, you (like your aircraft) are not invulnerable to other variables that might arise. Just as the aircraft is subject to mechanical factors, you as a pilot are subject to human factors. In fact, you're probably not even aware of all of these human factors or the profound effect they can have on your flying skills.

As you have discovered, simply knowing how to move the stick and rudder does not make you a safe or proficient pilot. As you gain experience, you realize that the more you recognize why the stick and rudder work, along with airfoils, engines, weather, hydraulics, and so on, the better (and safer) you are. The same holds true with understanding *how* your body and mind can be affected in flight as well as *why* you are affected. I can preach human factors, health, and flight physiology, but until you actually feel and sense these effects, you have little respect for the outcome. Furthermore, it is common for many physiological situations to occur at the same time, not a very comforting thought if you aren't even aware of what's happening!

In earlier days, pilots on TV and in the movies often seemed fearless, overcoming great odds in dangerous skies. They were flying planes that were falling apart as they neared their fateful destination, but they knew they could rise above the inadequacies of their mind, body, and machine. Even today, macho pilots believe they can drink up a storm, stagger out of the bar, and fly a perfect trip the next day. They pass off the effects of fatigue, dehydration, noise, hypoglycemia, and the myriad other factors associated with flight. Could you be in this group—even a little? If so, then it is definitely time for you to improve your understanding of human factors. Human factors are often the symptoms behind the diagnosis of pilot error.

The objective for you as the reader is to get a clear understanding and overview of the many varied physiological situations that can compromise safe flight. The military has long been an expert in flight physiology. This manual is not meant to "reinvent the wheel," and therefore it reiterates some material already presented in military publications. You are constructed the same way as military pilots, so the information is generic for everyone that takes to the skies. This manual is also meant to be a resource in your personal flying library. Future situations dealing with human factors and flight physiology will always pop up, and it's easier for you to refer to your own resources rather than depend on someone else's war story or uninformed answer.

When it comes to hypoxia, disorientation, jet lag, vision problems, etc., some pilots don't even know what these terms mean, and many don't care. Many pilots have little access to resources providing this insight. This situation doesn't mean that these issues are less important than flight proficiency or learning how to fly an ILS. They might not be as exciting or as challenging as sharpening your flying skills, but they all have a direct or indirect effect on your flying skills—and you might not even be aware that your skills are compromised. You might be the best pilot on the field, but not if you allow yourself to be subjected to and affected by the physiological factors that surround all pilots.

Flight physiology and human factors both have an impact on flight. Over 70 percent of aviation accidents and incidents are in some way related to human factors. Do you know when to say "I'm not safe!"? Do you fully understand hypoxia, fatigue, the effects of self-medication? The purpose of this manual is to help you understand the other part of flight—the human part—and to recognize when your body or mind is not in tune with the aircraft.

We all would like to expect ideal conditions. Good weather, working radios, no delays, instruments functioning, propellers turning. However, few flights are like that. Add to this the fact that your mind and body might not fully cooperate during a problem flight when all your physical and mental skills are needed. Now you become a setup for an incident or accident. Flying an approach to minimums with a faltering engine and an intermittent glide slope is stressful enough, but you probably can deal with the situation. However, being fatigued, disoriented, and suffering with an ear block makes your approach to minimums downright dangerous!

THE HUMAN FACTORS OF SAFE FLIGHT

Human factors in flight have a variety of meanings, depending on whom you ask. A psychologist defines it as how you deal with stress, how you communicate with crewmates and ATC, how you manage the variety of resources available to you in a critical situation (often called cockpit or crew resource management (CRM). A physiologist or physician expects you to be familiar with the effects of fatigue, hypoglycemia, illness, noise, and other medical issues. You might say it means the ability to perform under extreme conditions—how you judge what action to take when things turn sour. Everyone's objective is the same—getting you safely from point A to point B in a normally functioning flying machine.

Flight physiology is how your body and mind work in the flying environment. It includes such topics as understanding how your organs function, what keeps them from functioning, and what you can do to protect these functions before and during flight. Hypoxia, dehydration, fatigue, vibration, visual illusions, noise, disorientation, jet lag, self-medication, alcohol, smoking, and many more topics are included in the list. This list continues to grow as the aviation community recognizes more factors. Furthermore, defining and protecting your health is an important goal. Flight physiology might not be as exciting as learning how to make perfect landings, but it is not dull, nor is it just something that is "nice to know." It is essential to safe flight. Ask any pilot who has been disoriented or incapacitated with an ear block.

We tend to take these issues for granted because our bodies and minds are usually very tolerant and forgiving of the abuses to which we subject ourselves. Just once in awhile, don't you think that human factors happen only to other pilots, and they should have known? Denial of the importance of human factors compared to flight proficiency begins to take over our reasoning. The near miss or dumb incident usually gets our attention and brings us back to the reality of the significance of human factors. These pilots don't have to be told to learn—they know its importance. The very act of reading this manual means that you are, at the very least, curious about what all this human factors stuff is all about.

Flight physiology, therefore, is an integral part of human factors and safe flight. We expect our aircraft to be airworthy. We look to our mechanics to keep our aircraft airworthy. Before you fly you preflight the machine to ensure it is airworthy before you take off. Your expectations are high for that aircraft. You should have the same expectations for yourself and other flightcrew. You must also be airworthy—medically airworthy.

Safety is the prime goal of all flight for all pilots. Continue to read on. You might find some surprises, or at the least, a reinforcement of insight you learned years ago.

ARE YOU INCAPACITATED?

The ultimate objective of flight physiology awareness is the prevention of incapacitation, whether physical or mental. Incapacitation is defined as being unfit or unable to perform normal activity. Mental incapacitation is your mind's inability to use proper judgment, reasoning, or thought processes. Beyond that, mental incapacitation turns into neurological incapacitation, whereby the signals from your brain fail to use the signals from your eyes, ears, touch, smell, etc. Physical incapacitation refers to your body's inability to function in an expected way. The end result in any of these situations is an unsafe and poorly performing pilot.

A survey, originally conducted in 1967 and then repeated in 1988, revealed the following list of incapacitating symptoms as reported by professional pilots:

- Uncontrolled bowel action
- Nausea
- Vomiting
- Severe indigestion
- Earache
- Faintness
- Headache
- Vertigo/disorientation
- Back pain

- Dizziness
- Nosebleed
- Toothache
- Eye injury
- Chest pain
- Coughing attack
- Sneezing attack
- Leg or foot cramps

The following are a variety of classes of incapacitation, all leading to the same unacceptable result—an unsafe pilot.

Sudden incapacitation

The pilot collapses or slumps over the yoke. He might cry out in pain or have a seizure. The solo pilot is committed to whatever the plane now chooses to do. With a crew, the others can take immediate action to keep the plane flying—the first rule of safe flight in an emergency (fly the airplane!!). Because the situation is usually so obvious, there is no doubt that something has to be done quickly. Get the troubled pilot away from the controls and take over the flying, then declare an emergency and land. Do you feel you could determine if your crewmate is not in control and could you take over the controls without getting overly involved with the incapacitated pilot?

Subtle incapacitation

Subtle incapacitation can go unnoticed by you or your crewmates, which makes this a potentially dangerous situation. It's like driving your car and not knowing your brakes are out—until you need them. This pilot might be dazed, semi-conscious, or unable to move (as with a stroke). What do you do if this is a senior pilot, your captain, or a check pilot? At what point do you take over without being charged with mutiny?

Total or partial incapacitation

Total incapacitation means you are totally out of it, up to and including dead. There is no doubt that there is a problem that needs immediate attention. *Partial incapacitation* is more troublesome. Like *subtle*, you might not be aware of a deficiency. Or you don't relate the reason you aren't performing well to being fatigued or sick with the flu, or something else. In any case, you might not accept that you are incapacitated and won't admit this to yourself, your crewmates, or ATC. If this situation arises, who is going to intervene?

Distraction

The healthy pilot can be slightly incapacitated as a result of being distracted. This distraction can be worrying about a problem at home, concentrating on a yellow warning light, listening to an unrelated conversation on the flight deck, or any other scenario that virtually takes you out of the flying loop. Some call this a lack of situation awareness, not knowing or recognizing what's going on around you and your aircraft. Whatever the reason, distraction is always present and only you can get back on track—unless someone else, like ATC, brings your inattentiveness to your attention.

Pride often gets in the way of resolving situations that could turn into crises. Are you willing to admit you are having a problem if you think you can deal with it yourself? If there is a slim chance that pride could get in your way, then it represents another breakdown in use of cockpit and crew resources. Another unsafe situation is if you are unwilling to challenge another crewmate who is experiencing substandard performance, especially if you think it is possibly a result of some physiological problem. Assertiveness and self confidence becomes an important personality trait in good pilots and is a key topic taught in CRM courses.

You aren't expected to be an expert in human factors and flight physiology, but I'm sure you will admit that you must be knowledgeable about what can incapacitate you and your other pilot colleagues who are occupying the same airspace.

1

Your challenges in flight

"Off we go, into the wild blue yonder, flying high into the sky." These words from a popular Army Air Corps song decades ago express the desire to soar through the air with the birds. How often we have wished we had wings. And, as everyone has heard, if God had meant us to fly, he would have given us wings. Really BIG wings! Since you aren't flying with wings, how do you go off into the blue yonder?

There are three major components of flight: The plane (or "aerospace vehicle"), the pilot, and the environment in which you live and fly (the atmosphere). There is an interrelationship between all three, but it is the atmosphere that affects both the plane and you, often in unpredictable ways. Whereas your airplane might be right at home in thin air, you are not. Your airplane's engine might be more efficient at altitude, but your body is not. This chapter helps explain the atmosphere and how your body functions within it.

ATMOSPHERIC INGREDIENTS

The atmosphere is the gaseous envelope of air that surrounds the earth. It extends to about 25,000 miles above the surface of the earth. It rotates with the earth and its temperature and pressure are continuously changing. From a biological and physiological point of view, however, the composition of the atmosphere is constant. That is, no matter where you fly, the air is composed of the same relative kinds of gases. It's in what quantities these gases are present that you need to be concerned about.

There are a variety of layers of gases within the atmosphere (i.e., the troposphere, stratosphere, etc.), much like layers between water and oil

(Fig. 1-1). The composition of air within each of these layers is different. These layers can be divided physiologically to identify where the dangers lie for us as we fly from one elevation to another. All of these factors are directly related to known gas laws, which we all learned in high school. Understanding how your body is affected in these different layers is crucial to safe flight.

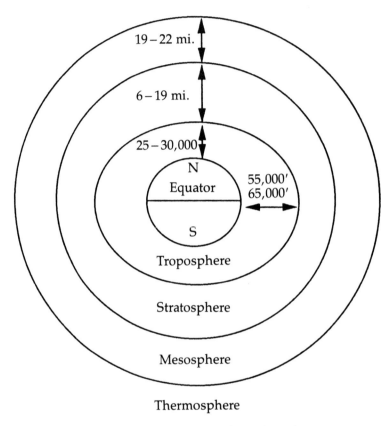

Fig. 1-1. The atmosphere is divided into layers based on temperature.

Because of these changing gaseous amounts in our flight path, the composition of the atmosphere is expressed in percentages and not absolute amounts. In other words, we say that the percentage of oxygen is about 20 percent of the total gases covering the earth. Yet the number of oxygen molecules, the actual amount of oxygen available to your body and all its parts, decreases with altitude. Furthermore, these percentages are affected by temperature, the presence or absence of water vapor, and many other variables.

Of primary importance to you is the oxygen and nitrogen you breathe and, to a lesser degree, carbon dioxide, ozone, and water vapor. Too much or too little of any of these gases could compromise not only your health but also your safety. Your body is not very tolerant of these wide variations of gas concentrations. Let's talk about each gas separately.

Oxygen

As a colorless, odorless, tasteless elemental gas, oxygen (O_2) is the most abundant of all elements on earth. It occurs as a free element in the atmosphere. Oxygen comprises roughly 20 percent of the total gases found in the atmosphere. The primary source of oxygen in our atmosphere is the process of photosynthesis, in which oxygen is generated from carbon dioxide and water. Of all the gases, oxygen is the most essential in maintaining life and permitting your bodily and mental parts to function. Any change in the oxygen levels that you breathe adversely affects how you fly. Lack of oxygen, or *hypoxia*, is discussed later.

Nitrogen

Another colorless, odorless, tasteless elemental gas in the atmosphere is nitrogen (N_2). At 80 percent, it is the most plentiful gas in the atmosphere. Consequently, the major portion of the total atmospheric pressure or weight is a result of this great amount of nitrogen. This gas can saturate the cells and tissues of your body, and too much in these tissues means you can experience problems like the bends.

Carbon dioxide

Although only 0.03 percent of the atmosphere, carbon dioxide (CO_2), which is also colorless, odorless, and tasteless, creates some of the most disabling physiological problems, especially in flight. A byproduct of our respiration, this gaseous compound is somewhat heavier than air. Because of our heavy use of fossil fuels for combustion, CO_2 is the only gaseous constituent of the atmosphere that has increased significantly during the past century.

Water vapor

Water vapor is not considered one of the components of the atmosphere. When we talk about humidity and dewpoint, we are talking about the water vapor in the air. The content of water in the air around you depends on how much water remains as a gas (not a liquid as in fog or clouds) as the temperature changes. Even at 100 percent humidity at

100°F, there is less than five percent water vapor relative to the other atmospheric gases. The percentage of water vapor decreases dramatically as you climb above the earth's surface. When you reach the stratosphere (see Fig. 1-1), it is virtually nonexistent.

Ozone

Ozone (O_3) is an unstable, pale blue gas with a characteristic pungent odor often noticed around electrical equipment and in thunderstorms. It is found in high concentrations at levels in excess of 5 miles. The ambient (surrounding) ozone concentration is dependent on the season, latitude, and altitude. Its concentration in the atmosphere is cyclic, changing over many decades. Ozone is not considered a component of the atmosphere; it's found in the stratosphere.

THE PHYSICS OF GASES

There are physical properties that can be universally applied to any gas or mixture of gases. The atmosphere is basically one large sack of gases surrounding the earth. These gases have a direct impact on how your body functions in flight.

Barometric (atmospheric) pressure is the weight per unit area of all the molecules of the gases (the air) above you. Therefore, this weight, or pressure, decreases with altitude because there are fewer molecules (same percentages, but less amounts). The pressure drop, however, is not linear because air is compressible. Density of a block of air now plays a role. The air near the surface of the earth is more dense, having more molecules of gases within a given volume. Therefore, as you near the earth's surface, a greater pressure change occurs.

A variety of physical properties of the atmosphere affect this pressure, in addition to its weight, including temperature changes secondary to the seasons, weather systems, and your location on the globe (the latitude and longitude of your location). To establish a base pressure from which you can calculate your various pressures used in flight, a standard atmosphere must be defined. The most commonly used base is the international standard atmosphere (ISA), which establishes a mean atmospheric pressure of 29.92 inches of mercury, or 760 millimeters of mercury (mm Hg), at a temperature of 15°C (59°F) in dry air at sea level.

The earth's surface, as you know, is heated by the sun, and in turn, reradiates the heat into the air above ground. This radiation causes little heating of the atmosphere at higher elevations. As you ascend from the surface, the temperature falls steadily and predictably throughout the troposphere. This temperature lapse rate levels off at the tropopause (about 35,000 feet). Additionally, the tropopause is higher in the summer than in the winter, which means you will notice different outside air temperatures as you climb during each season.

About 99 percent of the earth's atmosphere, in terms of the quantity of gases, exists below 32 kilometers (20 miles). The greatest pressure change encountered is from sea level to about 5,000 feet. Therefore, even in a pressurized aircraft, like an airliner, the problems associated with changes of pressure must be considered. Keep in mind that pressurized cabin altitudes often get up to 6,000 feet or more. That means you can become hypoxic!

From a physiological point of view, most pressures are expressed as standard atmospheric above sea level. However, because you fly at varying altitudes, you need to recognize that pressure is not constant. It is a variant of many physical properties, as explained in those gas laws you learned in school. This will be especially true as I discuss the physiology of oxygen/carbon dioxide exchange in your body, pressure breathing at altitude, decompression sickness, and ear blocks.

Remember, the composition and characteristics of the atmosphere is a mixture of gases and is subject to the basic gas laws of physics. If you are to understand how and why these gases affect your body, you must also have a basic understanding of the classic gas laws. So here they are.

Boyle's Law states that the volume of a gas is inversely proportional to the pressure, with temperature remaining constant (Fig. 1-2). This law

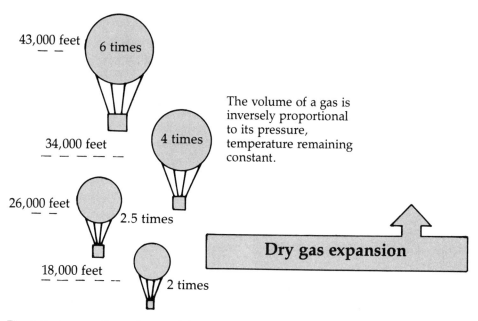

Fig. 1-2. Comparative volumes of dry gases at increasing altitudes and decreasing pressure.

Equivalent pressures, altitudes, and depths

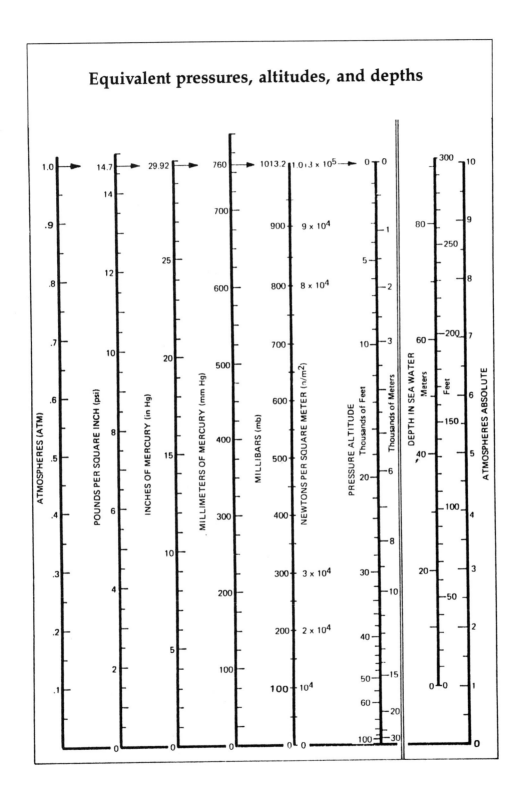

applies to all gases. However, in dealing with gas expansion in your body, a correction must be made for the ever-present water vapor. Such characteristics applied to your body explain the expansion of gases trapped within such moist areas as your middle ear, sinuses, stomach, and intestines. These areas are all actual or potential cavities within which moist air is present and can become trapped. Trapped gases are discussed later.

Because the atmosphere is a mixture of gases, and each gas has its own pressure at any given temperature within a given volume, it is important to know the physics of the combined pressures. *Dalton's Law* states that the total pressure of a gas mixture is the sum of the individual pressures (also called partial pressures) that each gas would exert if it alone occupied the whole volume. Each kind of gas exerts its own partial pressure, depending on the percentage of that gas in the mixture. Thus, even though the percentage of oxygen in the atmosphere is constant (about 20 percent), its partial pressure decreases proportionately as atmospheric pressure (expressed as barometric pressure) decreases.

Your body is affected by the pressure of gases surrounding you. In other words, as you ascend, the percentage of each gas in the atmosphere remains the same; but remember that there are fewer molecules at less pressure that your body can use (or get rid of). The lack of oxygen, for example, at a pressure necessary to carry it to your blood cells is what leads to hypoxia.

Henry's Law says that the amount of gas in a solution, not chemically combined, varies directly with the partial pressure of that gas over the solution. In other words, when the pressure of a gas over a certain liquid decreases, the amount of that gas dissolved in the liquid also decreases (and vice versa). Therefore, when equilibrium is reached, the dissolved gas pressure equals the partial pressure of the gas in the atmosphere to which a solution is exposed. Thus, as the pressure falls, as during ascent, the amount of gas that can be held in a solution is reduced. Open a bottle of pop. Watch the sudden release of bubbles as the bottle pressure equalizes with ambient pressure. This occurs as a result of Henry's law (Fig. 1-3).

The same thing can happen in your body. However, additional factors influence and modify the process of gas uptake and elimination, such as the varying types of fluids in your body, the circulation rate and volume of your blood, and the amount of hemoglobin in your blood.

Graham's Law says that a gas of high pressure exerts a force toward the region of lower pressure, and that if an existing permeable membrane separates these regions of unequal pressure, the gas of higher pressure will pass (or diffuse) through the membrane into the region of lower pressure. For example, this law explains the transfer of oxygen from one part

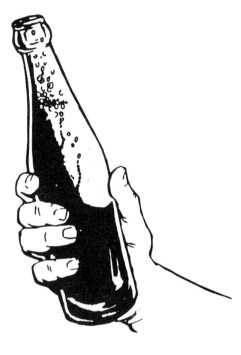

Fig. 1-3. The amount of gas dissolved in solution is directly proportional to the pressure of the gas over the solution.

of your body to another as it passes through your blood vessel walls and also in your lung's breathing tubes. Each gas behaves independently of the other gases in a solution and therefore can move in opposite directions to another gas of differing partial pressures. This sounds confusing, but the important thing to keep in mind is that oxygen in a solution can pass across or through your body's membranes to reach other tissues. More about this in the physiology of respiration in this chapter.

HOW THE ATMOSPHERE AFFECTS YOU

In addition to the pressure and temperature divisions of the atmosphere explained earlier, the atmosphere can also be divided into zones that can affect you medically and physiologically. When you are flying in any of these areas, you should raise your level of suspicion that any performance that is not considered acceptable to you or your crewmate could be a result of hypoxia or other conditions directly related to the content of the air surrounding you, even in a pressurized cabin.

The Physiological Efficient Zone, which extends from sea level to about 10,000 to 12,000 feet, is where your body is adapted or can be adapted to detrimental atmospheric changes. The barometric pressure drops by almost 300 mm Hg. The oxygen amounts (not percentages) are usually sufficient to maintain acceptable performance without supplemental oxygen—if you are healthy. However, rapid changes after prolonged time at altitude can result in a situation that could be incapacitating, such as experiencing ear blocks. Decompression sickness (or bends) is rare in this zone.

In the Physiological Deficient Zone, you run increased risk of developing problems, especially hypoxia, trapped gas, and evolved gas situations (the bends). This zone extends from the top of the Physiological Efficient Zone to about 50,000 feet. You cannot exist above this altitude unless you are in a pressurized suit or cabin. Therefore, above this altitude your body responds as if you were in deep space.

By understanding this hostile environment, you can respect your working conditions, which means reasoning for yourself what the risks really are and anticipating potential problems. Ear blocks and hypoxia are common. As long as you feel okay, you are often not aware of a potential problem simply because you are not suspecting anything. How you feel is often a poor predictor for being safe.

Despite war stories of pilots pressing on through the elements at all altitudes without supplemental oxygen, don't think that these pilots were not affected by conditions related to traditional gas laws—hypoxia, bends, ear blocks and other subtle situations. If you are in the atmosphere anywhere above the level from which you live, you are at risk. Simply being in flight invites potential and often undetected changes in your piloting skills. Flying at any altitude is safe and well tolerated if you are knowledgeable and protected, but the atmosphere is not forgiving if its physical properties are taken for granted.

HOW YOU ARE CONSTRUCTED

In this section, I briefly discuss each major anatomical system: brain, musculoskeletal, gastrointestinal, metabolic, and circulatory. This knowledge provides you some insight as to how the body should work under ideal and controllable circumstances. Even more important, it should raise your level of awareness of what can happen in less than ideal conditions. Then, and only then, can you take corrective action to either avoid unsafe situations or to be prepared to cope with the physiological and psychological challenges of flight.

When considering the abnormal body, we usually think of *pathology,* which is the medical term referring to anything that is not normal. One frequent form of pathology of any part of the body is an inflammation of that part. This can result either from an infection or from an irritation or injury. Every part of your body can be potentially inflamed. It is inflammation if the name of a body part ends in *itis*. In other words, when you hear such terms as tendonitis, tonsilitis, appendicitis, arthritis (*arthro,* meaning joint), meningitis (*menin,* meaning covering of the brain), carditis (*cardi,* meaning heart), and so on, you are talking about an inflammation. The intensity of the inflammation determines how impaired you are.

Let's talk about how your body is supposed to work—on the ground.

Your body's electrical system

The brain is the most important part of your total nervous system—also called your central nervous system (CNS). It controls all functions—physiological, mechanical, and mental— by sending electrical signals to the various parts of your body, much like a computer. Instead of using wires, a signal is transmitted via nerve cells. A row of these cells is called the nerve, often extending from the brain, through the spinal cord and to one of your body parts.

As explained above, various parts of your brain can become infected or inflamed. The same is true of injury. Because your brain is in a closed container (the skull), any impact to the skull can result in torn blood vessels, bruised brain cells, or swelling of your brain. A descriptive analogy to explain a closed head injury is to consider what happens to a fresh tomato that just fits inside a jar. Now rattle the jar. The tomato "bounces" back and forth (a rebound effect) within the jar with expected results—a softer tomato. Likewise, any closed head injury could represent injury to the brain and needs extensive evaluation and treatment.

A *concussion,* by definition, is any period of unconsciousness resulting from a blow to the head. If you experience any kind of loss of consciousness (LOC) for any reason, usually some brain damage has to be considered. This brain damage presents a potential risk for problems, especially in flight, ranging from a simple headache to convulsions, and at unpredictable times. Hypoxia is known to trigger unpredictable serious symptoms in anyone with a history of brain pathology. Therefore, any brain pathology is a potential risk to safe flying until it can be medically proven that there is little chance of a problem developing in flight.

The spinal cord is an extension of your brain, like a bundle of wires. Signals from the various parts of your brain are transmitted to the rest of your body by this cable of nerves. In addition, it brings back signals from your end organs (the body parts) as a form of feedback, which the brain then processes with the other data needed to function. For example, your brain tells you to turn the ignition on with your fingers. When the sound of the engine reaches your ear, that signal is transmitted back to your brain to tell you to release the ignition switch. All these signals pass through your spinal cord.

Any pathology in your spinal cord interferes with proper information getting to and from your brain. Any injury to your spinal cord could result in total loss of neurological control to your body parts. A nerve can be infected and inflamed like any other body part.

The peripheral nervous system is an extension of your spinal cord. The signals to and from your brain are transmitted to the various organs and parts of your body via the series of smaller single nerves in your peripheral nervous system. It's like a telephone trunk line coming into your house and then branching off into your extension phones in different rooms. Each muscle and organ cell has one or more nerves controlling its functions.

Control of your body functions is more complex than just a single nerve telling an organ or body part what to do. Many functions are autonomic. That is, they do not require a conscious effort on your part to initiate action. Functions of the autonomic, or sympathetic nervous system, include breathing, digestion, heart rate, blood pressure, internal temperature control, and many more. The feedback from your various organs, like a home temperature thermostat, tells your brain what it needs, and your brain responds without your intervention.

This is what happens in a fight-or-flight situation. When you are suddenly alarmed, scared, facing a dangerous activity, or in any situation requiring quick response, your brain senses the urgency and, in addition to sending electrical signals, also releases chemicals and hormones (commonly adrenaline). All of these activities increases your body's metabolism so as to be able to respond to the emergency. Often this is instantaneous. Everyone has experienced the rush of adrenaline: the rapid heart rate, tingling sensation, and other symptoms in a dangerous situation. Remember that near miss while driving in your car or the feeling when your doctor says your blood pressure is high?

Control of our senses is also automatic. You see, hear, taste, smell, and feel without having to consciously ask the brain to act. Your brain is always on, and you are continuously receiving cues from your organs of sense—especially sound, smell, and touch. And it's automatic. Pain is a good example. You can reach for a hot pan on the stove and pick it up through conscious commands. If it's too hot you automatically—instinctively— let go and pull your hand back, probably dropping the pan. This happens so quickly that you are usually unable to intercede before dropping the pan and consciously hanging on. What you do next now requires a conscious effort: Do you leave the pan alone, pick it up with gloves, throw water on it, or what?

Training and proficiency could allow you to hold onto the pan even if it is hot. This is a trained response. The same holds true in flying. Many actions and functions of flight are contrary to what your body thinks it ought to do without your input. It is very important to be familiar with those flight conditions not usually well tolerated by your body.

Your human airframe

Bones, tendons, ligaments, and muscles hold your body together and encase the organs that let you function. They make up the musculoskeletal system, and it packages your components and allow you to participate in life's activities. It's the tools you need to fly airplanes. Most of these parts are used in some way in some part of flight. Given the appropriate tools and controls, and the proof of performance through trial and error, many people can fly without a perfect body.

The covering, or skin, is actually another body organ. In fact, it's the largest organ in your body. Your skull houses the brain and most organs of your senses—smell, hearing, vision, and taste. Your chest contains the lungs and heart, and the pelvis protects the abdomen and supports the body by being attached to your legs. The rest of your bones are used to manipulate your body and perform a variety of functions (walking, sitting, picking up things—and flying airplanes).

Mobility of all your skeletal parts requires joints. Most are like simple hinges. Others, like your hip and shoulder's "ball and socket" joints, have a wide range of motion. All joints are held together with ligaments. Tendons are the linkage between your moving bones and muscles. One end of the muscle is attached directly to the bone and the other end using the tendon is attached to a variety of locations on the bone. Muscles can do only one thing—contract—and this contraction bends the joint. Muscle contraction is an active event that requires energy and strength.

You are born with the same amount of muscle tissue that you have now. You do not add muscles when you exercise, but you can increase the size of each muscle cell. The effectiveness of a muscle group is dependent on your physical condition and whether or not your muscles and tissues are getting adequate oxygen and nutrients. Therefore, exercise and a balanced diet are important beyond looking good and protecting your heart.

Injuries are the most common pathology to your musculoskeletal system. Your body is remarkably capable of rebuilding these tissues if you allow time to heal and protect the part from further injury or aggravation. Often, a pilot gets anxious and puts an injured part back to work only to be reinjured. Inflammation is another very common problem. Tendonitis, arthritis, and myositis are the usual results. Tendons and ligaments are particularly slow to heal because of their low blood supply. Because they have a large blood supply, muscles heal fairly quickly. Muscles, therefore, are easily bruised (a bruise is bleeding into your muscle tissues and under your skin).

Your working parts

The purpose of your gastrointestinal (GI) system is to provide and digest nutrients and fluids for metabolism into the tissue cells. Fortunately, eating remains one of the pleasures of life, and we often make excess of that pleasure. Foods and fluids that you ingest are transformed into energy, tissue rebuilding, and maintenance of your body functions.

Your *GI system*, or *tract*, is essentially one long tube beginning at your mouth and ending at the anus. Fluids are quickly absorbed through the GI tract walls and transferred to your bloodstream. The first part of digestion is that food is physically broken up with chewing, then converted into basic components (mostly glucose and amino acids) in the rest of your GI system. All waste products (undigested components) are passed out of the body through your large intestine.

Fluids are being absorbed and secreted throughout this entire process. The absorbed fluids replace those lost through metabolism, sweating, and urination.

Your large intestine (colon and cecum) is where undigested material is collected and compacted and then further broken down with bacteria. This bacterial action often generates gas, which can be passed out of either orifice. As this material, now called *fecal matter*, continues down the large GI tract, fluids are once again exchanged to maintain a soft consistency. Constipation results if there is not enough undigested fiber to absorb water. A bowel movement allows this material to pass from the large intestine, through the rectum, and out the anus.

Digestion is another part of your circadian rhythms. In other words, your internal rhythm tells your body when to expect food. This triggers hunger and stimulates your digestive juices. *Peristalsis* (the contractions of the bowel to assist movement of food through the GI tract) also begins. Digestion might not be efficient if your rhythms are out of synch.

Within the GI tract, the most common problems are intestinal flus, inflammation (gastritis), constipation, and hemorrhoids, all of minimal concern. Ulcers, bleeding ulcers, and tumors are of major concern.

Your metabolic system is what makes all your organs and musculoskeletal system work. Your nervous system supplies the information and direction, your musculoskeletal system is the container and does the mechanical work, your GI system processes the fuel and building material, and your metabolic system converts these resources into substances, chemicals, energy, etc., all of which support the activities of the body.

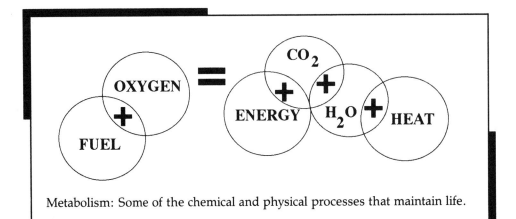

Metabolism: Some of the chemical and physical processes that maintain life.

Located in the upper righthand corner of your abdomen, partially under your rib cage, is the organ carrying most of the metabolic workload—your liver. This organ (sometimes called a chemical processing plant) is an essential part of metabolism. It makes glycogen (the body's storage form of glucose for future use), processes fats and proteins, removes waste products, and plays a role in the generation of heat for the body.

The liver is important in changing the simple chemicals absorbed from the GI tract into usable products. These products include vitamins, enzymes, bile and cholesterol. In addition, it detoxifies drugs, medications, and alcohol.

Your gallbladder, which is a small bag, stores bile made by the liver. However, it can also form stones, which can block the tube to the intestine and keep the bile from entering the GI tract. This backup can interfere with hepatic function.

From a metabolic point of view, alcohol is a toxin to the liver. As a result, there is often an increased production of certain enzymes used to detoxify the alcohol. These enzymes can be measured in blood tests, indicating that the liver is being affected.

Your kidneys (located on both sides of the spine just below the back of the rib cage) act like filters of blood. They take out impurities and some waste products. An important function is to maintain a fluid balance in the body. The kidneys therefore adjust the volume of blood in your circulatory system by conserving or excreting water. Furthermore, they adjust the composition of the blood to ensure the right balance of essential products. If there is not enough fluid (water) as serum within the blood, the kidneys conserve water by concentrating your urine. Concentrated urine is dark yellow as compared to pale yellow, which indicates adequate hydration.

Because your kidneys are capable of regulating urine concentration, you can rarely drink too much water. However, there is certainly the problem of too little fluids. In fact, dehydration is a real concern and results in prolonged concentrated urine.

A problem relatively common in aviation is kidney stones. Here, concentrated urine from dehydration over many months tends to form small sand-sized "stones." If small enough they pass without any symptoms. However, if a stone gets stuck in the ureter or at the entrance to the bladder, severe pain can suddenly result. Some people are more prone to making kidney stones. Therefore, once one stone is made, that person is at higher risk of making others. It is essential in preventing stone formation to maintain a high level of hydration, especially on long trips.

An important organ, the pancreas, is located to the left of the liver. Its primary function is to produce insulin. All body tissues require insulin for metabolism of glucose into energy. At certain times of the day, the pancreas is programmed to begin producing insulin. Thus there is also a circadian component that has a bearing on becoming hypoglycemic, a topic to be discussed later.

Diabetes is a disease where insulin, if produced at all, is produced in inadequate amounts. Insulin-dependent diabetics need to inject insulin into their bodies to maintain a balanced availability for use in metabolizing glucose. Some diabetics have the capability of making some insulin but need the help of an oral medication. This is a chemical (not an oral insulin) that stimulates the pancreas to make and excrete more insulin. Diet becomes a special concern in maintaining a proper balance because the pancreas is stimulated by the presence or absence of some key foods (such as sugar, carbohydrates, and fats). Exercise is equally important.

Your thyroid is a gland located at the front of your lower neck, right in the middle. It makes two different hormones, each of which play a significant role in establishing metabolic rate, or the speed with which your body functions and responds to activities. Too high a rate makes you "hyper," resulting in weight loss, nervousness, and a sense of warmth. Another hormone assists in the metabolism of calcium and bones.

Your hydraulic system

As I just discussed, your metabolic system is crucial in making everything work. However, it is the circulatory system that provides the energy and nutrients for metabolism to occur. It transports your blood, which in turn carries essential oxygen, nutrients, and waste products. This system includes fluid (blood), a pump (heart), tubing (blood vessels), and your body parts (organs) that require support of the system. Therefore, it is comparable to any closed hydraulic system, such as that in your airplane. It is this system that is of most interest to you because any change in oxygen levels immediately changes the performance of many organs, especially the brain.

The heart is the pump in this human hydraulic system. It is a closed structure, with blood flowing from your heart, into arteries, then through capillaries, which are then spread around the tissues. From there, your blood continues into the venous system, through the lungs, and back to the heart.

This pump is divided into four chambers, which take blood from a major vein and pump it into arteries (Fig. 1-4). The two smaller chambers on top (the atria) take in blood from the veins and pump it into the larger ventricles below. The ventricles then pump blood to the lungs and to the rest of your body. The heart is a muscle, and it responds just like any other muscle in your body. Every muscle fiber must contract at the same time to function properly. This contraction squeezes the blood through the one-way heart valves. The blood moves forward but not backward, so there is a moment when blood pressure goes down during this transition between contractions.

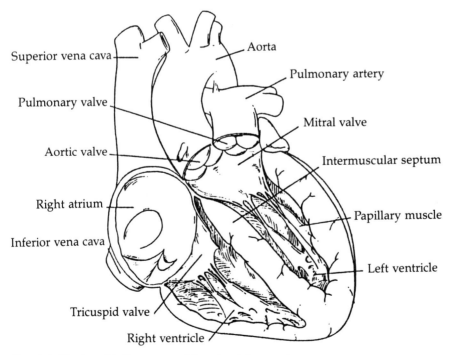

Fig. 1-4. The heart is the pump of the circulatory system.

Also, like any other muscle, your heart needs a blood supply. Blood is supplied via the coronary arteries. It is these arteries that become blocked in heart disease, sometimes leading to heart attacks or poor blood perfusion of the heart muscles (called ischemia). Oxygen needs to get to your heart muscle for energy. If it doesn't, the heart can fail or become less effective in pumping blood throughout your body. Total blockage of blood to your heart muscle leads to death of some of the tissues of your heart. Dead heart tissue is called a *myocardial infarction* (*myo*, meaning muscle, *cardia*, meaning heart, *infarction*, meaning dead) or *MI*. MI is another name for *heart attack*.

Risk factors for coronary heart disease

- Male sex
- Family history of premature heart disease
- Cigarette smoking
- Low HDL (<35 mg/dL)
- High total cholesterol (>240)
- High LDL
- Diabetes mellitus
- Hypertension
- Severe obesity (>30% overweight)
- Presence of arteriosclerosis

If your heart muscle fibers do not contract simultaneously, changes occur in the rhythm and contractility. *Fibrillation* is when your muscle fibers contract at different times. Any of these problems leads to heart failure.

The amount of blood that flows out of your heart per minute depends on several conditions: the heart rate (pulse), the volume of blood ejected from the heart, and the force of the contraction. Much of these activities are controlled by the autonomic nervous system; that is, you don't consciously have to tell the heart to function.

The lungs are where oxygen and carbon dioxide are exchanged between the ambient air and the blood. The alveoli is where this exchange takes place (Fig. 1-5). Your lung's structure is like an upside down tree. Air enters the lungs through your mouth or nose, then passes into your pharynx, trachea, and then to the main bronchus. This large breathing tube then splits into two bronchi, which further split into thousands of smaller bronchioles, or miniature breathing tubes. Therefore, all air inhaled ends up in tiny alveoli (tiny rubber-like balloons). Capillaries surround these alveoli and because both walls are so thin, gases can pass

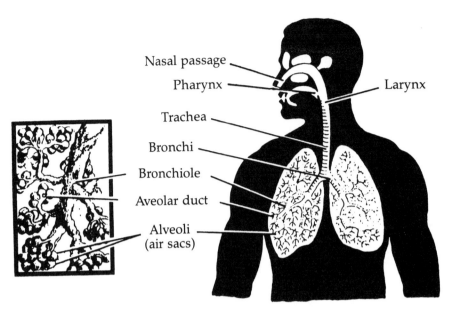

Fig. 1-5. The lung resembles an upside-down tree.

back and forth (diffuse) across these walls. Blood in these capillaries access the gases through continued diffusion.

Air is pulled into your lungs by decreasing the pressure within your chest cavity. The diaphragm is a muscular dome-shaped floor of the lower part of the rib cage which forms a closed container with only one opening—the bronchial tree. When this muscle contracts it flattens out, creating lower pressure and allowing air to fill the alveoli. This inhalation from the diaphragm contracting is an active event. Exhaling is passive because the diaphragm relaxes and returns to its dome shape. The muscles between your ribs also supplement this activity. The action of respiration is also an autonomic function, just like your heart. It's controlled by your brain. With exercise, both breathing and heart rate are increased without your thinking about it.

The "hydraulic" link between your heart, lungs, brain, and other parts of your body are the blood vessels (Fig. 1-6). Arteries carry oxygen-rich blood from the lungs to the tissues and are unique from other blood vessels in that they have muscle and elastic cells within their walls. This structure allows them to dilate or constrict, an effective way of increasing or decreasing blood flow to various parts of your body. For example, while running, your leg muscles need more blood. Arteries to these muscles automatically dilate to their full size, permitting a larger volume of blood to reach the tissues. The same process happens in control of your body temperatures, as is discussed in chapter 4.

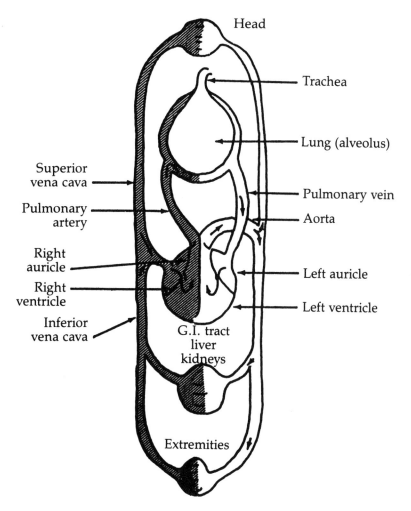

Fig. 1-6. Essential oxygen and nutrients are transported throughout the body by the circulatory system.

The elasticity of the artery wall helps keep your blood pressure constant during the relaxed period between heart contractions. The pressure within the artery resulting from this elasticity enhances and prolongs the pressure that is generated by the heart—like blowing up a balloon.

Veins are simple tubes without muscles or elastic tissues. Veins carry blood that is deficient in oxygen. Some veins in your arms and legs prevent blood from flowing backwards during the relaxed period defined above. This happens because they have one-way valves scattered throughout the length of the vein.

Blood pressure within your veins is very low. Muscles, such as those in your legs, surround the major veins. When the muscles contract, they compress the vessel's wall and "milk" the blood forward to the heart. This is often called the "muscle pump." Blood can pool in the extremities when you've been sitting for long periods of time, resulting in stagnant hypoxia.

Respiration is the exchange of gases between your body and its tissues and the outside ambient air. The main objective is to add oxygen while removing carbon dioxide. About 90 percent of blood is water (serum). Part of the nonserum blood is red blood cells, which physically carry oxygen molecules attached to a chemical on the cells called *hemoglobin*. The red blood cells become the transporters of oxygen through the use of hemoglobin. Any change in the hemoglobin, number of red blood cells, or diffusion of gases causes some form of hypoxia.

The darker color of venous blood is an indication of hemoglobin that has no oxygen attached. The bright red color of arterial blood results from the combination of oxygen with hemoglobin. The amount of oxygen carried by the red blood cells is normally about 95–98 percent of saturation of the cell. This is called the *oxygen dissociation curve* and indicates that available oxygen falls rapidly when the saturation goes below 90 percent (Fig.1-7). This is when hypoxia develops.

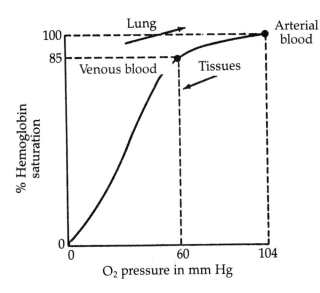

Fig. 1-7. Arterial and venous blood saturation for normal sea level conditions.

Gases move across the vascular membranes by the process of diffusion. Because of the physics of gas laws, a gas can move from an area of high pressure to an area of lower pressure. The same process of diffusion occurs at the tissue and cell level within your body (Fig. 1-8).

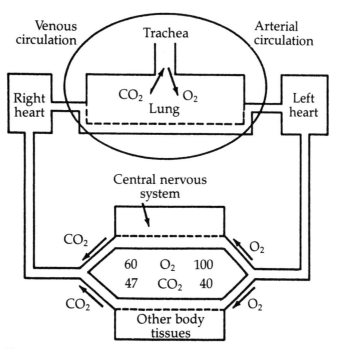

Fig. 1-8. The physiology of respiration. (The problem area in hypoxic hypoxia is circled.)

Obviously, your body is far more complex than what is described here. However, in order to understand how the physiology of flight can affect your performance, you must have a basic understanding of how the body works. Furthermore, anything that interferes with a normally functioning body—the status of your health—can also determine if you can pass FAA medical standards.

2

Flying above
5,000 feet AGL

Judy and her family left Des Moines for a skiing weekend in Colorado. Their sin-gle-engine Piper performed flawlessly, and they landed uneventfully at the Vail airport, in time for some late afternoon skiing. They felt tired but attributed that to the long, hard work week and the flight. After two days of skiing they headed home, except now they were very fatigued and Judy found it difficult to concen-trate and focus, even though she was never above 5,000 feet AGL. A nagging headache and general lethargy persisted. As the airplane continued on to Des Moines, she was able to get her aircraft below 5,000 feet MSL and she began to feel better. Although she was uncomfortable during the beginning of the flight, she also recognized that she was hypoxic from several days at an altitude that her body was not used to. She left her oxygen mask on for several minutes after get-ting lower. Had she not suspected hypoxia, she would have become more impaired than she did.

When people talk about "high-altitude physiology," they are com-monly referring to those conditions that affect your body as a result of being at an altitude where airliners fly. They think that only at extremely high altitudes should you be concerned about hypoxia, ear blocks, etc. However, in actuality, any time the human body remains at any altitude above where it is used to being, there is a risk of problems. Therefore, this chapter is not limited to airline pilots or flying above 18,000 feet, but is meant for all pilots, at all levels. This means recreational flying, helicopter flying, and low-level commercial flying as well.

Hypoxia, trapped gas situations, and decompression sickness—often called *the bends*—are the most common problems directly related to the physical properties of the different layers of the atmosphere. In addition, scuba diving has become very popular for all ages and complicates your decision to fly for yourself or your passengers. It is therefore essential for you to be able to identify the symptoms of any of these events as occurring in yourself and in your crewmate. Then, as a responsible pilot, you can maintain a high index of suspicion for potential high altitude problems and respond with immediate and appropriate action before you get an ear block or become hypoxic.

ESSENTIAL OXYGEN

The lack of adequate oxygen in your body's metabolism is called *hypoxia* (or *anoxia*, for the total absence of oxygen). It is this lack of sufficient oxygen to your body's tissues and cells that can impair you in flight. This situation occurs for reasons in addition to the reduced availability of oxygen in the air you breathe. These reasons include your blood's ability to carry oxygen, and the interference of drugs, alcohol, carbon monoxide, smoking, and illness, to name a few. Many incidents and some accidents are officially related to the pilot's inability to detect that he or she was hypoxic, even mildly so. That pilot's performance became unsafe because of compromised skills or judgment, pilot error, and a lack of respect or understanding of hypoxia and its effects. To fully understand the challenge in getting oxygen to the cell, you must understand the physiology of oxygen. Then you can understand and respect hypoxia, no matter what the cause.

Classification of hypoxia

No matter why you are hypoxic, the symptoms and effects on your flying skills are basically the same. The following classification is therefore intended only to review these causes so that your degree of suspicion of being hypoxic (or observing hypoxia in crew or passengers) is raised, especially when you are involved in flying situations that put you at higher risk.

Hypoxic (altitude) hypoxia. This term is the most commonly used when talking about hypoxia. It is, however, only one of four kinds. Hypoxic hypoxia is associated with lack of available oxygen in the air you breathe, such as experienced when flying at altitude in an unpressurized cabin. It means that there isn't enough oxygen available to bring into your lungs with sufficient partial pressure. This happens as you ascend. The number of molecules of oxygen decrease, despite the fact that the percentage of oxygen in the air remains the same. This situation is particularly evident in the physiologically deficient zone of the atmosphere.

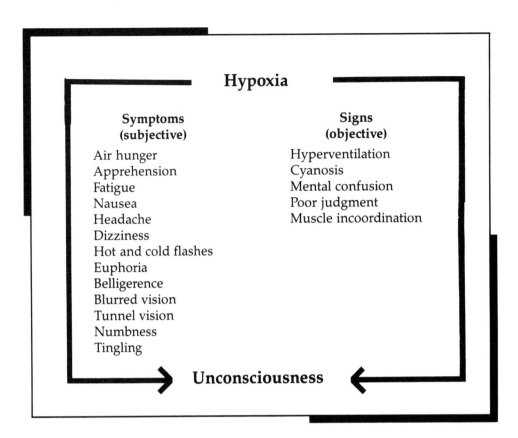

Hypoxia

Symptoms (subjective)	Signs (objective)
Air hunger	Hyperventilation
Apprehension	Cyanosis
Fatigue	Mental confusion
Nausea	Poor judgment
Headache	Muscle incoordination
Dizziness	
Hot and cold flashes	
Euphoria	
Belligerence	
Blurred vision	
Tunnel vision	
Numbness	
Tingling	

Unconsciousness

Strictly speaking, you are hypoxic even at a few thousand feet above the ground. In actuality, the symptoms do not become significant until about 5,000 feet, especially at night. The significance of the symptoms is related to many factors, which are explained later. Suffice to say, hypoxia must be considered to be present at all levels.

From a gas law perspective, hypoxic hypoxia exists when the partial pressure of oxygen in the atmosphere and the inhaled ambient air is reduced as it travels into your bronchial tree and lungs. In other words, the partial pressure of oxygen as it is made available to the blood within your lungs is too low to effectively transfer enough oxygen to the cells of your tissues.

Hypemic (anemic) hypoxia. Hypemic hypoxia occurs when the blood's ability to carry oxygen is the problem, even though there is adequate oxygen available to breathe. This type of hypoxia can occur for a variety of reasons. Anemia, or the reduced number of healthy, functioning red blood cells for any reason (disease, blood loss, deformed blood cells, etc.), means less capacity for blood to carry oxygen. Hemoglobin (Hgb), a chemical part of the red blood cell, physically carries (by combining with oxygen) more oxygen molecules than are dissolved in solution. Anything that would interfere or displace oxygen that is attached to the hemoglobin would obviously reduce the oxygen carried to the cell. This occurs most commonly when carbon monoxide is inhaled and the hemoglobin accepts it more than oxygen. Other chemicals cause the same combining interference to hemoglobin, such as sulfa drugs and nitrites (as in food preservatives).

Stagnant hypoxia. If the blood flow (the circulation of the oxygen-carrying hemoglobin in red blood cells) is compromised for any reason, then sufficient oxygen cannot physically get to your cells and tissues. *Stagnant* implies a diminished flow, not necessarily completely stopped. Such decrease in blood flow results from the heart failing to pump effectively, an artery constricting and cutting off the flow, or venous pooling of blood, such as in varicose veins of the legs. Sitting for long periods of time tends to enhance this pooling. Another cause, unique to flying, occurs during positive G maneuvers—pulling Gs—and long periods of pressure breathing at extreme cabin altitudes where oxygen masks are required. Another situation is in cold temperatures where blood supply to extremities is decreased. All these situations can lead to stagnant hypoxia.

Histotoxic hypoxia. *Histotoxic* means that the cell expecting and needing oxygen is abnormal or unable to accept the oxygen because of a toxin in the cell. In other words, the oxygen might be inhaled or reach the tissue or cell in adequate amounts, but the cell is unable to metabolize the oxygen once it is there. This hypoxia can occur when alcohol is present in the blood or in the cell and consequently prevents the utilization of oxygen by that cell. Alcohol becomes, in effect, a toxin to that cell. The same is true for some narcotics and certain poisons, such as cyanide.

Stages of hypoxia

The lack of oxygen—hypoxia—results in a variety of subtle and not so subtle symptoms, no matter what the reason is for oxygen not getting to and being used by the cell. The danger of hypoxia is that you probably are unsuspecting when you are hypoxic. The key to flying safe at altitude is to first recognize the conditions under which you could be hypoxic. Then the symptoms that you know are your individual indicators of being hypoxic must be respected by you. Equally important, you must be able to recognize and suspect it in your crewmate.

Most hypoxic symptoms are related, directly or indirectly, to the nervous system because your nervous system tissues have a profound requirement for oxygen, especially the brain (and eyes). If hypoxia is prolonged, serious problems develop progressively, and if it continues, evolves to ultimate death (Fig. 2-1). In extreme cases (prior to death), some brain cells are actually killed. Brain cells cannot be regenerated

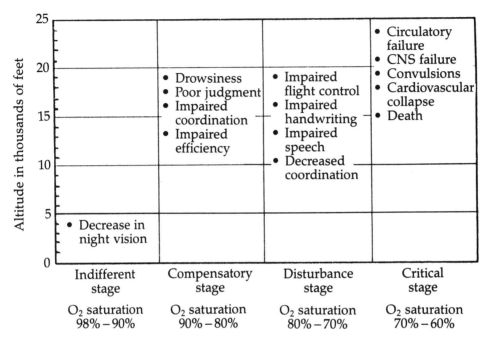

	Indifferent stage	Compensatory stage	Disturbance stage	Critical stage
				• Circulatory failure • CNS failure • Convulsions • Cardiovascular collapse • Death
		• Drowsiness • Poor judgment • Impaired coordination • Impaired efficiency	• Impaired flight control • Impaired handwriting • Impaired speech • Decreased coordination	
	• Decrease in night vision			
O₂ saturation	O_2 saturation 98%–90%	O_2 saturation 90%–80%	O_2 saturation 80%–70%	O_2 saturation 70%–60%

Fig. 2-1. Stages of hypoxia.

It bears repeating. Since hypoxia can be and often is gradual in its development, you must recognize its various stages, especially your own. Allow for some degree of anticipation should symptoms in the early stages be identified and you are in conditions conducive to hypoxia. The earlier hypoxia can be recognized, the sooner corrective action can be taken before you mentally become unable to act appropriately.

Keep in mind that, although altitude is the common denominator in being hypoxic, your health can affect your tolerance to the conditions leading to hypoxia. Other abuses such as smoking, alcohol, and stress can reduce this tolerance even if you are healthy. Therefore, hypoxia can be very unpredictable for you or your crewmates. Saying you had no problem at 10,000 feet last week does not mean you will be safe today at the same altitude.

Indifferent state. Because the eye is anatomically an extension of the brain, one of the earliest symptoms of hypoxia is its effect on your eyes.

Therefore, vision, especially your night vision, can deteriorate even at altitudes less than 5,000 feet. And you won't know you are having problems because you can't compare what you are seeing with what you should be seeing. For example, night vision decreases by 5 to 10 percent at 5,000 feet, 15 to 25 percent at 10,000 feet, and 25 to 30 percent at 12,000 feet. Other classical symptoms, in addition to impaired vision, can be present at lower altitudes if your body is not tolerant, as are explained later. Suffice to say, when flying at any altitude at night be aware that your vision and other mental skills can be compromised.

Compensatory stage. During this stage, your body and mind are quickly approaching the point where they can be severely affected and in increasing and subtle ways. However, your circulatory system and, to a lesser degree, your respiratory system, can provide some defense against hypoxia while you are in this stage. As a result of increased heart rate, enhanced circulation, and a more productive heart pumping blood, you can still cope. Respiration (breathing rate and depth) also increases. Although these body responses are automatic, you should not assume that you are recovering and neglect to take immediate conscious corrective action whenever you suspect hypoxia.

At 12,000 to 15,000 feet, the effects of hypoxia on the nervous system can become increasingly incapacitating, especially if you are unacclimated. As time at this altitude continues (as little as 10 to 15 minutes), impaired skills are very evident, especially to others. A variety of symptoms now develop, many of which compromise your flying performance and skills. Such symptoms as drowsiness, poor judgment, and frequent subtle errors in flying skills can occur. A more dangerous result to you is a feeling of well being and indifference (euphoria). Once again, the crucial characteristic about hypoxia, especially in this stage, is your recognition of an increasing oxygen deficit before you reach the point where you no longer care that you are in trouble.

Disturbance stage. At this stage, your probability of recovery is greatly diminished—you've missed your chance to intervene. Symptoms become more severe, including headaches, hyperventilation, impaired peripheral vision, marked fatigue, sleepiness, and euphoria. By now you might even recognize you are hypoxic, but you don't care and have little incentive to take corrective action, such as getting to a lower altitude or going on oxygen. You might actually be unable to physically reach for the oxygen and put the mask on, while mentally realizing that you should be doing something.

Critical stage. At this point, you have lost it—you're unconscious. All this can happen within 3 to 5 minutes after you failed to recognize you were hypoxic during the compensatory and disturbance stage. Some people faint as a result of circulatory failure or the failure of the central nervous system to function.

Symptoms of hypoxia

The following are some of the more common symptoms experienced by hypoxic pilots.

- Change in peripheral vision, even noting "tunnel vision."
- Visual acuity impairment, images appear slightly blurred, can't focus.
- Difficulty in visual accommodation, focusing from near to distant.
- Weakness in muscles, more difficult to change the airplane seat.
- Feeling very tired and fatigued, sleepy for no reason (not boredom).
- Headache, especially if hypoxic for long period (2+ hours).
- Light-headedness and mild dizziness, react poorly in tight turns.
- Tingling in fingers and toes.
- Muscular coordination decreased, sloppy at controls.
- Stammering, can't get the right words out to ATC.
- Impaired judgment, doing dumb things, slow thinking.
- Altered respiration, breathing faster and shallower.
- Reaction time decreased, you've lost your flying touch.
- Greatly reduced night vision (even at 5,000 feet).
- Euphoria; you settle for less, who cares?

Note that many of these symptoms are very subjective; that is, most are not definitive of how hypoxic you are. For example, a change in heart rate is objective evidence, but it can also change with exertion or stress. You might not think of being hypoxic. A common symptom is fatigue, another very subjective sign. How fatigued must you be for you to consider hypoxia? Are you fatigued from hypoxia or from the length of the flight? And if you are indeed hypoxic, you will be complacent about any degree of fatigue. Also, these symptoms are not listed in order of importance or ease of recognition. Some pilots experience a specific kind of headache, others only recollect being fatigued before they became incapacitated and lost control.

Hypoxia is an easy trap to fall into and it happens to all pilots, many times, to varying degrees. It is unfortunate, but the fact is that the human body does not have an effective warning system to alert you to the onset of hypoxia. Hypoxia is painless. Each pilot reacts differently to the same degree of hypoxia and experiences different symptoms and impairments.

These individual symptoms can also change with age. It is for these reasons that the military continues to expose flight crews to an altitude chamber ride about every three to four years. The main reason is for the individual pilots to experience their symptoms for hypoxia before they reach the disturbance stage and then cannot (or will not) recover or take appropriate action. No amount of lecturing or reading can prepare you for how to detect your own level of incapacitating hypoxia. Therefore, it is strongly encouraged that, at least once, early in your flying career, you take a chamber ride.

In summary, the signs and symptoms of hypoxia are many and varied, they differ from individual to individual, and they are unpredictable at any given time and altitude. Be aware, be suspicious, and watch your crewmates—and hope they are watching you!

Factors influencing tolerance to hypoxia

As mentioned before, it is impossible to predict exactly when, where, or how hypoxic reactions will occur in you because individuals vary widely in their susceptibility to oxygen deficiency. This susceptibility is related to many factors which, in many cases, you can control. Avoidance of these factors becomes part of your responsibility to preclude unexpected hypoxia.

Self-imposed factors. Although the cabin might be at less than 10,000 feet (pressure altitude), there is a "physiological altitude," an altitude that your body feels it is at. The presence of any of the following self-imposed factors raises this physiological altitude. Consequently, your mind and body react accordingly with some incapacitation. So instead of your body performing at a 10,000-foot altitude, it might respond as if it were at 13,000 feet.

Alcohol in your body can result in histotoxic hypoxia. Alcohol is a toxin. It has been observed that one ounce of alcohol equates to about an additional 2,000 feet of physiological altitude. It interferes with oxygen uptake and metabolism at the cell level. Furthermore, the usual depressant effects of alcohol on behavior can cloud your recognition of your own degree of hypoxia, adding to your decreasing tolerance.

When you are mentally or physically fatigued, you tolerate hypoxia poorly because you are already bordering on performance decrement. And since fatigue is a symptom of hypoxia, it becomes difficult to discriminate how hypoxic you are. You might erroneously reason that your fatigue is not a result of hypoxia and not consider taking preventative actions.

The carbon monoxide in cigarette smoke is a great threat to the pilot who smokes. Carbon monoxide has an affinity for hemoglobin more than 200 times that of oxygen, resulting in hypemic hypoxia (Fig. 2-2). As with alcohol, it has been noted by some that smoking three cigarettes in rapid succession or smoking 20 to 30 cigarettes in a 24-hour period prior to flight can saturate from 8 to 10 percent of the hemoglobin in the body. In addition, approximately 20 percent of a smoker's night vision is lost even at sea level. These factors can translate into a physiological altitude of an additional 3,000 to 5,000 feet.

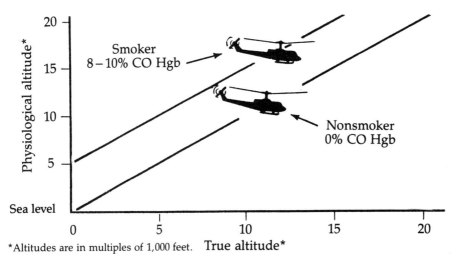

*Altitudes are in multiples of 1,000 feet. **True altitude***

Fig. 2-2. Smoking increases a pilot's physiological altitude.

If you are in good shape physically, that is, not overweight, have been exercising, and have a fairly nutritious diet, you are much more tolerant of the effects of low oxygen levels. The symptoms and potential incapacitation from hypoxia are still present, but you will find them less severe, and more important, you will be able to take appropriate action to recognize and avoid increasing hypoxia before you are truly at risk. Another way of looking at this is that the physiological ceiling is reduced. Also, keep in mind that it might be more than just improved tolerance. The healthy body itself might be more efficient in the use of oxygen and therefore require less oxygen in its metabolism. In any case, being in good medical condition is a true investment in safe flight. Being in less than optimum shape becomes a self-induced deterrent to tolerance.

Other factors affecting response to hypoxia

The following are other conditions that can determine the degree of hypoxia you can expect given the right circumstances. You have some control over these factors, but to a lesser degree, because they are a part of your flying environment and working conditions. When tolerance is described, it refers to how susceptible your body is to low levels of oxygen. In other words, as a result of the following, you could become hypoxic at lower altitudes than you would expect, even if your controllable risk factors are absent.

Acclimatization. People who live at high altitudes develop an increased tolerance to the conditions that would lead to hypoxia in people living at lower altitudes. Therefore, a pilot who lives in Denver (the "Mile High City") is more adapted when flying at a cabin altitude of 8,000 feet, or higher than someone who lives in Los Angeles. By the same token, the LA-based pilot who lands in Denver and has a layover there will already by slightly hypoxic when he takes off the next day.

Absolute altitude. The higher the altitude of the cabin (whether pressurized or not), the higher the risk of becoming hypoxic. Be advised that airline cabin altitude often reaches 8,000 feet. When the absolute altitude reaches a dangerous level, you must consider either lowering the cabin altitude or donning an oxygen mask.

Rate of ascent. The quicker your cabin climbs, the less effective your individual tolerance will be. Often, as a result of rapid ascent, you are even less aware of approaching hypoxia. The lack of time to notice suspicious symptoms can often lead you to experience some unexpected series of potentially incapacitating symptoms.

Duration of exposure. Staying at 8,000 feet for several hours (without supplemental oxygen) could result in the same symptoms of compromised skills as a half hour at about 16,000 feet. Symptoms are time-related, but also very unpredictable. As I discuss later, the higher the altitude, the shorter the exposure time needed before symptoms of hypoxia occur.

Ambient temperature. Temperature extremes in the cockpit, especially in smaller recreational aircraft and poorly air-conditioned pressurized cabins, make your body less tolerant to diminished oxygen levels. Shivering when cold uses body energy and this form of increased activity requires more oxygen. Coping with high heat and humidity is also a factor. Your body's circulatory system is working harder to maintain its "core temperature."

Effective performance time (EPT)

The Effective Performance Time (EPT)—formerly known as Time of Useful Consciousness (TUC)—is the period of time you have from the time oxygen becomes less available until the time when you lose your ability to take action, such as getting on oxygen or going to a lower alti-

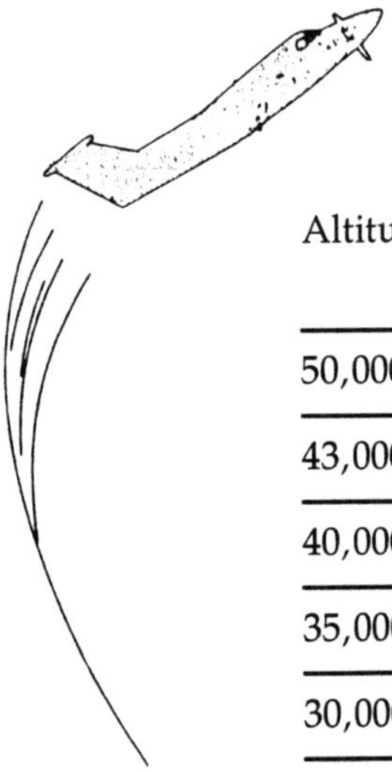

Altitude	Effective performance time	
50,000 feet and above	9 – 12	seconds
43,000	9 – 12	"
40,000	15 – 20	"
35,000	30 – 60	"
30,000	1 – 2	minutes
28,000	$2^{1/2}$ – 3	"
25,000	4 – 6	"
22,000	8 – 10	"
18,000	20 – 30	"

Fig. 2-3. Time of useful consciousness decreases as altitude increases.

tude (Fig. 2-3). As described earlier, a major symptom of hypoxia is euphoria. Therefore, if you go beyond your EPT, then you aren't aware that you are in trouble and will not take corrective action. The key word is *useful*. You might be conscious, but you're not making useful decisions.

The EPT decreases with increasing altitude and is dependent on the same tolerance factors defined earlier. The EPT can become very short but only at cabin altitudes not frequently experienced. However, decompression (sudden or slow loss of cabin pressure) still occurs in flight and you can quickly find yourself at altitudes in excess of 20,000 feet and not realize you have a shorter EPT. In fact, in a more rapid decompression, your EPT will be shortened by a third to a half. Of greater concern, and more likely to occur, is subtle decompression, where you are not aware that your cabin altitude is rising and that your EPT is diminishing. For example, if you are flying without supplemental oxygen in a cabin where the altitude is slowly climbing to about 18,000 feet, you can easily get into trouble and not be aware of it. At this altitude, the EPT is about 25 minutes. If you are very busy and are not keeping track of the time you are at that altitude, you can quickly approach your EPT.

Prevention of hypoxia

There is nothing remarkable about preventing hypoxia. As already discussed, avoidance of those conditions that increase the risk of becoming hypoxic is paramount. It's also prevented by maintaining a high level of suspicion any time your cabin altitude is above 5,000 feet, especially at night. Like maintenance on the aircraft, preventive management is more productive than crisis management. Waiting for symptoms of hypoxia to be observed before you take action is crisis management! Prevention of hypoxia, therefore, becomes anticipation of becoming hypoxic where hypoxia can happen. If you are a smoker, moderate drinker, and physically out of shape, you are at greater risk than a physically fit person who does not smoke or drink.

The obvious solution is to be in a pressurized cabin at an altitude of less than 10,000 feet or to use supplemental oxygen by mask. Although according to the regulations you are legal without oxygen at 10,000 feet, you can still be subtly incapacitated.

Treatment of hypoxia

If you suspect hypoxia in yourself or a crewmate, the immediate use of 100 percent oxygen is essential. Aside from the rare occurrence of oxygen toxicity, you cannot hurt anyone by giving them oxygen. If someone is hypoxic, they will have an almost immediate response and recovery. If improvement is not immediate, you must think of other causes for the symptoms. If supplemental oxygen is not available, then get the airplane or cabin altitude below 10,000 feet. Hypoxia is a valid reason to declare an emergency to ATC.

Hyperventilation

Hyperventilation is simply a matter of breathing too rapidly, which results in exhaling too much carbon dioxide during respiration. The symptoms are seldom completely incapacitating, but they do produce, at the very least, a potentially serious distraction, often in an already busy cockpit. Therefore, the problem is only further aggravated by increasing your anxiety level and breathing rate. It becomes a vicious circle.

Causes. Fear, stress, and anxiety can cause you to override normal automatic functions of respiration, such as breathing rate. As you become more stressed, you tend to breathe faster. Because you are more apt to observe the symptoms of hyperventilation in others than in yourself, this is another reason for depending on and trusting your crewmates.

Symptoms. Unfortunately, many of the symptoms of hyperventilation are similar to those experienced in hypoxia, fainting, and decompression sickness. They include, but are not limited to, tingling sensations in your fingers, toes, and around your lips; small muscle spasms; hot and cold sensations; visual impairment; dizziness; and, in severe cases, unconsciousness. The challenge is to make the proper diagnosis based on the symptoms and then take appropriate action.

If hyperventilation is suspected, trying to get voluntary control of your breathing rate is the most effective method of treatment. Normal breathing is about 12 to 16 breaths per minute. Recognizing that carbon dioxide is blown off by the rapid breathing, using the "paper bag" method also helps. Breathing into the bag gets you to concentrate on slowing your breathing rate as well as rebreathing carbon dioxide. Since hypoxia and hyperventilation have similar symptoms and hypoxia can cause one to hyperventilate, the initial treatment for these symptoms is the same—oxygen. A good rule of thumb, therefore, is to go on 100 percent oxygen and get your mind off your anxiety by working on something or mentally figuring out a problem. Even singing or talking has been suggested.

Final thoughts on hypoxia

It is essential that there be a mutual understanding and respect by all aviators for both hypoxia and hyperventilation. You should expect your crewmate to watch you just as you are obligated to keep your suspicions up in hypoxia-generating conditions. This is true for all facets of aviation, including helicopter flight, where there is a false sense of security as a result of the perception that you aren't going to get high enough to become hypoxic. Helicopters are flying higher all the time, often in excess of 20,000 feet! This is a common occurrence in mountainous areas, where you can leave sea level and quickly be at an altitude in excess of 15,000 feet. Although flying less than 10,000 feet AGL is common, remember that your physiological altitude can be much higher, especially if you are at the higher altitude for extended periods. Hypoxia happens, even to professionals. It needn't be a dramatic or obvious event. Subtle performance impairment takes place even with minimal hypoxia.

POISONS IN THE AIR

Carbon monoxide (CO)

The effects of carbon monoxide (CO) are subtle and deadly. Carbon monoxide poisoning is more common than poisoning by any other toxic gas. It is colorless, odorless, tasteless, and slightly lighter than air. Like hypoxia, carbon monoxide poisoning is painless and can incapacitate you before you know you are in trouble. Carbon monoxide is present in every smoker's body.

Effects of exposure. Relatively low concentrations of carbon monoxide in the air can, in time, produce very high blood concentrations. It is a cumulative problem. Such accumulations can occur in less than 30 minutes at carbon monoxide levels in the air of only 0.5 percent. Carbon monoxide competes with oxygen for attachment to hemoglobin. This situation leads to hypemic hypoxia even at lower altitudes.

Symptoms. Like hypoxia, the symptoms of carbon monoxide intoxication are often subjective. They include headache, weakness, nervousness, tremors, and ultimately unconsciousness. A loss of visual acuity also occurs; especially affected are night and peripheral vision (Fig. 2-4).

Percentage of circulating Hb saturated by CO	Symptoms (resting state, at ground level)
0–10	None noticeable.
10–20	Tightness across forehead and slight headache.
20–30	Headache and throbbing of the temples; breathlessness on exertion and perhaps nausea.
30–40	Severe headache, weakness, dizziness, dimness of vision, nausea and vomiting, collapse.
Over 40	Increasing liklihood of collapse, increasing pulse rate, irregular breathing, coma, convulsions, respiratory failure.

Fig. 2-4. Symptoms of carbon monoxide poisoning. R.L. DeHart: *Fundamentals of Aerospace Medicine*. Philadelphia, Lee & Febiger, 1985. Reproduced with permission.

Treatment. Like hypoxia, the treatment is immediate 100 percent oxygen. Unlike hypoxia, however, this treatment is an extremely slow process, taking several days for high carbon monoxide concentrations to be reduced to normal levels. Although the symptoms of hypoxia and carbon monoxide poisoning look alike, going to 100 percent oxygen will not immediately relieve carbon monoxide poisoning symptoms as it would with hypoxic hypoxia. This is another clue to determine why you or a crewmate is impaired.

CABIN DECOMPRESSION

Decompression occurs when cabin pressure is lost for any reason. The cabin altitude decompresses to the ambient pressure. In other words, if the cabin is pressurized to 6,000 feet and you are flying at 20,000 feet and a leak develops, your cabin can suddenly be at 20,000 feet.

A rapid decompression is characterized by a loud popping noise. Concurrently there is usually flying debris, paper, and dust, with some items being sucked out of the aircraft as the pressurized air rushes out the hole into lower pressure. Sudden fogging is very common and is sometimes confused with smoke. The temperature suddenly drops to equalize the outside temperature, often a significant change because ambient temperature at 35,000 feet is about $-67°$F.

Subtle decompression could be considered the most potentially dangerous in the sense that you might not be aware that your cabin altitude is going up. Not all pressurized airplanes give any warning about cabin ascent rate or that a dangerous altitude has been reached. Decompressions happen even with modern aircraft.

The most noticeable effects of all but the most subtle decompressions are first the sudden rush of air from the lungs. Trapped gas problems should not be significant unless it's an explosive decompression. Having a cold or flu increases the risk of problems. The primary concern is the sudden exposure to extreme hypoxic and cold conditions, especially at high altitudes. The treatment remains the same: get on oxygen, get to a lower altitude, and, of course, fly the airplane.

EAR BLOCKS AND OTHER PROBLEMS

Your body can withstand tremendous changes in pressure as long as the air pressure in your body cavities is able to equalize with the ambient air pressure. In other words, the pressure inside any part or organ of your body where gas is present does not cause any problems unless that pressure is not the same as the pressure surrounding that cavity. Problems occur when the expanding (or contracting) gas within your body cannot escape to allow ambient and body pressures to equalize. When gases within body fluids such as blood, escape from the fluid and enter your body as a gas (evolved gas), it also causes problems.

Dysbarism is a synonym often used for the bends and sometimes associated with trapped gas. It is no longer an accepted term since it is too nonspecific. It is better to use the terms *trapped gas, ear block,* or *sinus block.*

As a result of greater differential in pressure per thousand feet at lower altitudes, the risk of developing any kind of block is higher below

Usual ear clearing technique allows pressure to equalize.

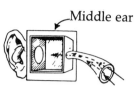

Middle ear

With ear blocked, pressure cannot be equalized.

Tube is swollen by a cold or collapsed by pressure.

Eustachian tube is okay.

Fig. 2-5. Common methods of clearing an ear block won't work if the block is the result of the mucous membranes being swollen from a cold or hay fever.

15,000 feet. In other words, a rapid descent from 30,000 feet to 20,000 feet often causes little or no discomfort, whereas a similar rate of descent from 15,000 feet to 5,000 feet causes great distress. The greatest pressure change (differential) is from sea level to 5,000 feet, and this is where most blocks occur. This effect is also noticed in scuba diving where the most significant pressure changes occur in the first 15 to 30 feet.

Middle ear block (Barotitis)

During ascent, as the ambient air pressure is reduced, the expanding air within the middle ear is intermittently released through the eustachian tube (Fig. 2-5). During descent the same process should take place, but in the opposite direction. This equalization of pressure on either side of the eardrum is essential for proper hearing since the flexibility of your eardrum must not be compromised. As the pressure increases in the middle ear, a small bubble forms which, after it reaches a certain size, escapes through your eustachian tube. You can often feel this equalization of pressure as the air bubble "pops" out.

This pressure equalization should be automatic without any conscious effort, especially under ideal conditions. Normal swallowing often clears the ears. Problems arise when your eustachian tube does not allow passage of air, usually a result of the mucous membranes inside the eustachian tube being swollen from a cold or hayfever. Often, the passage of air is only outward and not back into the middle ear—a type of one-way valve.

An unexpected, delayed cause occurs when breathing oxygen, as in unpressurized cabins at altitudes requiring oxygen breathing masks. Here, pure undiluted oxygen enters the cavity. If a block occurs and it is unable to be cleared, the cavity is now pressurized with oxygen which, in turn, is absorbed by the mucous membranes. Now, instead of high pressure, a lower pressure develops with equally disabling symptoms. This phenomenon is experienced fairly often by passengers who sleep through the flight, are not actively clearing their ears (their swallowing rate decreases during sleep), and during descent develop a mild block.

However, in all these situations, the real problem occurs a few hours later, when you are on the ground because the oxygen has been absorbed in the still blocked ear. The pain is now worse or it returns. Now it's time to see the doctor.

Symptoms. Inability to clear your ears (equalize pressure) can result in everything from mild discomfort to severe pain in the middle ear that often radiates to the side of your head—a true disabling earache. Anyone who has ever had an ear block never wants to experience it again. It is worse than a severe toothache. The pain becomes worse as the pressure changes and does not always go away even after you have landed. Sometimes, the trapped gas within the middle ear reaches a pressure high enough that the eardrum ruptures. The good news is that after a rupture the pain almost instantly goes away. The bad news is that now you have a tear in your eardrum, need treatment by a physician and could be grounded.

Generally, ear blocks occur on descent and often clear themselves on ascent. This is a result of the nasal end of the eustachian tube acting like a one-way valve for air passage.

Whatever the cause of the ear block, you are now disabled, potentially incapacitated, or at the very least, distracted from flying duties. The ear can be physically damaged, sometimes permanently. Despite continuing awareness of the causes of ear blocks and the dangers associated, pilots still get into trouble. A major cause is flying with a cold and delaying the use of techniques to clear your ears.

Treatment and prevention. As with many things in flying, the best treatment for a medical problem is to prevent it from happening. I'm sure you have heard that flying with a cold or congestion is asking for trouble, yet many pilots fly under these conditions. Admittedly, only a few develop a serious block, but that infrequent event is a major risk to safe flight.

In reality, if every pilot grounded himself for every sniffle, few would be flying. Therefore, if you have a mild congestion (and there is no good definition of *mild*), then taking some decongestant medication before you begin the flight might be appropriate. This medication must not contain antihistamines! Some long-acting cortisone-type nose sprays might also allow you to fly. The dilemma is that, technically, no medications are legal or safe if there is any possibility that side effects could compromise your performance or the condition you are treating. Most AMEs should be able to help you decide, but the ultimate decision and responsibility is yours.

If you are prone to early ear blocks, it might be wise to carry a small bottle of nose spray in your flight bag. It should be used only when you sense a block developing in flight—early enough that the spray has a chance to take effect, but only after all other measures have failed to relieve the block.

The safest and most common method of clearing an ear block is to move the jaw and swallow at the same time. Chewing gum is a great way to do this. Yawning, moving your head around, or a combination of both often clear the ear.

Another technique, and probably the most effective, is the Valsalva maneuver. Again, as soon as a block begins to develop (you sense some mild pressure in your ears), hold the fleshy part of your nose tight (as if you were going to jump into a pool of water). Then blow hard against your nose (as if you wanted to blow your nose). This maneuver often increases the pressure within the nasal area and forces air back into the middle ear through the eustachian tube. It is not likely that you can blow hard enough to injure the eardrum, so it's okay to blow fairly hard. This procedure is the same that scuba divers always use when descending.

If all these tricks fail, consider taking the aircraft (or cabin altitude) higher, to a level above where the block began. Then begin a very slow descent, using the techniques already mentioned, but now under controlled conditions.

If a block persists after landing, see your doctor. Unresolved blocks can lead to inflammation and sometimes infection. A middle ear infection will temporarily ground you.

Sinus block (Barosinusitis)

Basically, the same events occur with your sinuses except the openings to the sinus cavities are much smaller and the Valsalva technique is not as effective. The pain from a sinus block is as incapacitating as an ear block, and often more so. It is often said that a sinus block feels like an ice pick in the face. All the more reason to be cautious in flying with a cold or hayfever. Additionally, the sinuses are affected by both ascent and descent, unlike the middle ear.

Teeth (Barodontalgia)

Tooth problems are caused by cavities, abscesses, and inadequate fillings. Pain often increases with altitude and can become disabling. Descent usually brings some relief. Dental intervention is essential once such a block is recognized. Explain to the dentist what the circumstances are relating to the tooth pain. If it feels as if the entire top row of teeth are hurting, or if the discomfort occurs on descent, it is probably a sinus block rather than tooth pain.

THE BENDS

Evolved gas disorders, the physiological/physical event that occurs in varying pressures, is known by different names, and the entire issue is often minimized by the aviation community. Scuba divers are very much aware of what can happen to gases dissolved in the blood and released under lower ambient pressures. The physiology and anatomy is the same for flyers, and decompression sickness can and does occur in the flight environment, although slower and at much higher altitudes. The following are some of the terminology used when discussing evolved gas disorders.

DCS, or decompression sickness. Decompression sickness is the generic medical term used to identify all degrees and variations of evolved gas disorders. It does not include trapped gas disorders. DCS means only those conditions that result from gases dissolved within the blood and tissues that are released when the surrounding pressure decreases. It results in small bubbles now being transported by the blood to various organs and parts of your body.

Aeroembolism. By definition, aeroembolism means air (as a bubble) is acting as an embolism or blockage that can move throughout your body. An embolism often means a blood clot but generally can include anything that could obstruct a blood vessel, such as a bubble of air.

Bends. Bends is the most common term used in discussing DCS, especially in scuba diving. It is one kind of DCS, specifically involving the joints. It does not, however, refer to the other kinds of DCS, which are actually more dangerous. DCS usually refers to involvement of the nervous system. In actuality, bends is by far the most common type (over 85 percent) of DCS problems.

Basic physiology

Henry's Gas Law states that the amount of gas dissolved in a solution is directly proportional to the pressure of the gas over the solution. Observe what happens when you remove the top or pull the tab on a bottle or can of pop or beer. As you know, the contents are under pressure. When that pressure is released, so is the gas (in this case CO_2), and bubbles immediately form and come to the surface. Nitrogen dissolved in the blood responds the same way. As pressure outside the body decreases, gas—mainly nitrogen, which is 80 percent of air—is evolved from the blood and transported as bubbles throughout the body.

Of additional interest is the fact that fat tissue dissolves five to six times more nitrogen than blood. Any extra fat that a pilot has covering the body and internal organs now becomes an additional source of nitrogen and puts that pilot at increased risk of developing DCS problems at higher altitudes.

Physiologically, these gases, especially nitrogen, have the potential of being released into the bloodstream as pressures change over time. For example, inhaled air at sea level is absorbed into tissues and blood. After ascending to higher cabin altitudes (greater than 18,000 feet) and staying there for a few hours, some of those gases are released into the blood. If this continues, more bubbles are formed until the cabin altitude returns to sea level. The symptoms that result along with the effects on your body are what concern you when you fly at these altitudes.

Effects on the body

Circulatory system. These gas bubbles can act as a blockage within smaller vessels and are called *aeroembolisms*. Such blockage is of minimal consequence until the bubbles get larger or more vessels become blocked. The ultimate problem exists in your body's organs.

Musculoskeletal system. Pain will be noticed in the larger joints, such as the knee, shoulder, elbows, etc. It is often described as a "gnawing" ache, ranging from mild to severe, and obviously either distracting or incapacitating in the cockpit. This pain is also called the bends. The pain tends to be progressive, especially as ascent is continued. There is also the tendency for pain to recur in the same location during subsequent flights. It can involve several joints at the same time.

Paresthesia. By definition, paresthesia is involvement of nerves, causing abnormal sensations such as tingling, itching, and cold and warm feelings. It is thought that this reaction is from the bubbles forming locally around nerve tracts in the skin. Such symptoms are also found in hypoxia and hyperventilation, which means that you must be aware of the environment that you are in. You must consider which has the greatest chance of occurring before deciding if you are suffering from DCS or some other condition. Another term is *skin manifestations* of DCS.

Chokes. These symptoms are related to the chest (thorax) and lungs. Here the bubbles intrude on the pulmonary vessels (blood vessels carrying blood into the lung tissue). The first signs are a burning sensation mid-chest (sternum), which progresses to a stabbing pain accentuated by deep breathing. It is similar to the feeling after a sudden burst of exercise where it is difficult to catch your breath. There is an almost uncontrollable need to cough, but the cough is ineffective and doesn't come up with anything. Finally, there is a feeling of suffocation, with typical signs of cyanosis (decreased oxygen supply). Immediate descent is necessary because it is a potential medical emergency. If no intervention takes place, this condition leads to collapse and unconsciousness. In fact, after getting to the ground, there will still be fatigue and soreness about the chest for several hours.

Disorders of the brain (central nervous system). Although uncommon, these disorders are very serious. What is happening is that the brain and spinal cord are now involved with these nitrogen bubbles. The most common symptoms are visual, such as flashing or flickering lights. Other symptoms are headaches, paralysis, inability to hear or speak, and loss of orientation. Any of these symptoms (in the appropriate conditions of flight) should be highly suspect and are considered a medical emergency. As with other symptoms, these are easily confused with hypoxia and pulling Gs. Keeping a high index of suspicion is important if you are flying high over a period of time.

Prevention

DCS is very uncommon in typical flying. The bends do occur, however, in unpressurized smaller aircraft flying at altitudes above 15,000 feet, even though oxygen is being used. Therefore, if you are in conditions of high cabin altitudes or know you will be going there (even in a helicopter going from sea level to mountaintop rescues), anticipate that you could be affected. If you think you are susceptible, the following should help prevent problems.

Denitrogenation. Breathing 100 percent oxygen for 30 minutes prior to takeoff rids the body of some of the excess nitrogen. The amount of nitrogen lost is related to time but usually takes place within 30 minutes. This reduced partial pressure of nitrogen over a period of time helps prevent bubble formation. Denitrogenation takes place over several hours, but a large percentage is in the first half hour.

Pressurized cabin. Most cabins are pressurized to less than 10,000 feet. If there is no pressurization or it is lost through mechanical means (decompression), then you must be aware of the possibility of DCS.

Factors affecting severity

Time at altitude. The longer you are at excessive altitude, the greater the risk for developing DCS because more bubbles can form and be transported throughout your body.

Rate of ascent. The more rapid the ascent, the greater the chance of bubble formation because your body has little time to equalize the pressure changes.

Altitude. The threshold for developing DCS problems is usually above 18,000 feet. It increases more rapidly above 26,000 feet.

Age and obesity. Older people tend to be more susceptible to DCS. The same is true for obese people, whose fat stores more gas and nitrogen. It is also suspected that recent alcohol use can increase the risk.

Exercise and injury. Exercise is one of the most important factors influencing susceptibility. It is wise not to exert yourself prior to a flight or immediately after one at high altitude. A prior skeletal injury increases risk.

Repeated exposure. Taking several flights over a short period of time (48 hours) increases the chances of problems. Repeated insults to affected organs make them more susceptible.

In the real civilian world, the chances of developing DCS are small. However, being at altitude in IFR in a nonpressurized airplane or making several trips within a two-day period could lead to a situation that is ripe for DCS. Keep it in mind, especially if you are a scuba diver.

Scuba diving

DCS is a familiar term to scuba divers and is drilled into each diver continuously. The physiology is the same as for pilots at altitude, but the diver is more susceptible because there is a greater differential in pressure in water and in shorter distances. For example, pressure in water doubles at 30 feet whereas in flight you have to go from 18,000 feet to sea level to double the pressures.

What happens is that at only 33 feet in water, your body absorbs twice as much nitrogen from the scuba air tank (the tank does not carry oxygen; it's pressurized air). Every diver knows this and anticipates problems when returning to the surface. Prevention of problems is understanding the diving table, known to all divers, which determines the steps to take to prevent DCS. These steps do not include climbing into an airplane and further decreasing the pressure surrounding the body.

A rule of thumb: Don't take one more dive the same day before leaving for home in a plane whose cabin altitude is probably around 8,000 feet. The same situation is present as if you were flying at 40,000 feet unpressurized! The recommended waiting time is 12 hours after the last dive and at least 24 hours if you were part of a dive that required a controlled ascent (decompression stop dive). Current studies are suggesting that these times should be increased.

If DCS is suspected in a scuba diver, then that diver must get to a hyperbaric chamber (recompression) and be monitored by medical personnel. The dive shop should have the number of your closest chamber for treatment through an organization called DAN (Divers Alert Network).

Altitude chamber ride

This experience is common for military aircrew and is offered to the civilian pilot. Although not required, it is highly recommended that you have at least one chamber ride early in your flight training for a number of reasons:

- To experience the basic symptoms of hypoxia and decompression.
- To recognize personal symptoms before they become disabling. Because everyone responds differently to the same conditions, it is important to know what your unique symptoms are. Only through the chamber ride can you determine your signs and symptoms.
- To experience rapid decompression (R/D) in controlled conditions and realize that it is not the terrifying situation you might think it is. Also, it helps you realize the shock of R/D and how it can immobilize you and hinder your reactions.
- To gain confidence in and respect for high-altitude flight, especially for the insidious effects of hypoxia.
- To determine if you are prone to ear and sinus blocks.

The ride profile might vary, but basically you are taken to altitude, experience hypoxia and trapped gas, are shown the effects on other participants so that you can detect these problems in others, and then brought down (Fig. 2-6). The most useful part is to be able to recognize your own symptoms of early hypoxia so that you can take immediate action (getting on oxygen) before you are unaware that you are disabled or incapacitated. You are also shown the effect of hypoxia on night vision and what it is like to pressure-breathe.

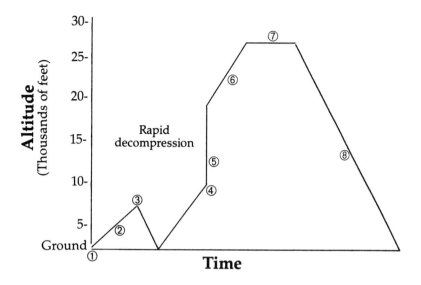

Altitude chamber flight profile

1. Preflight briefing.
2. Mask fitting and operation of oxygen regulator and intercom system in chamber.
3. Ascend to 6,000 feet and descend to ground level to determine proper clearing of ears and sinus cavities. Rate of ascent and descent is 3,000 feet per minute.
4. Reascend to 8,000 feet at a rate of 3,000 feet per minute.
5. Rapid decompression (8–10 seconds) from 8,000 feet to 18,000 feet. Masks will be donned during the decompression.
6. Ascend to 25,000 feet at the rate of 3,500 feet per minute.
7. Removal of masks at 25,000 feet to enable trainees to experience symptoms of hypoxia. Five minutes time limit off supplemental oxygen.
8. Descend to ground level at the rate of 3,000 feet per minute. Trainees will practice pressure breathing and discuss their hypoxia symptoms on descent.

Fig. 2-6. Every pilot should take at least one altitude chamber flight in his or her career.

3

Disorientation
in flight

. . . The captain had become so preoccupied with the dwindling airspeed that he failed to note that the autopilot, which relied exclusively on ailerons to maintain heading, was using the maximum left control-wheel deflection available to it to overcome the thrust asymmetry caused by the hung outboard engine. Even when the right wing began to drop, the captain didn't notice the bank on the attitude director indicator, despite the fact that the instrument was located right next to the airspeed indicator. When he finally did notice it, he refused to believe what he saw. By this point, the upset had already begun, and the captain and first officer were both spatially disoriented. What happened during the next two minutes and 20,000 feet is anybody's guess.

As previously stated, the greatest challenge to you and your fitness to fly is the prevention of a medical incapacitation. If you, your passengers, and the FAA could be guaranteed that you or your crew would not become incapacitated in flight—providing the airplane works—the aviation community would have few concerns about safety. One lingering concern, however, would be orientation.

If your plane works, and you are not impaired medically, then the only other significant ingredient in safe flight is maintaining orientation of the plane and yourself. Orientation is the key element in accident and incident prevention. *Situation awareness*, a term used in conjunction with orientation, includes the awareness of what's going on with other aircraft, weather, ATC, etc. Lack of orientation (or awareness of your situation) is *disorientation*, which is found in various forms. These include temporal, postural, vestibular, positional, rotational, auditory, and spatial, all of which, by themselves or in combination with others, can make an otherwise uneventful flight a memorable event.

Disorientation is a leading cause (not just a contributing factor) for more than 15 percent of aviation accidents and incidents. All pilots experience disorientation at one time or another, and most situations go unreported. This is true for both military and civilian aviation. In most cases, the pilot and crew recover from being disoriented and no one beyond the crew is the wiser.

Because few such scenarios are officially reported, disorientation does not show up in human factors statistics as frequently as it actually occurs. But if you listen to your colleagues talk in the crew lounge, you will recognize that disorientation is happening frequently, and not just with you. Knowing that disorientation occurs, it is your responsibility to respect this fact and to continue to take measures to prevent disorientation by maintaining an awareness of what affects orientation in the flight environment as well as keeping current in flight proficiency. Experiencing the effects of disorientation through unusual attitude flight or Vertigon simulators reinforces the power of this human factor on maintaining control of the aircraft.

Therefore, the objective of this chapter is to raise your level of awareness, to identify conditions that lead to the various kinds of disorientation, and to discuss measures to minimize the occurrence of disorientation. Intolerance to confusing signals from the body is increased even if you are only minimally impaired physiologically, increasing the risk of becoming disorientated. Put another way, you can easily become disoriented for a variety of reasons, which results in further incapacitation. Like a graveyard spiral, these cumulative factors eventually lead to a performance problem sufficient enough to cause an accident or incident.

TYPES OF DISORIENTATION

To be oriented is to be adjusted to a particular point of reference in any situation. That's a basic definition. It follows that if you aren't oriented to a particular situation, you must be disoriented. This is just plain common sense. The body uses several senses to orient itself. Vision is the most important, followed by vestibular (inner ear), and then proprioceptive (relative muscle position). I discuss each in terms of how they can give proper, accurate, yet occasionally misleading cues. Often there is a conflict between these cues from the different sources, thus creating more confusion.

Indications of loss of situation awareness

- No one looking out windows.
- No one flying.
- Expectations of event are not met.
- Pilot or crew unsure of condition of aircraft.
- Two or more sources of independent information don't agree.
- Confusion, questions, or statements of concern are not resolved.
- Attention of crew focused on one item, event, or condition to exclusion of all other activity.
- Consideration is given to using an undocumented procedure.
- Consideration is given to violating minimums.

Postural disorientation

A constant source of sensory input comes from your body's interpretation of the direction of gravitational force through proprioceptive signals—signals from various muscles and tendons in your body. Your mind is programmed to interpret these signals as being up or down, relative to the earth and its gravitational pull. This in turn determines your posture, your position relative to the ground. Concurrently, there are proprioceptive sensors within your skin, muscles, tendons, and joints that detect changes in relative position, pressure, and changes from up or down. Proprioceptive signals are those generated every time a muscle contracts or relaxes, tendons are pulled or released, or joints move. All these inputs continuously coming to your brain tell you what position you are in, usually relative to the common foundation of gravity. It's similar to INS navigation whereby avionics determine your plane's current position relative to where it started the flight.

Another source of signals defining posture is part of your vestibular system, the otolith organs, located in your inner ear. When your body is subjected to up and down changes, these signals play a role, along with proprioception, in determining your position.

Since gravity is "down" to the mind, any input from proprioception or the otolith organs is interpreted as either being "down" or a deviation from that position. Your largest source of such information is when you are sitting down. Comfortable postural orientation in flight is felt in a well-coordinated turn, where all postural signals are indicating that you are sitting upright, directly related to gravity. If your turn is coordinated, and doesn't disrupt your vestibular system, and your position is also confirmed visually, there is no impairment to your perception of performance.

However, in an improperly executed turn, especially in a climb, these signals become very confusing to your brain, giving false illusions as to your true posture. Rather than being pushed into the seat, your body is pushed sideways as in a skid or slip, giving the impression of tilting. In the absence of visual reference, the only sensation is your body being pressed into the seat, but not necessarily towards the ground. For example, recovering from such a situation in a climb gives the illusion of descending, causing you to pull back on the stick.

Positional disorientation

Positional disorientation basically means that you are lost, if even for a brief moment, and you don't know your position. You become disoriented until you can resolve where you are and where you are heading. In other words, for a while you don't know what to do. Do you keep going, go back, call for directions, or what? Positional disorientation is also referred to as geographic and directional. They all mean the same—you are temporarily lost!

All animals are creatures of habit, especially humans. Much of what you do, day after day, is a routine that you do the same way and usually without too much thought. Interrupt that routine and you are disoriented and don't know how to continue without having to think about it. Take for example how you take a shower (or bath). Most people wash the same way, each time starting at one part of the body and ending up at another. If you start with the front of your left shoulder, for example, that's how you start every time.

Next time you bathe, change the sequence. Start with your right foot. Now you have to think about what to wash next. This is no longer your routine and for a moment you are lost on your own body. You are briefly disoriented.

The same thing happens on familiar routes. You fly the same airways, talk to the same controllers, make the same approaches on all the legs of the trip. When you flew the route for the first time, you concentrated on maintaining your awareness of where you were. Then the trip truly became routine—nothing to break the monotony of the hundredth trip— and it became easy to fall into the trap of passing a check point, or flying right by it without knowing it. Now if ATC gives you a revised flight plan or changes your heading for traffic, you might miss the new clearance and continue on the same flight path you have always done before. Or you might set up your approach to the wrong airport or runway.

You become more susceptible to positional disorientation if you become distracted. You might be thinking about problems at home, concentrating on some activity in the cockpit unrelated to flying (reading a manual or listening to a commercial radio station), or involved in a conversation with a crewmate. Now both of you are out of the loop of maintaining positional awareness.

Another trap is the return flight or "get-homitis." It becomes more pervasive than the initial leg because there is the added distraction of anticipating what needs to be done at home. In any case, your checklists, which have been read many times before, become superficially reviewed. Distances, checkpoints, and waypoints become committed to memory (or so you think). Even familiar frequencies are part of this virtually automatic flight. Now throw in any deviation from the expected routine, or a malfunction of the aircraft, and you are easily disoriented. You have to spend time reasoning out what needs to be done to correct the problem and get back on course.

Pride often gets in the way when you think that you can get out of this fix without having to refer to manuals or maps. Certainly you might be reluctant to admit to ATC or even a crewmate that you are lost or that you forgot the controlling center's frequency. Consider how this situation could be amplified if, at the same time, you enter actual instrument conditions. This combination of positional and potential vestibular disorientation is an incident or accident waiting to happen.

Temporal disorientation

Disorientation relative to time (also called *temporal disorientation*) is subjective. How long an activity lasts in your mind depends on the level of activity and interest occurring at that time. Time can be perceived as being expanded; that is, you think you have more time to accomplish some action. On the other hand, time can appear compressed, with you feeling that more time has passed than actually has. This is common in monotonous, slow, and uninteresting activities.

There is little known as to why this happens in the mind. There is some suspicion that the amount of adrenaline flowing through your body determines how much time you perceive is available.

Adrenaline is the hormonal chemical that is released in fight-or-flight situations, allowing your body to respond to unexpected and emergency situations. With extra "emergency" adrenaline, blood flow is shunted to critical organs such as muscles, heart, and brain. Pulse rate and blood pressure go up. Your brain now becomes more intensely alert and processes information at an accelerated rate.

Whatever the reason, the perception of time expansion is real in your mind during the critical event. It becomes a concern because in an emergency situation you might take too long to react, thinking that plenty of time is available to try some other course of action.

The opposite is true during periods demanding minimal mental and physical activity. Here time drags on although you feel it is moving faster. This problem is less critical than time expansion because the actual prolonged time makes the trip even more boring but doesn't affect performance other than increasing the likelihood of positional disorientation.

Vestibular disorientation

As mentioned before, vestibular disorientation is the term commonly used for *spatial disorientation* and is also compared to the feeling of vertigo. While they are similar and often occur with each other, they are separate entities.

Vertigo is the feeling you recognize when you are actually experiencing vestibular disorientation. Disorientation from dysfunction of the vestibular system is probably the most severe and intense feeling of instability or unbalance. It is felt that this is the source of most motion sickness problems. In fact, even experienced pilots can get airsick under conditions of flight that interrupt their vestibular system. Although vision is still the most important source of orientation signals, the vestibular source of signals is the most difficult to cope with and the hardest from which to recover.

The vestibular system, located in the inner ear (Fig. 3-1) contains two distinct structures—the otolith organs, which sense linear acceleration and gravity, and the semicircular canals, which sense angular acceleration.

Otolith organs. Changes in the position of your head relative to the gravitational force cause the otolithic membrane to shift position on the macula, thus bending the sensory hairs and signaling the change in head position (Fig. 3-2). When your head is upright, a "resting" frequency of nerve impulses is generated by the hair cells. When your head is tilted, the resting frequency is altered to inform the brain of the new position of your head relative to the vertical.

Semicircular canals. This organ responds to roll, pitch, and yaw. It is similar to three gyros in three planes of direction perpendicular to each other (Fig. 3-3). Bending of the cupula results in movement of the hair cells situated beneath the cupula. (These hair cells move in the same way that sea grass moves with the water currents and wheat fields move in the wind. As the currents and winds change, so does the movement of the plants.) This movement in turn stimulates the vestibular nerve, whose impulses are transmitted to your brain where they are interpreted as rotation of your head.

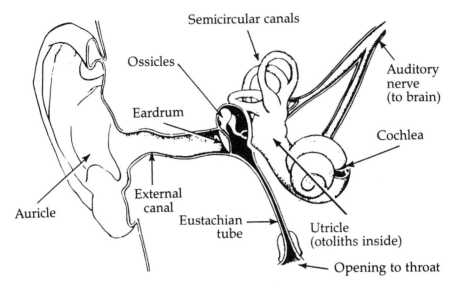

Fig. 3-1. Anatomy of the ear.

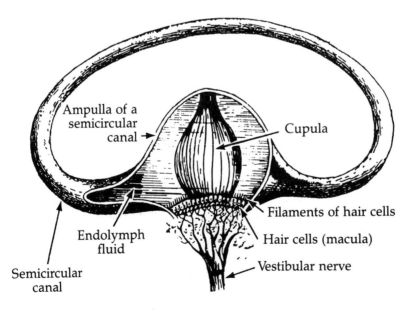

Fig. 3-2. Semicircular canal.

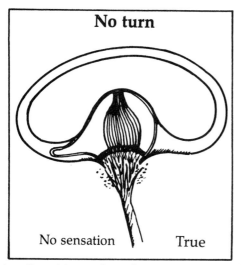

No turn

No sensation   True

Hair cell position and resulting sensation under nonacceleration conditions.

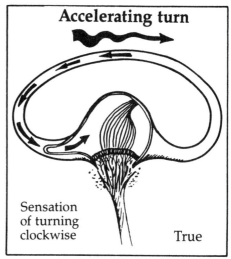

Accelerating turn

Sensation of turning clockwise   True

Hair cell position and resulting sensation under conditions of acceleration to the right.

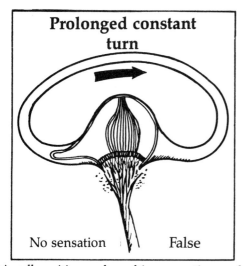

Prolonged constant turn

No sensation   False

Hair cell position and resulting sensation under conditions of prolonged constant turn.

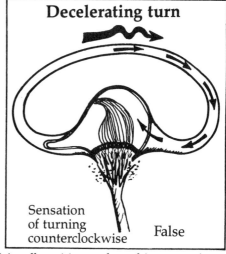

Decelerating turn

Sensation of turning counterclockwise   False

Hair cell position and resulting sensation under conditions of sudden stop or slowing.

Fig. 3-3. Hair cells change position during turns.

When no acceleration takes place, the hair cells do not move but remain upright and a sense of no turn is felt. When a semicircular canal is put into motion, as during the acceleration of a turn, the fluid within the canals moves but there is a lag in the response along the canal walls. This bends the hair cells in the direction opposite that of the acceleration. The brain interprets the movement of the hairs as motion, or a turn.

Vestibular illusions. The vestibular system, along with other sources of orienting sensations, works well in keeping you "balanced" with the rest of the world (Fig. 3-4). However, when subjected to the variables of flight's different forces on your body, these sources do not function in a manner that your body and mind are used to and can give you misleading information.

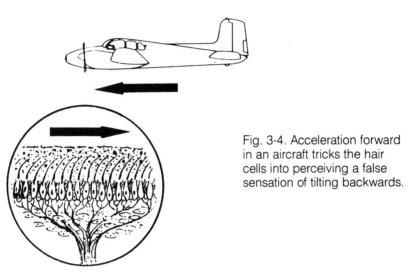

Fig. 3-4. Acceleration forward in an aircraft tricks the hair cells into perceiving a false sensation of tilting backwards.

False sensation of tilt backward.

Coriolis. This illusion is the most dangerous because of its often overwhelming sense of disorientation, and it can occur in any phase of flight where some type of climbing or descending turn is initiated. In weather, coriolis is the effect on wind as it passes over a rotating earth. In physiology, it represents the tumbling of your internal gyros or the semicircular canals (Fig. 3-5). Some pilots describe the sensation as resembling a giant hand taking over their instruments, fighting their urge to move the stick.

When you and your airplane are straight and level and without acceleration, the fluid in your semicircular canals is in equilibrium, not moving. Now, when your aircraft turns and banks, the accelerative force on the fluid tells you there is a change. If you stay in that turn, the fluid once again reaches equilibrium and does not move. In other words, only when there is change does the fluid move and give out a signal. All three planes of the canals are affected to varying degrees depending on the rate and degree of turn.

The coriolis illusion

If a semicircular canal is rotated in one plane until the fluid is going the same speed as the canal walls, then the canal is tilted out of the plane of rotation. The fluid flows briefly in the canal while it is in its new plane.

The resulting sensation is one of rotation in the plane of the new position of the canal, even though no actual motion has occurred in that plane.

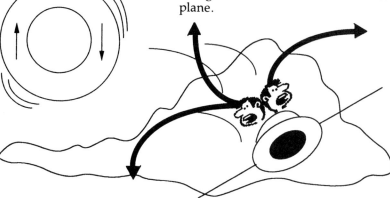

Fig. 3-5. If a pilot moves his or her head abruptly during a prolonged turn, the coriolis effect can cause an overwhelming illusion of change of aircraft attitude.

If the turn is coordinated and not abrupt, minimal misinformation goes to your brain. If, however, during this maneuver, you turn your head in a different direction from the turn, such as downward, one of these planes is disrupted—tumbled—and sends a misleading cue as if the plane is in a roll or yaw. The coriolis illusion makes you perceive your aircraft to be doing maneuvers that it is not actually doing. This illusion can also be induced in turbulence during a climb or a descending turn. It's the sudden change to the vestibular apparatus that causes this illusion.

Without a visual reference to the horizon, this illusion can overpower your recognized need to recover, creating a conflict between the sensation expected in the maneuver and the requirement to control the aircraft against that sensation. It is easier to demonstrate this illusion than to describe it, and this is why unusual attitudes are practiced in flight and why it is recommended that a ride in a Vertigon (a simulator that demonstrates coriolis) be experienced.

Leans. This illusion is the most common and occurs when you sense a bank angle when the aircraft is actually in level flight (Fig. 3-6). If you

The leans

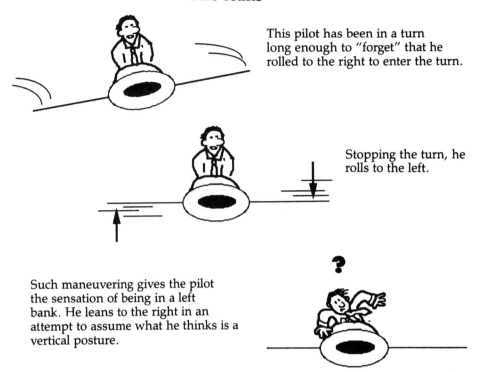

This pilot has been in a turn long enough to "forget" that he rolled to the right to enter the turn.

Stopping the turn, he rolls to the left.

Such maneuvering gives the pilot the sensation of being in a left bank. He leans to the right in an attempt to assume what he thinks is a vertical posture.

Fig. 3-6. The leans.

maintain the level attitude of the aircraft (as you should), you still feel compelled to align your body with the perceived vertical. In doing so, you actually lean in the opposite direction of the perceived turn.

The leans can easily occur if your attention is removed from the instruments for even a short period of time. If during this distraction your aircraft begins to turn slowly to the right, for example, undetected by you, the canals respond accordingly. After a period of time in the turn, your brain "forgets" that it is in a turn. When your attention is again directed back to the aircraft and instruments and you return to level flight, you will have a false sense that the aircraft is banking to the left. If you react to your senses rather than the instruments, you will roll your aircraft to the right.

Oculogravic illusion. When your aircraft accelerates or decelerates in level flight, your otolith organs sense a nose-high attitude relative to gravity (Fig. 3-7). If you react to that sensation without cross checking instruments, you might pitch the aircraft down. Deceleration causes a similar sensation of a nose-low attitude.

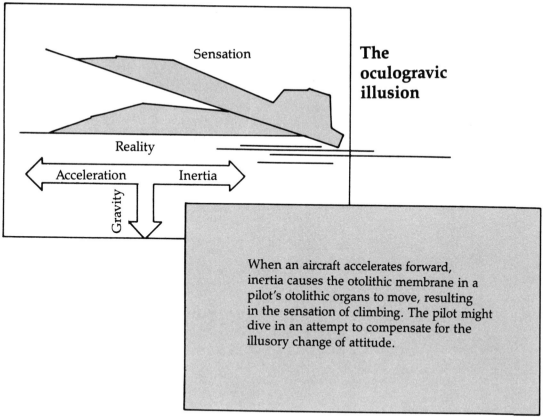

The oculogravic illusion

Sensation

Reality

Acceleration — Inertia

Gravity

When an aircraft accelerates forward, inertia causes the otolithic membrane in a pilot's otolithic organs to move, resulting in the sensation of climbing. The pilot might dive in an attempt to compensate for the illusory change of attitude.

Fig. 3-7. Oculogravic illusion.

Rotational illusion. Also called *angular motion illusion*, rotational illusions result from misinformation from a constant rate turn, as in a spin. If the turn is at a constant rate, the fluid in the canals returns to its original position of equilibrium. This results in your perception that the turn has stopped. When the turn slows (a change as in acceleration) or your aircraft levels off, the fluid is once again displaced but this time in the opposite direction.

The "graveyard spin" is a condition most likely to affect fixed-wing aircraft pilots (Fig. 3-8). Upon recovering from the turn (or spin in this case) as just described, you undergo deceleration, which is sensed by your semicircular canals and interpreted as a spin or turn in the opposite direction. Your instruments tell you that you are not spinning, but you have a strong sensation that you are. If there is no outside reference to the horizon and you disregard or don't believe the instruments, you are tempted to make control corrections against the falsely perceived spin so that you re-enter a spin in the original direction.

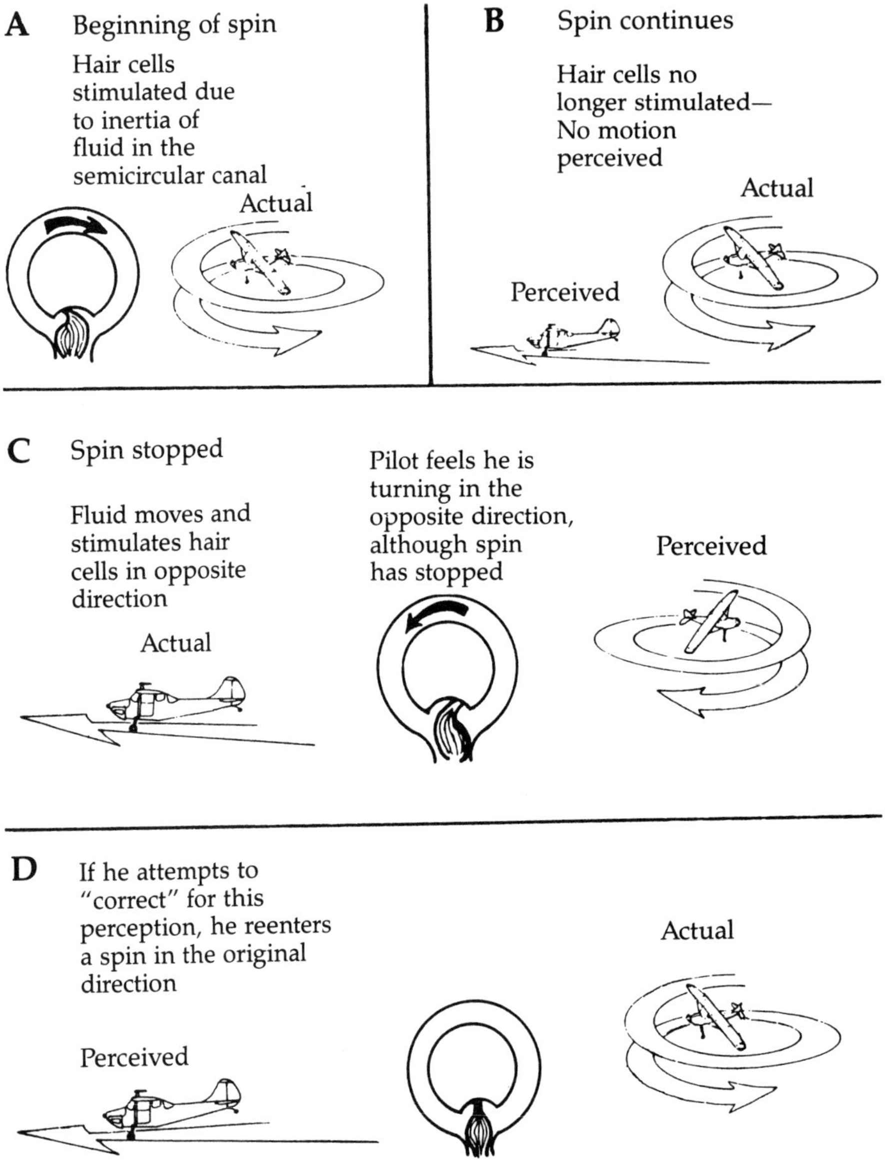

A Beginning of spin

Hair cells stimulated due to inertia of fluid in the semicircular canal

Actual

B Spin continues

Hair cells no longer stimulated— No motion perceived

Actual

Perceived

C Spin stopped

Fluid moves and stimulates hair cells in opposite direction

Actual

Pilot feels he is turning in the opposite direction, although spin has stopped

Perceived

D If he attempts to "correct" for this perception, he reenters a spin in the original direction

Actual

Perceived

Fig. 3-8. A graveyard spin illusion is a type of rotational illusion that is most likely to affect fixed-wing pilots.

This action is compounded by you noting a loss of altitude as the spin develops and applying back pressure on the controls and adding power in an attempt to gain altitude. This tightens the spin to the point where recovery is nearly impossible.

Spatial disorientation

Spatial disorientation defines illusions associated with relative motion, often called *vection illusion*. Furthermore, *spatial* infers a visual orientation; how you are oriented to the horizon as either straight and level, in a turn, or climbing or descending.

Treatment of spatial disorientation

- Get on the instruments and develop a good cross-check.

- Never try to fly both VFR and IFR at the same time.

- Delay intuitive actions long enough to check both visual references and your instruments.

- Transfer control if two pilots are in the aircraft. Seldom do two pilots experience disorientation at the same time.

Of all the senses available to provide input to your brain, vision provides the most valuable data. Some have determined that 90 percent of usable cues for orientation comes from vision. Your visual acuity comes from your central vision (foveal or focal), and your peripheral vision (ambient) supports your perceived position in space. This peripheral vision is so strong in relaying your body position to the brain that it is estimated that 90 percent of visual effects on orientation are from the peripheral vision. You can see the potential conflict in instrument conditions, where central vision is used to read your instruments and virtually no peripheral vision senses exist to establish spatial orientation.

Recognizing that peripheral vision is a powerful source of determining balance and orientation, it should be easy to recall the fact that everyone experiences spatial disorientation, whether in a car or an airplane. Looking straight ahead and concentrating on where you are going or scanning instruments maintains direction. However, take some visible objects, such as another airplane waiting next to you on the ramp, or flying through snow or rain and you feel the effects.

For example, you're sitting at an intersection in your car, waiting for the light to turn green, and you suddenly perceive your car moving backwards. You slam on your brakes only to realize your car is stationary. It's the car next to you, creeping forward in anticipation of the traffic light.

Your peripheral vision was telling you how to react with the relative motion of the two cars.

For helicopter pilots, the same illusion is apparent when hovering over tall grass, for example. The wave action of the moving grass gives you the sensation of moving, when in fact you are not. Flying in clouds with strobe and other anticollision lights generates the same confusing cues.

Instability varies, depending on many conditions. One of the intents of maintaining flying currency is to be able to suppress inputs from your peripheral vision and to increase dependency on your central (or focal) vision. Unfamiliarity with the aircraft also increases vulnerability to your peripheral vision cues.

Spatial disorientation, as described here, becomes a serious source of disorientation, especially in instrument conditions. If you are physiologically impaired (tired, hypoxic, using OTC drugs, etc.) you lose your ability to suppress inputs from your peripheral vision. You can quickly become incapacitated as a result of conflicting spatial senses.

VISUAL ILLUSIONS IN FLIGHT

Visual illusions affect what you perceive through vision, which in turn determines how you respond. It is more of a misguidance in a flying activity (such as landing and judging distances), as opposed to the "illusions" of disorientation, where your body automatically responds to physiological cues from your vestibular system and peripheral vision. They are obviously related in that they both can lead to incapacitation, especially when the events occur concurrently.

Autokinetic. Autokinesis is the perception of false movement when you look at a static source of light for a period of time (minutes) in the dark (Fig. 3-9). This moving reference point (an illusion) could lead you to follow it. Prevention is a combination of realizing the eye must focus on other objects at varying distances, not fixating on one target, and basic scanning.

Oculogyral. Oculogyral illusion was previously described under physiological disorientation. From the visual point of view, this illusion is more apparent at night, when vision is already compromised. You perceive the apparent movement of an object in the visual field as a result of stimulation of your semicircular canals. Therefore, in the early stages of a turn to the left, for example, the target appears to move rapidly to the left. After the turn is established and then stopped, the target object appears to move in the opposite direction, to the right. You might correct your aircraft accordingly unless you are scanning your instruments and confirming that you are tracking an illusion.

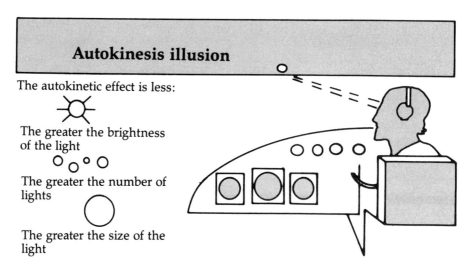

Autokinesis illusion

The autokinetic effect is less:

The greater the brightness of the light

The greater the number of lights

The greater the size of the light

Fig. 3-9. To a pilot suffering from autokinesis illusion, a static light, stared at for several seconds, appears to move.

Oculogravic. Also called *somatogravic illusion*, oculogravic illusion is a perception of tilt induced by stimulation of your otolith organs. From the visual perspective, the illusion to you is either a climb or a descent when you have no visual reference to the horizon. With a climb, your eyes try to compensate with a downward tracking, as is common when flying through an updraft. This illusion is also called an *elevator illusion*. The opposite illusion, familiar in helicopter flight in an autorotation, is the intuitive response of the pilot to change direction or altitude, which can decrease airspeed to below a desired level.

Visual cue illusions

In addition to how your body responds to cues from a variety of sources (disorientation), there are also strictly visual illusions that mislead you into erroneous actions. These are not physiological events as associated with the semicircular canals. It is the interpretation by your brain of an image as a result of the illusion of misleading visual cues. The greatest chance of these illusions affecting flight is in the landing phase and, to a lesser degree, in cruise where outside visual cues can be misleading.

Fog and haze. Depth perception, the ability of your brain to determine relative distance from visual cues, is compromised by any atmospheric conditions that interfere with light transmission. In addition to obscuring the ground and nearby outside obstacles for avoidance and orientation, fog and haze refract light rays differently than clear air, leading to out-of-focus acuity. Contrast is reduced, which is important in defining size and shape. It becomes difficult to judge distances, especially height above ground and distance from the end of the runway. Light from ground lights, including REILs, VASI, and runway and taxiway lights, are diffused, losing the detail necessary for a precision approach and landing. Penetration into fog can create the illusion of pitching up.

Water refraction. Rain on the windshield refracts incoming light rays, which misleads you concerning the position of the horizon. The perception is the horizon is below where it actually is, especially on an approach, resulting in a lower approach.

Landing visual illusions. Runway width that is narrower than usual or expected tends to make you think you are higher than you actually are and to therefore fly a lower approach. A runway width that is wider than expected has the opposite effect, with the approach being too high.

An upsloping runway or surrounding terrain can result in the illusion that your aircraft is higher than it actually is, resulting in a lower approach. Downsloping runways have the opposite result; the glide path appears low and the approach might be high.

The absence of ground features such as buildings and trees with which you can relate distance can cause you to think you are higher than you are. Flying an approach over water, for example, without frequent referral to instruments, results in a lower approach height.

Recognizing the importance and power of peripheral and central vision inputs to your brain, it should be respected that visual cues can be disorienting in addition to misleading. It should be obvious that the scan and cross-check of instruments becomes a critical part of any flight activity. Only practice and currency overcome these illusions.

COPING WITH DISORIENTATION

If a healthy pilot can become disoriented, and visual illusions affect everyone, then it must be recognized that a less-than-healthy pilot is at greater risk. Any one or combination of the following can degrade your performance, especially during critical phases of flight.

The following are all discussed in other chapters and are identified here to reinforce their importance. Conditions that can reduce your tolerance to overcoming the effects described previously include use of alcohol (even hours before a flight), hypoglycemia, fatigue, use of medications, illness, and hypoxia. If you know you are suffering from any of these conditions, you must be particularly careful about instrument scans and attentive to all communications and also maintain a high level of awareness and cross checking to monitor performance.

You can cope with these situations of disorientation and illusions by maintaining currency in familiar aircraft. Flight proficiency is also absolutely essential. The lack of either or both reduces your tolerance to these potentially incapacitating events. Every pilot knows that he or she is rusty in performance skills, often after only a few days of not flying. Flying instruments only once in a while puts you at high risk of unacceptable performance when eventful instrument conditions arise. There is no substitute for training and maintaining currency.

FLICKER VERTIGO

Flicker vertigo, a poorly understood sensation, is probably not as serious or frequent as one would expect. Some pilots, especially in helicopters, suffer a variety of symptoms from light that has a strobe-like flashing or flickering to the eyes. It occurs as light from the sun or other source is reflected off a propeller or rotor blades or interrupted in the same cycle by the props. The rate is about 4 to 20 cycles per second and can produce unpleasant and potentially dangerous reactions. Nausea, vomiting, and fatigue can result. In extreme cases in highly susceptible pilots, neurological reactions occur, such as convulsions and changes in levels of consciousness. The pilot who suffers from the previously mentioned conditions is also at higher risk. There is a great deal of anecdotal information but little scientific data to confirm actual "flicker vertigo."

THE AIRSICK PILOT

The vestibular system appears to be the source of the symptoms of motion sickness (airsickness). Any pilot subjected to the right combination of unusual attitudes or flight conditions can become airsick. In other words, if the semicircular canals can be "tumbled" in a way to which you are not adapted, then you become sick. There is no doubt that familiarity with the aircraft and its typical maneuvers, currency, and self-confidence are the best deterrents to airsickness.

Passengers (or pilots not in control of the aircraft) are easy subjects. New pilots are also susceptible. Some of the additional common causes include heat discomfort, anxiety, observing or smelling someone else who is airsick, and eating foods that are nauseating.

Most people know if they are prone to airsickness. Even so, there is no known dependable prevention technique or adequate treatment to help. Much research is being carried out because motion sickness is a prime concern in space travel. Some suggest that there is more chance of becoming airsick if one flies on an empty stomach. Therefore, you should eat simple foods that you know you can tolerate well, including adequate fluids. A variety of medications are available both over-the-counter and as prescriptions. However, there is little reliability or predictability from one person to another and side effects often accompany common drugs.

4

Flying in heat and cold extremes

"It was a balmy 72-degree February day when our crew left Kansas for a five-day trip to Alaska. The reality of where we had landed hit us square in the face when we opened the hatch upon landing and experienced −50 degrees (which was actual temperature—no wind chill added). After unloading our gear, I had to sit in the cockpit while the aircraft was towed (power off). It was the worst 15 minutes I had ever spent in a cockpit. My body began to shiver almost uncontrollably. I couldn't move switches because I couldn't grab them. All of my mental and physical actions slowed down as I tried to move as little as possible. After returning to the hotel I remembered how exhausting those 15 minutes were—I could hardly get my winter clothing off. On the return trip, we were in such a scramble to get through the preflight and get airborne that after takeoff I noticed that the fuel panel switches had been improperly positioned, all because we had rushed."

Few places on earth have a constant weather system, no matter where you live. Temperatures, winds, dewpoints (humidity), and rain are continually changing. Some parts of the world have weather extremes that last for months, allowing inhabitants to acclimate to the season. Those of you living and flying in the northern latitudes of the northern hemisphere adapt to cold winters, whereas those of you living in the hot humid areas would find the conditions in the north during winter not only unbearable but dangerous.

Your body and mind have the metabolic resources to respond to these variations and extremes, which allows you to continue to perform. On the other hand, your body also reacts in adverse ways, which interferes with expected performance, again, both physically and mentally. This interference equates to impairment of your piloting skills, making you less than safe and, in effect, incapacitated.

Today's flying machines now take us great distances, not only within our own country but also around the world, all in a matter of a few hours to 1 to 2 days. Therefore, as the pilot of those machines, you are exposed to variations of extremes of weather conditions without the advantages of adapting or becoming acclimated. Furthermore, you are often unprepared to cope with these extremes because you might be flying without adequate protective clothing or in less than ideal physical condition. Depending on the aircraft you fly, it might not be uncommon for you to depart from a cold, dry, windy airport and arrive several hours later at a hot, humid, calm destination. And you might stay there only a few hours or days before heading back or continuing on to yet another location of variable extremes.

BASICS OF HEAT EXCHANGE

Just as you often resort to basic stick and rudder skills during complex situations, let's start our discussion of how the environment impacts your piloting skills by reviewing the basics of temperature extremes. The first thing to realize is that the definition of cold is the absence of heat. Absolute zero temperature ($-459.67°$) means there is no heat, no energy. As the energy of heat is added, the temperature rises. Therefore, in any discussion of temperature-related situations, it's important to understand that we are talking mainly about the transfer of heat.

What happens in your body is essentially the same physics as occurs in your home. Warming up the building means adding heat to the circulating air. Cooling means removing heat. How this heat is exchanged depends on other physical properties of heat transfer (Fig. 4-1).

Heat that is transferred by direct contact with another object is called *conduction*. Conduction can happen within the same object, like an airplane, by going from one part to another (heat from the engine warming the airframe). The more common situation is when a part of the body, like hands or feet, comes in contact with another object that is colder or warmer, like sitting in a cold seat or leaning against the wall of an airplane sitting on the ramp in the middle of summer.

Convection is the most common way to transfer heat. Here heat is moved within gases or liquids as it flows from one object to another. This type of transfer is what happens in a building or airplane cabin. Air is heated by a flame or hot object (engine) and the airflow carries this heat to another part of the building or aircraft. You feel warm as the heat is transferred from the air to your skin. Depending on the ambient temperature,

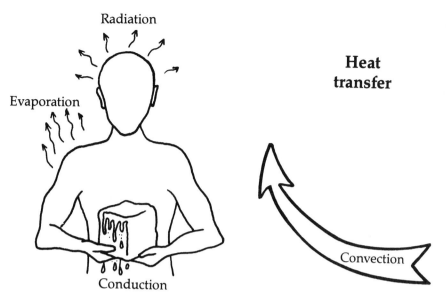

Fig. 4-1. The first law of thermodynamics states that heat is transferred from hotter to colder objects.

the relative flow of air as it moves across your body also becomes a major factor. This flow can be from a fan or from your body moving itself. If there is no difference between the temperature of the moving air and your body, you still feel colder because of wind chill, described later. Within your body, heat transfer by convection is performed by warm blood carrying heat from one part of the body to another.

When heat is transferred from one object to another of different temperature without being carried by a gas or liquid (and you're not touching anything), it is called *radiation*. The transfer is in the form of electromagnetic waves. The sun is the most obvious example. You often feel the warmth from the sun on your skin even though the ambient temperature is low. The amount of heat transferred depends on the size of the radiating object, the relative difference of temperature, and, like light, exponentially on the distance from that object. Radiation also initiates the greenhouse effect in the cockpit of an airplane sitting on the ramp in the sun or your car in the driveway.

Another form of heat transfer, evaporation, requires energy or heat to change a liquid to a gas. Mechanical refrigeration with a compressor uses this physical property when heat is taken away from the container (refrigerator) as the refrigerant expands. The same holds true with your body. Sweat, for example, evaporates off the skin and in doing so takes heat away from the skin.

How you feel, how comfortable you are, also determines how effective you are when performing your job. If you feel too hot or too cold, your performance might be substandard. This comfort factor is dependent on all these forms of heat transfer and to varying degrees and combinations. For example, in a small cockpit or small airplane, radiant solar heat warms the air and body without heat from any other source. The greenhouse effect can raise the temperature 10 to 15 degrees Celsius higher without any other source. Convected heat (or lack of heat) from air vents and heaters supplements the radiant energy. Sitting in a hot or cold seat conducts heat to or from the body. And if you are sweating from the preflight activities, evaporation adds to the discomfort (or comfort). It's subjective, and each pilot responds differently and unpredictably.

TEMPERATURE CONTROL IN THE BODY

Quick—what is the proper temperature of your body? 98.6°F, 89.6°F, or somewhere between the two? If you said 98.6°F, you are on your way to understanding core temperature. The core defines critical organs such as the brain, heart, liver, lungs, and some of the senses of vision and hearing. This core of organs must be kept at a constant temperature (average of 98.6°F) if you are to be kept in good spirits. This characteristic distinguishes you, a warm-blooded animal, from cold-blooded animals, whose core temperatures stay close to ambient temperatures. Failure of warm-blooded animals to keep the core temperature within this range (96.6° to 99.5°F) results in depressed performance and ultimately total incapacitation.

Therefore, the goal of your body's temperature-control system is to maintain a constant body core temperature, often at the expense of other parts and organs of the body. It requires a properly functioning body in good physical condition. Temperature control incorporates all the physics of heat transfer and flow, heat generation, air (blood) conditioning, and heat/cold regulation.

Heat is generated by virtually all activities of your body and is the ultimate form of energy. In fact, it is estimated that so much heat is created that if it weren't dispersed, the core body temperature would rise to 190°F! Your body, therefore, has a vast resource of available heat. When heat is needed and not externally available, how does your body respond? It shivers, which is its way of involuntarily increasing muscle activity and generating more heat. All muscle activity requires internal calories from the energy of ingested food. It follows, therefore, that during periods when heat is needed, more food must be eaten to provide adequate fuel.

The skin (the largest organ of the body) is considered the heat exchange component because of its large surface area. The more blood that reaches the skin, the more heat that can be dissipated, provided the heat is taken from the skin either by convection or evaporation. The amount of blood reaching the skin is controlled by the ability of the arteries to shunt blood away from or to the skin. Here is where vasodilation and vasoconstriction of arteries play an important role.

In a hot environment, your body must get rid of excessive heat in the core or prevent the core temperatures to rise. It does so by opening the vessels to the skin and within the skin, getting more blood to the surface area of your body and allowing it to be dissipated. The skin becomes red and flushed as a result of the superficial blood vessels getting wider (a bad landing can sometimes generate the same effect). The reverse is true in a cold environment. To preserve the core temperature, blood is shunted away from the cool skin and concentrated in the core, resulting in pale and blanched skin color. Shunting leads to poor warming of extremities and other outer body parts, such as the nose and ears.

Efficient blood flow is dependent on an efficient circulatory system and a healthy heart. Therefore, those in poor physical condition are less effective in tolerating any temperature extremes. Also, self-induced stresses (alcohol, self-medication, dehydration, poor nutrition, etc.) can seriously compromise adequate coping with temperature extremes and reduce effective acclimatization.

Your body can generate heat and get excess heat to the surface of the body to be dispersed. However, heat removal by radiation or convection is not efficient enough. Heat also has to be taken from your skin by evaporation of sweat on the skin. Since evaporation requires heat, this process is effective in using the heat in the skin.

Just as additional fuel is needed for generation of heat through increased muscle activity, your body obviously needs more water under conditions of increased sweat production. This internal need means fluids must be available within the body to be effective. Because sweat includes some electrolytes (mainly sodium and potassium chloride), you must be aware of depletion during high losses of sweat.

Most of what I have discussed so far takes little or no conscious effort on your part. The thermoregulatory center takes input from your body's receptors and then generates heat by either increasing muscle activity, which warms the blood, or increasing sweat production, which cools the blood. The center then regulates the flow of blood between the core and the skin to either conserve heat or to dissipate heat to the core. In extreme conditions, some conscious effort must be taken, however, to assist your body's own actions.

Apparent temperature

Because both temperature and humidity act in combination with one another, there's a system for measuring their combined effects on the body. It's called the *heat index* (formerly known as the *temperature humidity index*).

The heat index (HI) couples the temperature and relative humidity into an "apparent" temperature. If, for example, the temperature is 90°F and the relative humidity is 65 percent, the HI, or apparent temperature, would be 102°.

The HI is a more accurate means of gauging the effects of heat and humidity on the body's cooling system. Increasing temperatures cause the body to sweat more, and increasing humidity decreases the air's capacity to absorb the sweat and facilitate cooling.

When the HI is in the 80 to 90° range, fatigue is likely during prolonged activity; when it is in the 90 to 105° range, sunstroke and heat exhaustion are possible; 105 to 130° indicates that sunstroke and heat exhaustion are likely; 130° or higher indicates that heatstroke is likely.

Local weather forecasts often report the HI.

FLYING WHEN HOT

As mentioned earlier, when your body's thermoregulatory center senses that the core temperature is going up, certain functions begin to take place. Blood supply is shunted to the core where heat is accumulating. The heated blood is taken quickly to the skin where the dilated blood vessels warm the skin relative to the amount of heat being dissipated. The more heat, the higher the skin temperature. Concurrently, sweat volume is increased from the sweat glands for evaporation. Stay in this hot environment too long and as much as 4 to 16 quarts of water can be lost through sweating and respiration in an active person.

Obviously this fluid must be replaced. From a comfort point of view, a pilot given enough water can function all day at a temperature of 115°F with a relative humidity of 10 percent. If, however, the relative humidity is raised to 80 percent, that same person can be incapacitated within 30 minutes. Dewpoint is sometimes a better indicator of anticipated discomfort. If the dewpoint is above 60°F with outside air temperatures at any level above that, you will be uncomfortable, which could be as disabling as the physiological conditions to be discussed later.

Some of the conditions that make a person less tolerant to heat extremes include increasing age, excessive alcohol intake (alcohol dilates blood vessels and prevents efficient shunting), lack of sleep, obesity, and previous history of heat stroke (the more serious kind of heat stress). Being inadequately acclimated makes you much more susceptible.

General symptoms of heat stress

As your body temperature increases (hyperthermia), and struggles to maintain a constant core temperature, some symptoms have a direct effect on your piloting performance. These symptoms include less reliable short-term memory, an increase in error rate, erosion of motor skills, and general decrease in performance skill. Heat stress increases your irritability and diminishes insight into judgment skills, creating a tendency to overreact and make more mistakes. Heat also increases the susceptibility to motion sickness, hypoxia, and any degree of G forces. In addition, fatigue becomes apparent after several hours of coping with heat.

Specific heat stresses

In addition to the previously mentioned generalized symptoms, the following are physiological stages of heat stress that need to be recognized. As each stage evolves without recognition and treatment intervention, you become increasingly impaired to the point of becoming completely incapacitated.

Heat cramps. (Also called *minor heat stress*—body temperature of 99.5 to 100.5°.) Painful muscle cramps of the extremities, abdomen, and back are common in heat. Some feel cramps are due to a lack of adequate electrolytes, but it is related more to the early stages of fluid depletion. Identification of this stage is important because it is the first indication of the body's struggle to maintain its own temperature control. Treatment consists of rest, getting out of the heat environment and into shade, and forcing fluids as much as can be tolerated. Electrolyte-type "athletic" beverages might be helpful.

Heat exhaustion. (Body temperature of 101 to 105°F.) Heat exhaustion is the first serious stage where you body begins to be unable to keep up with controlling core temperature. The thermoregulatory center is still working and the body is responding with proper shunting of blood and enough sweat to evaporate. However, if the conditions are severe with high heat, high dewpoints, little or no shade, and a high level of activity, then the body will be unable to keep up without rest and more fluids.

Symptoms include headache, confusion, incoordination, loss of appetite, nausea, and cramps. Because the heat control system is still functioning, there is sweating, which means the skin is moist and still relatively cool. But the cardiovascular system is working harder to keep up with the increased heart rate necessary to overcome the dilated vessels during the transport of heat from blood flow.

The treatment is to help the body's heat exchange function and to get the body out of the heat. Rest in the shade or in a cooler setting is mandatory. Fluids are especially important. Water is probably all that is needed at this stage. Do not be overly concerned about salt replacement. You cannot take in too much water; however, when taken too quickly, it can cause nausea and vomiting. Continual sipping of cool water is ideal.

A key point is that if you are ever in this condition, you have reached the limits of your body's attempt to control core temperatures. You are "behind the power curve." Therefore, returning to work or flying is not safe for several hours.

Heat stroke. (Body temperature above 105°F.) Heat stroke is the last phase of inadequate temperature control and the most serious. It is a medical emergency when identified. Your body is no longer capable of defending itself. Its thermoregulatory center has broken down and is unable to control the body temperature control functions and keep core temperatures acceptable. You'll find yourself already significantly impaired and might become unconscious in a short time.

Heatstroke

Causes:

- High temperature and high humidity
- Changes in climate
- Inadequate solar protection
- Exertion
- Past incidence of heat stroke
- Dehydration
- Medication
  (certain drugs interfere with perspiration)
- Illness
- Skin problems

Prevention:

- Water!

The key to this diagnosis is the lack of any body cooling activity. Sweat is no longer being made and therefore no evaporation is taking place. The skin is dry and hot. The temperature might reach as high as 106 °F, which is life-threatening. The body is literally burning up.

The first step is to get to a cool place. Treatment includes calling for medical assistance along with any methods to cool the body down, such as immersion in cool water, or spraying or pouring any liquid over the body to help cooling by evaporation.

In general, when in hot conditions, whether on the ground or in the air, be suspicious of extreme conditions and look for potential symptoms in others as well as yourself.

As with any other medical problem, prevention is the best cure. Heat stress could be considered self-induced because you have control of prevention. The most important part of prevention is drinking more than enough fluids. That means drinking water before subjecting yourself to heat extremes. In other words, maintaining hyration is the single most important goal. In hot weather, an average person requires 2 to 3 quarts of fluid per day in addition to that supplied in a normal meal. By the way, fluids do more good in the stomach than being poured over the body to cool off. It might make you feel cooler, but the body's heat control system needs the water to replace evaporated sweat. Thirst is a poor indicator of need because you are already dehydrated when the feeling of thirst appears.

Avoid those fluids known to contain diuretics—caffeine and alcohol—especially prior to being subjected to heat extremes. Tea, as in iced tea, is particularly bad since there are two diuretics present—caffeine and theophyline. If you are not acclimated to the environment, salt can be added to food, but salt tablets are not generally required. Most Americans consume more salt than is healthy anyway.

Protective clothing is important, provided it still allows for circulation of air over the skin. White, loose, lightweight clothing is preferable. Protection of the head is also important to protect the scalp from a heat load.

It might seem overly stated to consider heat stress a problem to pilots who are in flight. However, consider the fact that you might also spend a lot of time out of the airplane—preflight, loading, waiting, often on a hot ramp in humid weather. You might be dehydrated before showing up for the flight. If you're behind in fluids and now jump into the hot cockpit, the body continues to be heat-stressed with the same symptoms as if you were still outside. After sitting in a hot cockpit as a result of the greenhouse effect, it could take more than 20 minutes just to recover after the cabin finally cools.

Before being acclimated, your capacity to work in heat or cold is impaired. Your body senses the change in climate and adjusts its thermo-regulatory system, which alerts the body to prepare for more efficient use of body fluids and heat generation. Subjectively, you cope better in hot environments and can be more active both physically and mentally without undue impairment.

It takes 2 to 3 weeks to completely adjust to a new environment. Therefore, if you live in a climate that turns cool in the fall and travel to a hot humid location for a few days, you will not become acclimated in that time and will therefore be at high risk of developing heat stress. Conversely, living in warm climates and trying to cope in below-freezing conditions is equally impairing.

FLYING WHEN COLD

Ever preflighted your aircraft on a really cold day? It's been said that the length of the preflight in cold conditions is directly proportional to the temperature. Coping with the cold is basically generating and conserving heat. Enough heat is generated by your body if the body is active and has enough caloric fuel. The primary goal, then, is to protect your body from losing too much of the heat that is already present.

Hypothermia symptoms

In the early stages of hypothermia, you feel obvious discomfort leading to distraction. As you get colder, you might experience muscle stiffness and weakness, fatigue, and sometimes drowsiness. Thought processes are dulled and stuporous. As the cold increases, shivering begins uncontrollably. These early symptoms are the first signs of clinical hypothermia, and corrective action must be taken. As heat is taken away from the core (by the futile attempts of the body's heat conservation system plus the loss of heat from lack of protection of the surface of the body) the body begins to become generally impaired, unable to keep up. It's just the opposite of trying to keep the body core cool.

The same heat-transfer process is taking place. In order to conserve heat, blood flow is shunted away from the surface at the expense of the extremities and other nonessential body parts. Muscle activity is increased involuntarily. As the body loses this battle, the core temperature continues to go down.

Hypothermia symptoms are less subtle than those of hyperthermia, and in most situations are more easily controlled, if you are prepared. The degree of heat loss is dependent on your physical condition, the environmental conditions (temperature and wind), and the protection of your body.

Loss of body heat

All the physical properties of heat transfer are in effect in cold extremes, but with variations from that associated with heat. Radiation now becomes the leading cause of heat loss through any uncovered skin. The scalp is especially vulnerable because of its highly vascular anatomy (that's why there is so much bleeding when anyone gets a laceration of the scalp). Hats, therefore, are an essential piece of cold-weather clothing.

Conduction is also important as one is in contact with cold seats and instruments and other unheated objects. Wet, cold clothing can remove heat 25 times more rapidly from the body than dry. Sweating soaks the clothing next to your skin. This exposed moisture is cooling as it evaporates, resulting in heat loss from the body first through conduction then convection. Loose clothing is therefore important.

Convection plays a big role in heat loss especially when surrounded by cold air or cold water. When cold air passes over exposed skin, heat is lost rapidly. This factor is called *windchill* and is the product of temperature and wind velocity (Fig. 4-2). Not only is heat lost in a short period of time, but local areas of exposed skin on the extremities and other locations where blood has been shunted away (ears and nose) can freeze. Any liquid can cause the same problem, including aviation fuel.

WIND SPEED		TEMPERATURE (°F)																				
CALM	CALM	40	35	30	25	20	15	10	5	0	-5	-10	-15	-20	-25	-30	-35	-40	-45	-50	-55	-60
KNOTS	MPH	EQUIVALENT CHILL TEMPERATURE																				
3-6	5	35	30	25	20	15	10	5	0	-5	-10	-15	-20	-25	-30	-35	-40	-45	-50	-55	-65	-70
7-10	10	30	20	15	10	5	0	-10	-15	-20	-25	-35	-40	-45	-50	-60	-65	-70	-75	-80	-90	-95
11-15	15	25	15	10	0	-5	-10	-20	-25	-30	-40	-45	-50	-60	-65	-70	-80	-85	-90	-100	-105	-110
16-19	20	20	10	5	0	-10	-15	-25	-30	-35	-45	-50	-60	-65	-75	-80	-85	-95	-100	-110	-115	-120
20-23	25	15	10	0	-5	-15	-20	-30	-35	-45	-50	-60	-65	-75	-80	-90	-95	-105	-110	-120	-125	-135
24-28	30	10	5	0	-10	-20	-25	-30	-40	-50	-55	-65	-70	-80	-85	-95	-100	-110	-115	-125	-130	-140
29-32	35	10	5	-5	-10	-20	-30	-35	-40	-50	-60	-65	-75	-80	-90	-100	-105	-115	-120	-130	-135	-145
33-36	40	10	0	-5	-15	-20	-30	-35	-45	-55	-60	-70	-75	-85	-95	-100	-110	-115	-125	-130	-140	-150
WINDS ABOVE 40 HAVE LITTLE ADDITIONAL EFFECT.		LITTLE DANGER				INCREASING DANGER (Flesh may freeze within 1 minute)					GREAT DANGER (Flesh may freeze within 30 seconds)											
		DANGER OF FREEZING EXPOSED FLESH FOR PROPERLY CLOTHED PERSONS																				

Fig. 4-2. Windchill is the product of temperature and wind velocity.

Treatment should be obvious. Get out of the cold, immediately remove wet and cold clothing, and begin rapid warming of the body (hot bath or shower). Drinking hot beverages also helps. Get the person into warm clothes and try to get some muscle activity going.

Frostbite

Frostbite is a more extreme condition of heat loss from a local area. Tissues are actually frozen, and the degree of injury is related to how deep the freezing goes. Tissues that are frozen die as a result of the crystallization of tissue and cellular fluids.

The symptoms vary. The first sensation is numbness, not pain. Grayish or white spots might show up on the skin before freezing actually occurs. After awhile there is no feeling and the tissues are hard to the touch. All this occurs because there has been no internal warming by the blood that has been shunted to the core.

Frostbite to fingers and toes is common to pilots who are on the ramp in slush and spilled fuel. Doing a preflight without gloves, hat, or other additional protection leads to other areas at risk for frostbite or hypothermia.

Treatment includes immediate warming. Do *not* rub with snow! Ideally, the affected parts should be immersed in water that is warm to the touch. Be advised that as the tissues thaw, the pain becomes severe. The pain is not an indication to stop warming. If the injury is this severe, medical attention should be obtained.

Prevention of cold stress

Once again, as with coping with heat stress, prevention is the most important action you can take. In this case, prevention means not only awareness of keeping warm and preventing heat loss, but also preparedness—having access to and wearing adequate cold-weather clothing when you know you are going to a colder destination.

The specific and obvious measures to follow are:

- Be aware of the temperatures, winds, and wind chills at your present location and at your various destinations.
- Limit the amount of time of exposure.
- Keep the body and clothes dry—if you're sweating and spill water or fuel on your clothes, get them off and get on dry clothes.
- Use the layered look wearing several layers of loose clothing that can be removed or added as comfort levels change.
- Keep your activities below the sweating level.

A word on alcohol: Remember that alcohol is a vasodilator and might make you feel warm (and flushed) because it keeps surface blood vessels wide open. However, the body is trying to do just the opposite—to shunt blood away from the skin. Nutrition is equally important. The body needs calories to generate heat in cold conditions. Eat high-calorie meals.

DEHYDRATION

Dehydration is very common in flying and not just when related to temperature extremes. The lifestyle of the traveling pilot and the cockpit environment lend themselves to increased risk of becoming dehydrated. Hours of increased dehydration is one reason kidney stones are relatively common in pilots who fly great distances in a dehydrated condition.

Why? Because most pilots do not drink water enroute. More often than not coffee is the fluid of choice, although the trend is towards decaffeinated coffee. Pressurized cockpit humidity approaches less than 5 percent, 20 to 30 minutes after takeoff. Even if the pilot is physically inactive during flight, insensible water loss from respiration and skin runs about 1,000 ml per day in ideal conditions, more so in dry conditions.

Consuming a lot of coffee (or tea, including iced tea) before the flight and urinating more than one has consumed is another problem. This, by the way, can be monitored by observing the color of urine. The darker the urine, the more dehydrated the pilot is.

Dehydration has symptoms similar to those experienced with heat stress. Headache, dizziness, and especially fatigue are the most important and are very common and occur in varying stages, from mild to incapacitating. Unfortunately, pilots tend to wait for symptoms instead of practicing the common-sense approach of prevention. Thirst is an indicator, but as noted, only after dehydration is present.

RADIATION

Radiation comes in many forms, and each form has a different effect on the body (Fig. 4-3).

Various portions of ultraviolet (UV) light or radiation wavelengths can affect the eye, specifically the cornea (UVB 200 to 315 nm), lens (UVA 315 – 400 nm), and to an uncommon degree, the retina (UVC 400 to 700). Most UV radiation from the sun is filtered out by the ozone layer in the atmosphere, especially UVC waves. Increasing evidence, but little proof, indicates that the ozone layer is being depleted, which could increase the risk of UV radiation damage, especially to pilots flying at high altitudes for long trips. This damage is limited to eye changes, such as cataracts. It

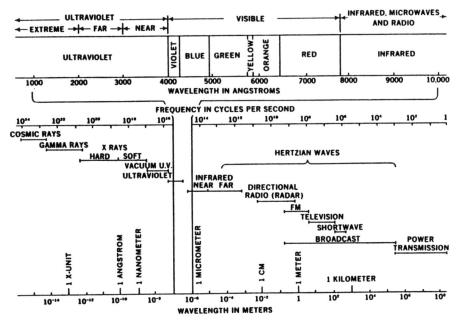

Fig. 4-3. Electromagnetic spectrum of radiation.

is easily prevented by ensuring that all prescription glasses and sunglasses, have a UV coating that filters out UV radiation. It is important that the full UV range (200 to 400 nm) is filtered out. Check the label on the glasses.

Exposure to UV radiation also affects the skin, resulting in the all-too-common sunburn. UVB causes most of the damage, but studies now show that UVA (found in tanning booths) adds to the effect of UVB, but is not as severe as UVB. Few pilots have avoided the symptoms of sunburn, and most can remember that a good burn is at best distracting. Despite increasing evidence about the relationship between UV radiation and sunburn with skin cancer, tanning still is a summer ritual for some. One can acclimate the skin through gradually increasing exposure.

The best protection from sunburn, especially for unacclimated skin, is to use sunscreens. There are now many on the market in a variety of combinations. The key ingredient is PABA (para amino benzoic acid). The more PABA, the greater the protection. Some people's skin is more sensitive to the sun and requires greater protection.

5

Self-imposed
medical problems

Tony had a cold and his doctor put him on medication to help and advised him not to fly. He called in sick for the trip, which meant his chief pilot had to fly. Two days later Tony's cold wasn't much better, but now the chief pilot had a cold and the next trip would have to be canceled unless another pilot could be found. Wanting to make points with his boss, Tony suddenly got well, telling his chief pilot that he was over his cold and would fly the trip for him. Tony's cold symptoms were still there, however, so he doubled up on his medication before he took off just to be sure he wouldn't get plugged up in flight. Two hours later, making an approach to his destination, Tony was so light-headed and unsteady (from the medication—it was an antihistamine) that the landing was too hard and he veered off the runway.

Temperature extremes, illness, noise, weather and several other factors beyond your control can affect your health and performance. However, many factors that affect your health and performance are under your control. How well you fly is compromised as a result of how you abuse your health or live your life, including playing doctor—making a self-diagnosis and then using self-medication. Also, subjecting yourself to overindulgence of alcohol, nicotine, caffeine, and the like can easily impair your body's functions and your mind's ability to function safely.

PLAYING DOCTOR

The primary reason that you see a doctor is because you are in pain, uncomfortable, or unable to work or play. You are looking for relief so you can go back to your activities. The doctor, who is eager to make you feel better, has the added responsibility of finding out why you feel bad. More important, he must determine what conditions could be serious to your health and which ones must be ruled out. Once this has been accomplished, the doctor can treat the cause, if it's treatable, and then, and only then, treat your symptoms. Unfortunately, the doctor is often bypassed because you don't want to take the time to see a doctor unless you are really sick. Here are some of the more common disorders for which you may be tempted to play doctor.

Colds and flus

Colds and flus are commonly caused by viruses. Antibiotics do not cure viral infections as they do bacterial infections. Therefore, there is no cure for the cold or flu. Only time and allowing your body to fight off the viral infection can end the malady.

The symptoms of a cold or flu are what get your attention, ranging from a simple sore throat and cough to generalized aches and pains, fatigue, headache, and congestion. Such symptoms, which are often limited to your respiratory system, are sometimes caused by bacteria and therefore respond to antibiotics. Therefore, if your symptoms don't begin to clear on their own in a few days, seeing a doctor is the next step. Antibiotics could help in this situation.

Flus often have the same symptoms as a cold, if the flu virus affects the respiratory system. However, many flus are associated with the gastrointestinal (GI) tract with resulting nausea, vomiting, diarrhea, and stomach cramps. Sometimes these symptoms include a generalized malaise (achy, tired, "feeling rotten"). However, these same symptoms can result from problems with your gall bladder, appendix, liver, and other organs. Symptoms are not very good diagnostic tools.

For whatever reason, these are the variety of symptoms that pilots often try to take care of themselves. Self-medication becomes easy because the marketing statements on the packages of over-the-counter (OTC) medications imply that they clear up those symptoms and, by inference, cure your problem. If you feel that you aren't too sick, then it is very tempting to assume you're okay as long as you can take care of the symptoms with these OTC medications. But now you have three strikes against you: the effects of the cold or flu, the potential side effects of the medications (especially in flight), and the possibility that you made the wrong diagnosis.

Hayfever

Hayfever affects just about everybody to varying degrees, depending on geographic location and type of activities. Even though you might not consider you have hayfever (or allergies), mild allergic symptoms are often mistakenly thought to be caused by a mild cold. The significant difference between the two is that a cold is an actual infection and has additional symptoms, such as fatigue, that are potentially unsafe in flight.

Injuries

Because of your eagerness to fly, some injuries that are not serious (minor broken bones, cuts, sprains, etc.) are often minimized. These include arthritis and tendonitis, which, although not injuries, are experienced by just about everyone at one time or other, especially as they get older. Commonly, the diagnosis of arthritis is relatively obvious for most people. Persistent symptoms from any of these conditions, however, are often an indication that more is going on and a doctor should be informed.

A variety of OTC medications are available to treat the symptoms of these and other conditions and to control the discomfort. Keep in mind, however, that medications are often used with the thought that in time the cause of the problem will go away. Therefore, you can rationalize that by relieving the discomfort, you can return to flying. Furthermore, taking away the symptoms might mask the only signal the body has to alert you to a continuing problem.

There is a conflict, therefore, between your desire to fly and your willingness to accept that you might not be safe. A simple statement from a doctor saying that your medical condition shouldn't interfere with flying could be misleading because many doctors are not familiar with the unique requirements for flying. That statement from a well-meaning doctor might give you a false sense of safety, when, in fact, you are not safe. For example, a sprained ankle after several weeks is still weak, but you might not realize that until you try pushing a rudder pedal in a crosswind landing.

Also, because others have been known to put up with the illness, use self-medication, and then fly without apparent difficulty, you assume it's okay for you to do the same. It reinforces the rationalization that you are safe to fly. Looking at the labels on OTC medications complicates the situation because of their claims of making your symptoms go away—the quick fix. The eagerness to fly the trip now overrides the potential of being unsafe during the flight.

A rule of thumb to keep in mind is that if you have any medical situation for which you feel you need any treatment, even for the symptoms and including OTC medications, then you probably aren't safe and should reconsider flying. Mild symptoms from known causes might be the exception, but only if you are sure of your diagnosis and acceptable safe treatment.

Self-medication

There is a huge market for medications and drugs that the public can purchase without a prescription or visiting a doctor. Over-the-counter (OTC) medications are a multibillion dollar business in the United States alone. Although the Food and Drug Administration (FDA) is charged with protecting the public from medications and chemicals whose labels mislead or imply false results, it is a continuous struggle to keep ahead of the false or misleading claims with factual information. Current programs of enforcement by the FDA to ensure legitimate labeling is helping consumers.

Pilots especially are vulnerable to the hype of the many ads for quick-fix medications. Although not deliberately seeking unsafe or unhealthy therapy, you are often swayed into judging that you know how ill you are and that you can fly safely. Thus you self-diagnose and self-medicate. Would you take a sleeping pill to cure a cold? You are when you use OTC medications. Read on.

Flight surgeons and AMEs are often asked if it is okay to take a certain medication and still fly. The initial response technically has to be no. There is no list of approved drugs or medications that you can use, prescription or over-the-counter, without approval by a flight surgeon or AME. Obviously, many medications and treatments have their place, even OTC, but you must use them with the full knowledge of both you and your doctor as to why the medication is needed and the effect of this medication on safety and performance. It's a situation of risk assessment. Because civilian aviation does not have a close relationship to the aviation doctor, you must assume responsibility for determining what course of action to follow. That's stated in FAR 61.53, which says that you must not have any disqualifying medical problems to be legal to fly. In other words, you must be healthy enough as if you had to pass an FAA medical before you go flying. If in doubt, check with your AME.

Marketing claims

The labels on the containers of these OTC medications are often very revealing, and sometimes the claims are very creative. It's uncommon to find any comment about cure or coping with the cause of the symptoms. And, of course, you'll find the ultimate disclaimer to see your doctor if symptoms persist.

Consider some of these claims for OTC drugs:

- Symptomatic relief! Some symptoms are relieved, but sometimes at the expense of causing significant side effects, especially in a flight environment. "Symptom relief" is an effective statement because that is precisely what you are looking for in the medication.
- Temporary relief! Temporary relief could mean a few minutes to a few hours. It does not mean permanent relief as would be expected if the medication were curative.
- Extra Added Ingredients! This claim implies greater potency or more reliability in meeting its claims, even though that extra ingredient could simply be caffeine! Here is where the FDA is cracking down on claims that these added ingredients really do what is claimed. The label will tell you what that ingredient is.
- New and Improved! Compared to what? The ingredients probably are the same, but the amounts might be slightly different, or perhaps the only difference is the shape of the pill or the color of the liquid. It doesn't mean the drug is any more effective than the previous drug.

It would be a good exercise to read labels just to see how creative marketing people can be to get you to buy their product.

Basic ingredients

There are over 450 different drugs and OTC medications made from a combination of one or more of the following chemicals. These eight ingredients make up a high percentage of all of the usable chemicals that are allowed in OTC drugs (Fig. 5-1). There are others, of course, but these are certainly the most common. In addition to discussing the effects and side effects, look at the half-life for each chemical. *Half-life* is that amount of time that half of the chemical needs to have to get out of your body. For example, if you ingest 1 gram of a drug and its half-life is 10 hours, then in 10 hours 0.5 gram will still be in your body.

Antihistamines. Antihistamines are the most popular ingredients in allergy and cold OTC medications. There are several kinds of antihistamines and several that are by prescription only. Some of the more common antihistamines used are Brompheniramine, Chlorpheniramine, Doxylamine, and Diphenhydramine. Note that each generic name ends in -ine.

Chemical name	Half life*	Actions and side effects
Caffeine	Varies	Stimulant (adrenalin-like) Diuretic (urine loss) Fatiguing Withdrawal "anxiety"
Aspirin	20 minutes	Analgesic (pain killer) Antipyretic (fever) Anti-inflammatory Tinnitus (ringing ears) Gastritis
Acetaminophen	3 hours	Analgesic Antipyretic
Dextromethorphan	Varies	Antitussive (cough)
Ephedrine and Phenylphrine	3 hours	Decongestant Stimulant (like caffeine)
Chlorpheniramine	6 hours	Antihistamine (allergy) Sedative Drying agent (secretions) Vertigo Blurred vision Increased heart rate Decreased coordination
Phenylpropanolamine	6 hours	Decongestant Stimulant Anorectic (appetite) "Amphetamine"-like Increased blood sugar Increased blood pressure

* = It takes about five times the "half-life" to clear the body

Fig. 5-1. Ingredients contained in a majority of over-the-counter medications.

Effects. Primarily, antihistamines help dry up secretions from upper respiratory mucous membranes (nose and sinuses) that cause the sniffles and post nasal drip (often also leading to a mild cough). They also thicken secretions. In addition, some of the associated itchy nose and eyes and sneezing is controlled. However, antihistamines are usually effective only with allergies, not infections. There is some dispute as to whether or not antihistamines actually help in a cold.

Side effects. Drowsiness and sedation is, by far, the most serious problem with any OTC medication that contains antihistamines. There are countless stories of pilots who were incapacitated in some way as a direct result of taking such medication. There are some prescribed antihistamines that, according to studies, do not cause drowsiness. If such treatment is necessary in keeping you flying comfortably and safely, then your doctor must be a part of that treatment and monitoring.

Antihistamine's recognized side effects
(In susceptible individuals)

Chills	Drowsiness	Confusion	Heartburn
Irritability	Fatigue	Delusions	Nausea
Headaches	Weakness	Hysteria	Constipation
Muscle twitching	Anorexia	Paralysis	Nightmares
Rapid heart rate	Impaired judgment	Neuritis	EKG changes
Tremor	Hypertension	Tinnitus	Hypotension
Insomnia	Nasal stuffiness	Blurred vision	Dermatitis
Hypertension	Dry mouth	Dilated pupils	Anemia
Euphoria	Hypoglycemia	Vertigo	Sugar in urine
Delirium		Double vision	

There are many other side effects of OTC antihistamines that are unacceptable in flight. These include decreased coordination, reduced visual accommodation, dizziness, depression, and some cardiovascular effects (rapid heart rate, reduced vascular shunting response, etc.).

Sleeping medications. It is important to note here that virtually all OTC sleep medications are antihistamines. Drug companies have simply changed the name of the product and put a different label on the bottle and box, and the antihistamine has become a sleeping pill. Consider the comment made earlier. Would you take a sleeping medication to treat your cold so you could fly? That's what you're doing if you take OTC antihistamines to treat a cold.

Decongestants. Generally, decongestants are well tolerated by the body. They are found in OTC medications, separately and in combination with antihistamines and other chemicals. They are often the active ingredient in most nose sprays. Common decongestant chemicals are phenylephrine, ephedrine, and pseudo ephedrine.

Effects. Mucous membranes usually swell during colds, flus, and allergies. This swelling causes congestion and plugging in the nose, eustachian tube, and sinuses. The congestion is what creates problems in flight—ear and sinus blocks—and decongestants are effective at reducing this swelling. They do little to reduce secretions.

Side effects. The major problem with these drugs is their stimulant effects, similar to that of caffeine. Included are such effects as making you nervous, jittery, and overactive plus keeping you awake when you are trying to get needed sleep. Most people are quite tolerant to these effects, but it is difficult to predict what happens to an individual in flight. An already heavy load of coffee, plus the symptoms for which you need a decongestant, might increase impairment. Furthermore, pilots who have borderline high blood pressure should be aware that decongestants can aggravate blood pressure elevation. It is wise (and expected of you) to confirm the use with your flight surgeon or AME.

Nose sprays. Nose sprays help reduce the congestion of the mucous membranes of your nose. Frequent use of short acting (less than 3 hours) nose spray decongestants can lead to what is called *rebound*. The spray itself can be an irritant to the mucous membranes of your nose. In other words, as the expected favorable decongestant action begins to diminish in a few hours, you take another shot of the nose spray to keep your nose clear. Over a period of a few days, the irritation of frequent use causes its own swelling and congestion. This is rebound. Longer acting sprays (over 8 hours, as with oxymetazoline) might be better tolerated, especially if used for no more than a few days; however, rebound can still occur.

Another issue is the recommendation by some doctors to keep a long-acting nose spray in your flight bag as a "get me down" treatment, when you get caught in flight with an ear or sinus block. This is not recommending using the nose spray prior to flight because of a known cold or allergy because, as stated elsewhere, if you think you need treatment before flying then you should not be flying. Keeping a nose spray available during flight for emergency use probably outweighs the risk of imprudent use. If there is doubt, don't fly—and ask your AME.

Analgesics (pain relievers). Analgesics are sold alone for the reduction of pain or in combination with other cold and flu medications. Discomfort (whether pain, achiness, or general malaise) generally is why you seek help from an analgesic, but your symptoms could also be nature's way of telling you something isn't safe. Therefore, it is more important with analgesics that you consider why you need the medication. Unless you know for sure why you hurt, you need to discuss your problem with your doctor.

Aspirin. One of the most common of pain relievers, aspirin is a medication that has several other effects. It is also an *antipyretic*, or *fever reducer*, and an effective anti-inflammatory medication frequently used for arthritis and other inflammation problems. It is relatively safe if used as directed—taken with food or an antacid, not taken more than recommended, and avoided if there is any history of previous stomach distress or gastritis.

Acetaminophen. This is often the ingredient that competes with aspirin in marketing OTC medications. It is an effective pain reliever for some people and is also often found in combination with other chemicals in cold and flu medications. It is not as effective in anti-inflammatory treatment. It appears to be tolerated better than aspirin in those who have problems with gastritis.

Ibuprofen. Ibuprofen was once only a prescription medication, but now pills containing comparatively small doses are sold OTC. The prescribed medication is usually used for inflammation and the OTC pills for pain (the analgesic properties were found as a side effect when it was used initially as a prescription). This is also relatively well tolerated in most people, but others do notice side effects such as stomach distress.

Cough suppressants (antitussive). In most cases, cough suppressants contain dextromethorphan, a fairly innocuous chemical that can assist in relieving coughs in some people. It has few if any significant side effects. This is not the only ingredient used in cough medicines, and you should keep in mind, that derivatives of codeine are sometimes found in prescribed cough medication. Codeine, used in this formula, is a very effective antitussive agent, but it is considered a narcotic, is mood altering, can cause drowsiness, and will show up in drug testing programs.

Extra added ingredients. Extra added ingredients include a variety of other chemicals that may or may not enhance the other ingredients in a product. The FDA is watching closely to see if these additions do any good. Caffeine is one of the most popular added ingredient and is commonly found in combination with aspirin and diet pills. Another is an antacid, which basically helps overcome some expected side effects such as stomach distress. Alcohol is another common example and is used as a solvent for the other ingredients. Up to 25 percent or more of some OTC medication is alcohol—that's a 50 proof drink.

Phenylpropanolamine (PPA). Phenylpropanolamine (PPA) is becoming well known in the industry as causing some very undesirable side effects. It's a common ingredient in a variety of OTC medications—diet pills, cold and flu relief, and allergy control. It acts as an antihistamine, a decongestant, and an anorectic (appetite suppressant). Depending on how it is packaged, it can do one or all of these functions. However, PPA is also a very strong stimulant to some people, giving them a real "high" similar to amphetamines. It can have a severe effect on blood pressure, often elevating normal blood pressure to the point where the diagnosis of hypertension is made. PPA can interfere with sleep and cause headaches, dizziness, rapid heart rate, mood changes, and nausea. The FDA is taking special interest in this chemical because of its many adverse side effects.

Review

There are some concerns that bear repeating when discussing OTC medication or self-diagnosis. The most important is, read the label. You will find the above mentioned chemicals and ingredients in just about all of the common drugs used for symptom relief. You will notice that they are in varying doses and often associated with different symptoms. This description is often in small print. Since the scientific name of most of the chemicals of concern end in -ine, you can have a better idea of what you can expect in terms of helping or hindering. The bottom line is this. If the symptoms that you choose to diagnose as being a result of a cold, or flu, or whatever are sufficient to treat with OTC medication, you probably are not safe. If in doubt, check with your AME or ground yourself for a few days.

CAFFEINE

Caffeine, no matter where you find it, is a drug that can have adverse effects on your body. It also ends in -ine, which indicates it could affect your performance as a pilot. In some people its use becomes a mild addiction, or at the very least, a strong habit. Caffeine, like alcohol, when used to excess in some people, can cause problems, resulting in a variety of physical and mental dysfunctions or impairments. It is one of the most underrated, readily available mood-altering drugs available.

Caffeine increases heart rate and rhythm, affects coronary circulation, constricts blood vessel diameters, increases urine production and excretion, and disrupts normal mental processes. There is a variation of tolerances among different people, some noticing few if any side effects, others noticing significant unwanted symptoms, even with only one cup of coffee.

Sources

The main sources of caffeine are coffee and tea (Fig. 5-2). Regular brewed coffee has an average of 100 mg of caffeine per cup. Decaffeinated coffee has only about 4 mg. Tea has about 70 mg per cup (or glass of iced tea). Others include a cup of cocoa (50 mg), cola drinks (40-70 mg per 12

Substance	Amount (mg)
Coffee, 5 to 8-oz. cup	
Decaffeinated, instant	2
Decaffeinated, brewed	2–5
Instant	40–110
Percolated	65–125
Drip	110–150
Tea, 5 to 8-oz. cup	
Bag, brewed for 5 minutes	20–75
Bag, brewed for 1 minute	15–50
Loose, black, 5-minute brew	20–65
Loose, green, 5-minute brew	15–60
Iced, canned	25–35
Cola drinks, 12-oz. glass	
Pepsi-Cola	38
Coca-Cola	33
Tab	32
RC Cola	30
Diet RC	25
Diet-Rite	17
Other soft drinks	
Mountain Dew	54
Dr. Pepper	38
Cocoa, 8-oz. cup	50
Milk chocolate, 1 oz.	3–6
Bittersweet chocolate, 1 oz.	25–35

Fig. 5-2. Caffeine content of various beverages.

ounces), and chocolate (15 mg). Caffeine is also present in many OTC medications, as previously mentioned.

Occasional intake in excess of 250 mg is symptomatic in many people who have not built up a tolerance over the years. Symptoms become more noticeable in very sensitive people. Some pilots are not aware that some of their fatigue, headaches, and nervousness could be secondary to their caffeine intake. Others notice a change in their heart rhythm, in addition to heart rate, after just one cup. This rhythm disturbance will often show up on their FAA EKG.

Caffeine is a strong stimulant, which is the reason most people drink coffee. One to two cups is usually well tolerated and for some people does diminish fatigue, improve mood and alertness, and may temporarily increase mental and physical work capacity. However, the withdrawal effects after a trip where a lot of coffee has been ingested can be counterproductive.

Side effects

Because caffeine is a stimulant to the central nervous system, some people are unable to sleep if they ingest caffeine several hours before retiring. This can be a real dilemma if the pilot uses coffee to stay awake on a long trip and then subsequently tries to get to sleep on the layover. For some people, just one cup of coffee or tea is enough to keep them awake.

Caffeine is also a strong cardiac stimulant, acting like adrenaline to the heart muscle. Arrhythmias, such as skipped beats, and other irregularities might show up on a physical exam or an EKG, such as with a company or FAA exam. Other possible causes must be ruled out. Pilots have been grounded for this situation until the evaluation is completed satisfactorily and no other problems are discovered.

Caffeine is also a diuretic (increases urine production and excretion). In other words, one cup of coffee could result in urinating two or more cups of water, a negative fluid balance that makes dehydration an even bigger problem. Because of an additional chemical (theophyline), a cup of tea can be a stronger diuretic than the same amount of coffee. One can see that iced tea, especially during the summer, can be refreshing, but it can also be more dehydrating in an already dehydrating environment.

One of the most serious yet subtle side effects is on mental functions, often called *caffeinism*. It can cause anxiety and panic disorders, worsen premenstrual syndrome, and create headaches and nervousness. This becomes particularly true during withdrawal from caffeine. Swings of heavy intake, as on a trip or studying for exams or checkrides, to minimal amounts during routine days often generate problems not usually considered to be associated with caffeine. Yet these symptoms must be considered abnormal until proven otherwise, which means yet another medical evaluation.

Tolerance

Low amounts of caffeine are generally well tolerated by most people. However, over a period of years your body builds up a tolerance for greater levels. That is, you might not be aware of symptoms of too much caffeine, but your body is still reacting to those high levels and expects this added boost every day. If you are drinking more than three cups of coffee (or iced tea or cola products) per day, then you can assume you could be at undesirable levels, especially in the environment of flight.

A good policy to follow is to have your one cup of regular coffee in the morning but then either dilute subsequent cups or substitute decaffeinated coffee or tea. Actively increase your water intake to several glasses of water, especially during flight. Substitute juices, herbal teas known to be safe, or just plain hot water (or hot lemonade, etc.) Recognize that you probably don't need that third cup of regular coffee and find something else to take its place.

MISCELLANEOUS ABUSES

Hypoglycemia

Hypoglycemia is not a disease in the traditional sense. It's a condition of having low blood sugar for any number of reasons, often the result of the inability to find adequate nutrition, limited many times to calories from a vending machine. Restaurants, coffee shops, and fast food places aren't always open when you need them, you're in a hurry and don't have time in the morning, or the expected meal is not available on board the airplane. Missed meals is a problem with unpredictable results. Furthermore, you might not be able to control the unexpected lack of adequate and nutritious food. However, there are creative ways of "bagging" food that you can keep in your flight bag or suitcase. This can range from a roll of candies to bags of peanuts or trail mix (peanuts, raisins, and candy) to a bag of easy-to-eat vegetables. And don't forget your large glass of water. Admittedly not as nutritious as a regular meal, it does resolve the symptoms of hypoglycemia for the short term and is certainly better than toughing it out.

By recognizing the symptoms of hypoglycemia, such as headache, stomachache, nervousness, or shakiness, you can take appropriate corrective action, including some form of instant calories, such as candy or peanuts. Prevention is still the best therapy, respecting the body's need for adequate calories that will last for several hours. Avoid empty-calorie food (sweet rolls and colas) to take the place of any meal.

The cola and candy bar, especially when substituted for breakfast, can lead to a blood-sugar rebound effect (sugar high followed in a few hours by a sugar low). Try to find snack foods that are high in protein. These provide energy over a longer period of time.

Smoking

Aside from the risks to your health as described in the chapter on health, smoking also puts carbon monoxide into your blood system and cells. As explained in the chapter on hypoxia, this carbon monoxide interferes with the transportation of oxygen, leading to even higher levels of hypoxia. Smoking up to three cigarettes prior to flight increases your body's hypoxic symptoms as if you were 2,000 to 3,000 feet higher—an increased physiological altitude. It becomes a significant factor with night vision, which is dramatically affected by hypoxia.

Smokeless or chewing tobacco is a significant source of nicotine. It puts more nicotine into your body than does smoking. It greatly increases your risk for other medical problems. A wad of tobacco in the mouth generates a lot of saliva, which must either be swallowed or spit out.

Self-imposed stress can spell death for pilots.

Drugs
Exhaustion
Alcohol
Tobacco
Hypoglycemia

Prescribed medications

Although not self-imposed since your doctor feels you need to be on medication, it's important to know that there are situations when you can fly and still be on prescribed medications. Essentially, when deciding if you are safe, it is a combination of why you need the medication along with any side effects that would be present, just like with OTC medication. Remember, at altitude your symptoms might be different than at ground level. It is wise, therefore, to ground yourself for several days, determine if the medication is doing its job and whether or not it causes side effects. Sometimes unwanted effects disappear after several days on the medication. If the illness is under control and you experience no significant side effects, then returning to flight status might be okay. In any case, if the illness is significant enough to require medication, this situation must be coordinated with your treating physician and your AME or flight surgeon before flying.

Another problem is your schedule interfering with the timeliness in taking your medication. Or you just plain forget to bring your medications along on a trip. If you are supposed to take your pills four times a day, that doesn't mean one every hour for 4 hours in the morning before you take your trip. Your medication must be taken as directed on the container. Furthermore, it is important that you understand the required dosage and frequency. Be sure to tell your personal physician what your duties are in flight and then consider if flying is safe. It is essential that you fully understand the potential side effects, so you know what to look for and your doctor can advise you about your performance degradation.

ALCOHOL AND OTHER DRUGS

Before continuing on with the topic of alcohol and drugs, it is essential that you have a clear understanding of FAR 91.17, which applies to all pilots. "Drugs" could include OTC medications, in addition to the traditional definition of illicit drugs. Because "using any drug that affects" and "influence of" refers to alcohol and drugs, this FAR takes on more significance for the pilot even after the legal 8 hours. It reads:

    a. No person may act or attempt to act as a crewmember of a civil aircraft—
      1. Within 8 hours after the consumption of any alcoholic beverage
      2. While under the influence of alcohol
      3. While using any drug that affects the person's faculties in any way contrary to safety or
      4. While having 0.04 percent by weight or more alcohol in the blood.

The remainder of this regulation refers to your passengers and you submitting to testing for alcohol and drugs. Keep these regulations in mind as you consider whether or not you and your crewmates are truly legal and fit to fly.

Alcohol

Alcohol is found in a variety of places, ranging from food additives, components of medications, and, of course, beverages. Alcohol is alcohol, no matter where it is found, and it has the same effect on you whether it is in highballs, beer, wine, or punch. This might seem simplistic, but many people feel that beer is only a beverage to quench thirst—they do not equate their beer intake to the fact that several beers is the same as several highballs. The saying "if you drink a lot of beer, you drink a lot" is very true, although few summer beer drinkers would admit that they drink a lot of alcohol. The same holds true for wine. There is the same amount of alcohol in a 12-ounce beer, a 1.5-ounce shot of vodka, or a 5-ounce glass of red wine.

Physiology

Ethanol (or *ethyl alcohol*) is the chemical name for the alcohol in beverages. It is readily absorbed in your stomach and small intestine. From there it immediately goes to your brain, where most effects are noticed, some expected and desired, others unexpected and undesired. Other tissue cells become "intoxicated" with alcohol, which sometimes replaces water in the cell structure. Ninety-five percent of the ethanol is then ultimately metabolized by your liver into carbon dioxide and water through a complex process. Prior to being broken down, it is changed to glucose in your body, as a source of energy. Alcohol, therefore, is the ultimate empty calorie because it has no other elements of nutrition.

A full stomach often delays absorption, although the alcohol will then last longer in your body. Liquors are absorbed more quickly than beer. It is also recognized that carbonation, as well as sugar in the mix, increases the absorption rate. These variables make it difficult to determine how an individual responds to any given amount of alcohol. To say your body can tolerate greater amounts because some of these variations are controllable is naive. You are still under the influence.

Some alcohol is excreted unchanged in the urine and some from the lungs. The smell of alcohol on your breath is an indication that a significant amount of alcohol is still in your bloodstream. Even after your blood level reaches zero, you still experience impairment from the effects of hangover and other physiological changes.

Basic physiological effects

Ethanol depresses the central nervous system and is probably the greatest kind of impairment to a pilot. Fatigue and sedation are closely related. Loss of inhibitions, increased euphoria, and a general sense of well being are examples of how you feel and react with alcohol in your system. You talk more and are more sociable. Performance-wise, even at low doses, alcohol causes a loss of fine movement of muscles and touch and diminished concentration.

Ethanol is also a diuretic, especially in the early stages of drinking. As you approach intoxication, your kidneys tend to make less urine. The darker color of your urine is a good indication as to the amount of water that has already been lost thru diuresis—the lighter the color of the urine, the more fluids you are losing. Eventually, your urine becomes a deep yellow or orange, indicating that you are dehydrated. This variation in the amount of fluids remaining in the body—the degree of dehydration—after the drinking is finished might have some effect on the severity of the subsequent hangover. Some studies indicate that fluid retention and blood vessel dilatation cause the headaches and other symptoms of a hangover.

Vasodilatation, or widening of the arteries, especially within the skin, is another effect. This makes you feel warm and gives some drinkers the ruddy or flushed complexion. However, as noted in the chapter on heat and cold stresses, alcohol is counterproductive in coping with temperature extremes because it interferes with the body's attempts at controlling internal body temperatures.

Effects on the body. Ethanol is a toxin to the body and to the liver, altering and killing tissue cells. For example, heavy drinkers lose about 100,000 brain cells per drinking day, which is about 10 times the normal attrition. We have billions of brain cells, so in most cases only minimal damage is being done. The same is true with the liver, in that the cells are altered, eventually turning into scar tissue. This condition is called *cirrhosis*, and in severe cases it is incompatible with a productive life, let alone normal metabolism. These changes to the liver (and the kidneys) can be detected by changes in blood tests that include liver and kidney function measurements.

The cardiovascular system is affected by an increased heart size and elevated blood pressure and heart rate. Blood lipid levels (cholesterol, LDL, etc.) are also increased. A doctor seeing a patient with unexplained hypertension, rapid pulse, and elevated cholesterol might suspect alcohol abuse and look for further evidence. Irregular heart rhythms are common with intoxication and become chronic with heavy drinkers, even long after the last drink. This includes heart blocks, extra beats (PVCs—premature ventricular contractions), conduction defects, and tachycardia (rapid heart rate).

Alcohol is an irritant to the lining of your esophagus and stomach, sometimes resulting in gastritis or bleeding ulcers. Gastritis is common with drinkers, often requiring large doses of antacids to overcome. A medical emergency exists when you begin vomiting blood.

Ethanol also induces hypoglycemia after the last drink and for several hours later. This effect, in combination with other nutritional short cuts usually taken during the party and the morning after, makes you even more susceptible to the symptoms of hypoglycemia. Good nutrition with lots of water is the best way to help your body recover.

Histotoxic hypoxia, where your body's cells are unable to use oxygen, is often caused by alcohol. Within the cell, alcohol is a toxin, interfering with metabolism, especially with oxygen usage. This is why your body acts as if it were at a higher altitude. Some have said that two drinks adds between 4,000 and 8,000 feet to the physiological altitude at which your body is trying to perform.

Your vestibular system is also affected by alcohol, even for many hours after your blood alcohol level is zero. Your sense of balance and orientation is impaired. Dizziness is noted, especially during intoxication. When trying to lie down, the dizziness gets worse because the semicircular canals are "tumbled." These later effects include a marked reduction in the tolerance to G forces (even mild) and linear forces as experienced in a turn.

Effects on performance. The most significant effect is impairment of your fine motor skills and mental processes unique to flying. You are taught to fly straight and level, but the greatest emphasis in your training is how to react in emergency situations. You must react instinctively and at the same time respond to rapidly changing situations. Rapid decisions and actions are necessary in a potentially deteriorating scenario. Alcohol and post-alcohol impairment interfere with every mental and physical activity associated with the skills necessary for a safe recovery.

Some of the impairments include increased reaction time, such as taking longer to make an evasive maneuver or correct an unsafe trim setting. Tracking is impaired, which equates into an inefficient and unproductive scanning of instruments. Judgment of distances and heights is compromised, leading to inadequate situation awareness on approaches.

Visual acuity is diminished, making charts difficult to interpret, closing traffic difficult to see, and increasing the likelihood of using improper settings of radios and navigation equipment. Coordination skills are seriously eroded, preventing you from doing several activities at once, as in making a simple turn while adjusting throttle settings.

The most subjective problem is your inability to think clearly and to make sound decisions. As with hypoxia, you are unaware that your performance is impaired. As most pilots do, you are always monitoring yourself, seeking perfection. When that self-monitoring process is diminished by alcohol, you are a prime target for unsafe situations. Alcohol interferes with that process and allows you to do ill-advised things without even recognizing the seriousness of your actions or inactions.

When under the influence of alcohol, the usually conscientious and careful pilot loses his or her normal attitude of caution when he or she sees a change in his or her performance—especially in evasive maneuvers. Poor judgment is a byproduct of this progressively dangerous situation.

All these impaired performance and judgment skills can be occurring at the same time and at blood alcohol levels less than 0.04 percent, the legal FAA allowance. You might think you are doing better when in fact you aren't. And how are you going to tell? Even experienced pilots are impaired when faced with multiple tasks. And again, like being hypoxic, you are unable and unwilling to recognize how impaired you are and thus cannot and will not take corrective actions or let someone else fly.

Many more unsafe situations occur even when blood alcohol content returns to zero, and for many hours afterwards. Couple this with the additional effects of a hangover, and you are looking at an accident waiting to happen.

Hangover

Scientists refer to a hangover as *post alcohol impairment*. The symptoms include tremors, thirst, nausea and vomiting, heartburn, sweating, dizziness, and of course, headache. More subjective effects are increased irritability, anxiety, and mental depression.

With heavier drinking, these symptoms are more severe and mental function impairment is less subtle. Performance is affected in critical phases of takeoffs, landings, and emergency situations. There is marked reduction in your ability to perform nonroutine tasks. These impairments are noted even 14 to 24 hours after blood alcohol content (BAC) is zero.

A major problem even after blood alcohol content is zero is fatigue. Alcohol is known to reduce REM sleep, which means that the drinker is not getting a restful sleep. You might be passed out or sleeping heavily, but it is from depression of brain activity, not sleep.

Preventing a hangover is related to decreasing the amounts and rate of ingestion of alcohol and reducing the absorption in the GI tract. High protein foods, such as dairy products and meats, stay in the stomach longer and slow absorption of alcohol. Gulping drinks increases not only the total amount consumed in a given period of time, but also causes alcohol to enter the bloodstream and your brain more quickly. Carbonated beverages, including beer, tend to make your stomach absorb alcohol more quickly. Mixes with juices and water instead of soda water are less likely to lead to hangover. The slower the absorption, the slower the alcohol gets to the cellular level.

It should be obvious that 8 or even 12 hours "between bottle and throttle" is not nearly adequate to prevent the varied impairments from alcohol, especially from the effects of a hangover. Impairment depends on the total amounts, the time over which alcohol is ingested, and the tolerance built up by the drinker. You could still be under the influence, even if your blood alcohol content is zero.

Hangover and other headaches
(Independent causes in susceptible individuals)

Hangover:
- Excessive alcohol
- Red wine
- Cheap wine

Chinese restaurant syndrome:
- Monosodium glutamate (MSG)
- Excessive salt

Hot dog headache:
- Sodium nitrite preservatives

Fermented cheese & salami

Dark chocolate

Aspartame

Caffeine (Withdrawal)

Consider: How often are two or more of these causes occurring at the same time?

The only cure for the effects of a hangover is the passage of time, sometimes up to 36 hours. Coffee and oxygen have no effect on reducing the symptoms or improving performance. Caffeine might make you feel better, but it still disrupts skills. Oxygen is not part of the metabolism of alcohol. However, the act of "sucking on oxygen" might make you feel you are doing something to overcome the effects.

Tolerance to alcohol

Over time, the body can develop a tolerance to very high levels of alcohol. Studies indicate that you cannot judge that you are impaired or that your blood alcohol is zero by how you feel. In fact, as noted previously, some problems arise even when alcohol is no longer present in your blood. Many pilots actually think they are safe to fly only 4 hours after their last drink, despite facts to the contrary. Often this is a perception based on their increased tolerance.

Recognizing a problem drinker

It really isn't that difficult to recognize a problem drinker if you are honest with your observations. However, few want to be a snitch, nor do they feel competent to pass judgment on someone they suspect has a problem. After all, what is the definition of a problem drinker or one who is truly dependent on alcohol? Is it someone who drinks more than you, or are there distinct criteria? Anyone with a blood alcohol level of 0.15 percent is considered to be intoxicated, but how often must a person be intoxicated before being considered dependent?

The problem drinker has a little of all these indications. You must keep a high index of suspicion when observing someone you know slowly develop a lifestyle that has an increasing drinking pattern. Don't count on the flight surgeon or personal physician to intervene. It is estimated that less than 10 percent of referrals of alcoholics to treatment come from the doctor. Usually it's from concerned family and friends along with business and flying colleagues and managers.

Specialists in alcohol problems have specific guidelines to be used in determining if there is a potential dependency. The following are a few danger signals. In the right combination, these could also be diagnostic of alcoholism and cause for FAA medical disqualification.

A. Any one of the following factors
   1. A clinical diagnosis of "alcoholism"
   2. Evidence of withdrawal from alcohol
B. Any two of these major criteria which indicates that alcoholism is definite and a diagnosis of a history obligatory
   1. A medical history of liver disease
   2. A medical history of central or peripheral nervous system involvement
   3. Psychological dependence on alcohol is demonstrated by either admission or by history
   4. More than one conviction for an offense involving alcohol, including nonhighway arrests
   5. Known to various health and social agencies in the community through contacts related to alcohol problems
   6. Treatment at an inpatient facility devoted to alcohol rehabilitation

C. Minor criteria from which any three or four fulfilled or one major and two minor criteria
    1. Accidents involving injury or property damage that may be presumed to be related to alcohol
    2. Known to have a history of troubled relationships in employment
    3. Known to have a history of troubled relationships within family
    4. Known to have troubled relationships with banks or creditors
    5. Intoxicated more than four times a year
    6. At any time a blood alcohol level of greater than 0.2 percent
    7. A history of blackouts
    8. Odor of alcohol on the breath at the time of medical certification
    9. Evidence of social and behavioral distruption.

These criteria are used as a guide to assist in determining the degree of use of and dependence on alcohol and whether or not there is a problem that could interfere with meeting FAA standards. Many of these criteria are also a sign of poor judgment in the use of alcohol.

The two biggest indications for suspicion of alcohol dependency are increased tolerance and denial. The denial is the hardest to define because the alcoholic is a master of denying that there is a problem, even when confronted by other people.

Addiction, dependence, and alcoholism mean somewhat the same thing for our purposes. The problem drinker cannot control his or her intake, or is unable to say "enough." The problem drinker is unable to stop after the first drink. Frequency of use is often daily, with careful avoidance prior to work or flying. The amounts consumed are often staggering (literally), a quart of vodka or a case of beer per day not uncommon. The deception to the drinker and those around him or her is the perception that he or she doesn't appear drunk or impaired—but is. The problem drinker has developed a tolerance to large amounts.

Dependency is the main concern when discussing alcohol use, especially in aviation. The combination of being impaired (and not recognizing that fact) and the denial that there is a problem leads to the pilot often flying under the influence, even after blood alcohol content is zero. Therefore, identifying the problem drinker by keeping a high index of suspicion that dependency is present becomes the responsibility of everyone. Some things to look for:

- Increased tolerance to alcohol (probably the most important), resulting in drinking more and more rapidly than others.
- Gulps the first drink or two.

- A personality change over a period of time.
- Increased absenteeism and use of sick time.
- Increase in complaints about family life or management, often trivial and with a suspicious nature.
- Frequently drinks alone and avoids nondrinking friends.
- Increase in irritability, becomes more argumentative.
- Denial of increased alcohol intake and of the problems just noted.

Treatment of dependency

The first step in treatment is recognition, by both pilot and those around the pilot. This was just discussed but the challenge remains—few will take the step of recognizing that there is a problem. This combination is often called *enabling*—allowing the problem to continue by enabling the drinker to continue.

Once a problem is recognized and action is decided upon, the next step is intervention. Although it is hoped that the problem drinker will seek help, this is usually not the real world scenario. An intervention is where concerned individuals participate in a structured confrontation, an action that essentially corners the drinker into hearing what is happening to him and then what needs to be done. There is only one way out, only one solution for the drinker—to enter treatment (which must already be arranged). Intervention is often done by professionals along with family and colleagues. More information relative to this step is best obtained from treatment centers, Alcoholics Anonymous representatives, or company employee assistance programs.

Treatment for a dependent pilot must be at an FAA-accepted treatment center and usually on an inpatient basis (admitted into the center for the full term of treatment and not allowed to "commute" home). The techniques of treatment vary from center to center but generally follow the 12-step program developed by Alcoholics Anonymous (AA). Also, there is comprehensive testing, both medically and psychologically, counseling with professionals, and sessions with groups. The details can be obtained from the same resources just mentioned. It is recommended that you become familiar with the scenario to better appreciate how you can help.

Alcohol, especially when associated with dependency, is a major problem within all aviation. Often the only way the pilot with a problem can be identified, treated, and returned to flight is through the combined efforts of those around him. The FAA will participate in this program if it sees the proper and appropriate efforts and results. Therefore, you are not ruining a pilot's career or flying status if the above-mentioned procedures are followed. There is no reason, in reality, to avoid intervening. If you suspect someone has a problem, seek advice from your company's employee assistance department or union, or call the FAA to obtain advice. (No names need be mentioned; you're seeking recommendations on whom to contact to get directions to help.)

Illicit drugs

Illicit means *illegal*. Pure and simple. A pilot using illicit drugs is in violation of the law and federal regulations. It's not a matter of when they are used, how much is used, or how impaired you are. If you are caught, you have no excuse. You broke the law!

That aside, there are some facts that pilots need to know, especially to recognize why these drugs are dangerous before and during flight. A prime problem with these drugs is their highly addictive properties. Furthermore, you can become more dependent on these chemicals than on alcohol, which means increased difficulty in achieving successful treatment.

Kinds of drugs. All these drugs are called mood altering and are often associated with being a stimulant, depressant, or hallucinogenic. Hence, there are a family of drugs that are tested for in most drug programs: amphetamines, marijuana, cocaine, PCP, and opiates.

Marijuana is probably the most common of these drugs, although cocaine is equally common in some cultures and parts of the country. The active ingredient is THC (delta 9 tetra hydrocannibinal), and it is this chemical that is tested for in urine. THC causes temporary euphoria and relaxation. However, more than alcohol, it distorts perception, weakens critical judgment, and interferes with the ability to concentrate.

THC also increases heart rate and the incidence of cardiac arrhythmias. Short-term memory is impaired, IQ is thought to be diminished, and there is a decrease in reaction time and tracking (similar to alcohol). In severe cases, there is marked depression and some hallucinations.

Physiologically, THC is stored in fat tissue, which means it can be slowly released at unpredictable rates long after THC is first taken into the body. The same effects can then develop, with the greatest threat to the brain, and can occur up to 30 days after taking in THC. Because most THC is taken in by smoking, it should be noted that this smoke is far worse in producing cancer than regular smoking. THC might also cause genetic changes and damage and interfere with the body's immune system.

Testing. Using the current testing programs, there are no false positives. The common procedure is a two-phased test for these five drugs in the urine. The first part is a screening test, and it is here that false positives can occur; that is, some other chemical might show up as being positive for one of the five drugs. But this positive is not officially reported, and a confirmatory test is automatically done. This test is a gas chromatography and mass spectrography analysis, which generates a unique curve for every known chemical.

Furthermore, it is necessary that the amount of the drug found must exceed a predetermined level. In other words, the test is not only qualitative but quantitative. For example, if 90 units of THC were suspected in the screening test and the level to be considered positive is 100, then that part of the test is reported as negative. If above 100, then the confirmatory test is done. Again, there is a level above which that drug must be present before being reported as positive.

In conclusion, you have a lot more control of your health and how you perform in flight than you might recognize. Common sense, moderation, and recognition of self-imposed stresses can keep you out of trouble. Furthermore, you can assist others by advising them of the facts of self-imposed medical problems.

6

Vision

John, only 42 years old, had never worn glasses and had passed his FAA exams without difficulty. He did notice, however, that is was more difficult to see the bottom line for near vision, but neither the nurse nor the doctor said anything about it. And since there was no limitation on his medical, John never thought he would have any problem reading for a long time yet. But tonight was different. He was tired from flying 9 hours across the Pacific as the copilot. The cruise was uneventful at FL390. The cockpit and instrument lights had been turned down because there wasn't much to do. Yet he was having increasing difficulty reading the CRTs. The letters weren't clear and he had trouble telling 8s from 0s and 3s. Even the approach plate he attempted to read in anticipation of arrival was less than sharp. Finally, he turned up the lights and noticed an improvement. The captain noted the difficulty and offered his reading glasses to John. "Wow," he said, "does that make a difference! But I'm too young to be wearing these 'cheaters.' What's wrong?" All the captain said was to take a look at the cabin altitude and consider how long they had been flying under night conditions.

Of all the senses used by the human body and mind for flying, vision is by far the most important. In addition to supplying nearly 90 percent of your cues for orientation (vestibular and proprioceptive is about ten percent), vision supplies data for monitoring your instruments, searching for traffic, reading your written materials, and determining visual references for taxiing, takeoffs, and approaches to landing. Put another way, any disruption of your vision can incapacitate you, and impaired vision increases the likelihood of an unsafe flight.

Most people take vision for granted, as long as they can read and see distant objects. But without testing for visual acuity, you have nothing by which to compare your vision and might not be aware that what you are seeing is not as clear or sharp as it could be. A common comment by children who begin wearing glasses for the first time is that they now realize that brick walls have lines. Until they began to wear corrective lenses, the bricks were a blur, but with nothing to compare this image to, they assumed that there were no lines.

The same holds true for older pilots (over age 40) who begin to wear reading glasses for the first time. It's almost startling to them to see how clear their approach plates and CRT characters really are. They might have been able to pass the FAA vision test, but that didn't mean they were seeing near objects clearly.

Furthermore, pilots with 20/20 day vision might not possess adequate night vision as a result of the physiology of how the retina converts light energy into electrical energy for the brain. There also appears to be an individual variation in pilots of how light energy is perceived by the brain and translated into data necessary for flight. In other words, with the same visual acuity, one pilot sees better and uses vision more effectively than another.

LIGHT AND LENSES

Light is defined as radiant energy that excites cells of the retina of your eye and produces an electrical current that is transmitted to the visual cortex of the brain for interpretation (Fig. 6-1). Visible light is only a small part of the radiation spectrum, ranging from the color of violet at 380 millimicrons (one millionth of a millimeter) to red, which is 760 millimicrons. Longer wavelengths (infrared) cause heat and are a source of increased energy. Damage to your eye, especially the retina, is dependent on degree and duration of that energy.

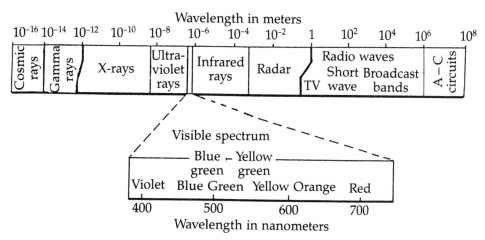

Fig. 6-1. The electromagnetic spectrum.

Light rays reach your eye either directly from a light source or indirectly, as reflected from a source back to your eye. There are individual light rays reaching the eye from the light source (or reflected from an object). These rays are virtually parallel to each other beyond 20 feet from your eye. Light rays originating closer than 20 feet come to your eye at an angle.

Anatomy of the eye

Light is focused onto the retina after it enters your eye through the cornea and passes through the lens (Fig. 6-2). The retina translates this radiant energy into electrical energy by photosensitive cells called *rods* and *cones*.

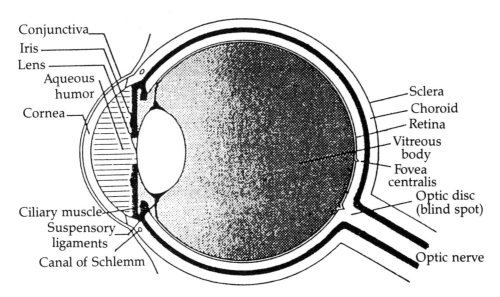

Fig. 6-2. Anatomically, the eye is an extension of the brain, so, like other brain cells, the cells of the eye are adversely affected by fatigue, hypoxia, and alcohol.

The outer layer of cells of the eyeball is the cornea. The transparency of the cornea can become affected permanently with age and temporarily with overexposure to ultraviolet radiation.

Like in a camera, the lens refracts light rays as they enter your eye and focuses each ray onto the retina, which is analogous to the film in a camera. If the focal point is in front of or behind the retina, the perception will be a blurred object. Because the lens of a camera is hard, a camera changes the position of the focal point by shortening or lengthening the distance of the lens from the film. The lens of your eye is soft and moldable, and its shape is changed by the ciliary muscles that surround the lens. When these muscles contract or relax, the lens changes from fat to thin, allowing for more or less refraction of the light rays. Therefore, focusing is accomplished by changing the shape of the lens rather than changing the distance. How well your lens can be changed in shape determines how well your eye can clearly focus an object onto the retina.

The lens can become opaque in some people as they age, resulting in cataracts. Also, as you age, your lens begins to stiffen, which prevents sharp focusing and slows down the rapid change of focusing from distant to near objects (accommodation).

The iris is the colored membrane seen in the front of your eye and determines the color of your eyes. The center portion is called the pupil, and like a camera's aperture, the size of the opening can be changed to allow more or less light to enter your eye. This gives your eye more flexibility to control the amount of light reaching the retina, wider in low light, smaller in bright light.

The brighter the light, the smaller the pupil, which like a camera, increases the depth of field. Depth of field is the distance from the lens within which everything is in focus. Therefore, in low light conditions, the depth of field is very short because the pupil is larger. Squinting duplicates this action to a small degree and allows for some focusing.

The retina is the film of your eye, using photosensitive cells to detect light energy in place of light-sensitive silver nitrate crystals in photographic film (Fig. 6-3). A big difference is the distribution of two different kinds of cells within the retina. Each of these cells connects to a nerve, which in turn ends up in a bundle of nerves called the *optic nerve*.

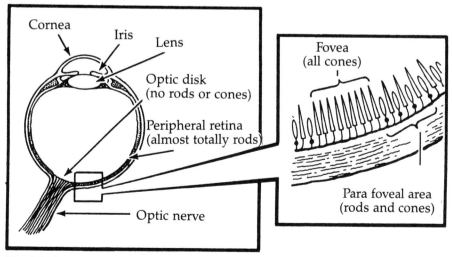

Fig. 6-3. Anatomy of the eye.

One kind of cell is the *cone* cell, which is sensitive to bright light and colors as well as clarity. They are thus used primarily in daytime and provide the most accurate visual sensing. Cone cells are concentrated in a small area called the *fovea*. This is the spot on the retina where most visual objects are focused. This is your central vision.

Rod cells are reactive to low light but not to colors and thus are more suitable for night vision. Surrounding the fovea is an increasing number of rods and a decreasing number of cones until the periphery, where there are no cones. This peripheral vision is more suited to orientation and is supplementary in night-vision techniques.

There are no cones or rods where the optic nerve is formed on the retina. This lack creates a blind spot in vision but is compensated for by having two eyes, each one overcoming the other's blind spot.

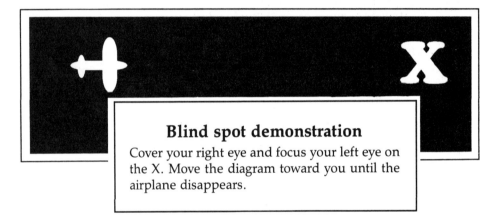

Blind spot demonstration

Cover your right eye and focus your left eye on the X. Move the diagram toward you until the airplane disappears.

Optics and physics of light

A single light ray has a variety of physical properties that are associated with vision. *Refraction* is the property of a lens to bend the light ray so as to reach a given point (on the retina). Several light rays must also remain in focus through the same lens. Furthermore, the lens must be able to focus on near as well as distant objects. This is called *accommodation*, where the refractive powers of the lens are continuously changing, allowing for uninterrupted focus—as opposed to a camera, which has to change its focal length.

Several other properties determine the clarity of the perception of these images. These include brightness, contrast, and color. Reaction time, or the time from seeing or identifying an object and recognition by the brain, must also be considered. In addition, atmospheric conditions such as fog, haze, rain, etc., can also interfere with light ray transmission and its diffusion through the atmosphere.

The brighter the light, the easier it is for your eye to gather light rays onto the fovea. As with sound, low sources of energy result in a poor signal, or lack of clarity. The opposite extreme is too much light and glare, which interferes with proper acuity and is uncomfortable.

The greater the difference between an image of an object and its background (contrast), the easier it is to distinguish what the object (or character) is. If the edge is fuzzy for any reason, the object appears out of focus. Look at a painting and you will notice how the artist has clarified edges by outlining them with a darker color. Fog and haze interfere with this contrast and lead to poor acuity and clarity as well as visual illusions.

Color also affects acuity. Each color is refracted differently through a lens, as evidenced by the rainbow effect from a prism. Therefore, some colors (other than white light, which contains all colors) will not be in focus, relative to other colors. Red, for example, is refracted much less than others, which leads to unfocused perception by you. It will not be as clear as an image illuminated by other colors or with white light. Therefore, using red light in the cockpit is not recommended because small characters on maps and checklist will not be clear and sharply focused and can be misread.

Two objects of the same brightness can be distinguished easily if there is a recognizable color contrast, even in low light. The clearest is black against white. However, few situations have such a clear definition. If you are not sure what is being visualized, you will take more time than necessary to discern what the object or character really is.

GETTING TO 20/20

Several variations of the lens affect acuity. *Acuity* means the sharpness or keenness of vision, with *perfect* meaning that your eye sees or perceives exactly what the object is, whether it is close to or distant from your eye. Because focusing and accommodation are relative to the status of the curvature of the lens, you can enhance the curvature with artificial lenses (glasses or contacts).

Variations of acuity

Testing for acuity is accomplished by comparing what you can see clearly in actual conditions to what a normal eye with perfect vision can see in the same conditions. The eye doctor will have you distinguish various characters of different sizes. The bottom line of the eye chart (20/20 or 20/15, depending on the chart) can be read without difficulty by a normal eye. However, as the ability of your eye to see well diminishes, the characters must be larger, as in the second line (20/30). The poorer eye can only see a character size at 20 feet that a normal eye can see at 30 feet. These tests are also done under ideal conditions with bright light and black and white contrast.

Myopia (nearsightedness) is the most common acuity problem (Fig. 6-4). Myopia means distant objects are out of focus without correction. Optically, the focal point of the lens at rest is in front of the retina.

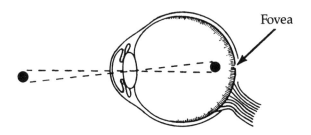

Fovea

Fig. 6-4. Myopia (nearsighted-ness).

Astigmatism is the unequal and variable curvature of the lens and the cornea that prevents an equal focus of varying distances. For example, a vertical light pole might be in focus, but the horizontal power lines might be out of focus. If one has a perfectly spherical cornea and lens, there is no astigmatism.

Presbyopia (farsightedness) is a predictable change to your lens, occurring as you get older. The lens stiffens and is unable to accommodate effectively. The focal point at rest is behind the retina. It affects near vision which requires "reading glasses" while distant vision remains unchanged. There is also less light passing through the older lens, which further interferes with depth of focus. It is common for the older pilot to have uncorrected distant vision remain at 20/20 but need glasses to read.

Refractive error

The refractive powers of the lens can be measured to determine how well it can focus. This is accomplished by using a variety of different strength artificial lenses placed in front of your eye. You then tell the doctor which supplemental lens makes a character clearer on a chart. Corrective lenses can be ground using this refractive error when stated as a prescription.

Corrective lenses

Once the refractive error is defined, lenses can be ground to make up for this error of refraction, allowing the focal point to be on the retina and in focus. This correction can be in the form of frame glasses or contact lenses. There are trade-offs. Frame glasses are generally more easily tolerated, but contact lenses allow for better peripheral vision. Also, as you get older and near vision changes, you will need to wear glasses for near. If you already have distance glasses, then bifocals are needed.

Bifocal glasses (upper part of the lens ground for distant and the other lower part for near vision) are common. Furthermore, as it becomes more difficult to accommodate, even middle distances might need correction, hence trifocals. Your glasses might have to be specially ground in order to effectively accommodate to focal lengths not common outside the cockpit. Many pilots are reluctant to wear glasses, especially for reading. However, the sooner such glasses are worn as a habit, the easier it will be to adapt to the correction.

NIGHT VISION

Vision under low light is a different physiological activity than vision under bright light. There is a chemical change within the cells of the retina that process light energy. During the day and in well-lighted conditions, most light rays are focused on the fovea, which is concentrated with cone cells. Such cells have a chemical called *iodopsin* that allows the eye to be immediately stimulated.

Another chemical (*rhodopsin* or *visual purple*) is found in the rods. However, the chemical must be made by these cells whenever light levels are low. Time is required for this chemical to be formed, which means it takes longer (up to 45 minutes) to adapt to low light than to bright light (about ten seconds). Therefore, the retina has the ability to adapt to different light conditions by changing the amount of low-light-sensitive chemicals found in the rods.

Types of vision

Because of the varying resources the eye and retina has to adapt to changing light conditions, your vision is divided into two types, depending on the amount of light available.

Photopic vision. This is daylight conditions with relatively sufficient light to activate your foveal cells (cones), either from sunlight or from artificial illumination. Here color is easily discerned and images are sharp because of the use of the fovea (central vision). Cones are found in the fovea, but the visual purple chemical is bleached out by the light. Thus, photopic vision is primarily through use of cones and central vision.

Scotopic vision. This occurs in low-light conditions, either at night or in darkened environments. Here, cone cells are ineffective, resulting in poor resolution of detail. Peripheral vision, with rods, is used. Visual acuity decreases considerably, sometimes as much as 20/200. Color vision is totally lost.

Dark adaptation

Dark adaptation is the process by which your retinas increase their sensitivity to decreasing levels of available light. The chemical change occurs in the rods as the cones becomes less effective. The lower the starting level of available light, the more rapidly the adaptation will occur.

It takes about 30 to 45 minutes for this adaptation in minimal light conditions. The brighter the surrounding light, the longer it will take to adapt. This also is dependent on ideal conditions during which there is exposure to bright light, even for brief periods. This "bleaches" the changing chemical in the rods, which then has to be re-adapted. A very bright light, such as a flashlight directly into the eye for even a second, or the strobe lights on aircraft, can seriously impair night vision. Recovery could take several minutes.

Preserving night vision

The obvious technique to preserve night vision is to avoid bright lights and to stay in a darkened environment for the time it takes for the rod cells to adapt. There is another method to protect your night vision, and that is by using red light for illumination.

Rod cells in the retina are least affected by the light wave length in the red range (longer wave lengths). A red light source will not "bleach" the chemical rhodopsin as do other colors of shorter wavelengths. It follows that the use of red light, once vision is adapted to night, would not alter the status of the retina and the rods. For this reason, wearing red goggles in certain situations prior to actual flight and in preparation for a night trip might be helpful.

There is a trade-off, however. Red light refracts less than the other colors of white light (remember that white light is a combination of all colors). Objects are no longer in focus using only red light, and it is more difficult to accommodate from near to distant vision. Red light also masks any red-colored objects, instruments, or map markings. As more and more CRT (cathode ray tube) displays are used in "glass cockpits" with multi-colored and multi-hued characters, red light (or any light source other than white) becomes counterproductive and should not be used.

A good compromise would be to use red light only when trying to enhance the adaptation process, but not during actual flight. Low-level white light on the instruments and within the cockpit is the best, provided the intensity can be controlled. As darkness outside increases and the eyes adapt more to low light, this white light source can be reduced.

Techniques for improving night vision

There are significant changes in how the eye perceives any level of light as darkness increases. Central vision is compromised because of its dependence on cone cells. Peripheral vision becomes the primary source of visual cues (Fig. 6-5). Therefore, off-center vision must be used. Off-center vision involves looking at an object about ten degrees away from the object. Your peripheral vision becomes the source of light signals to your brain. Another challenge is the observation that if an object is visualized for more than 2 to 3 seconds, the retinal cells can become "bleached out," which can result in the object not being seen. Continuous scanning or changing the position of your eyes on an object can prevent this occurrence (Fig. 6-6).

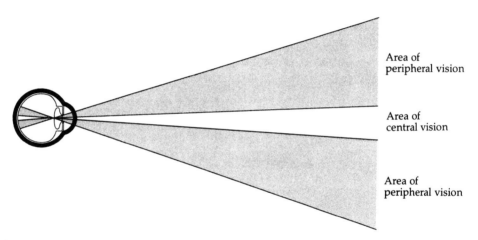

Area of peripheral vision

Area of central vision

Area of peripheral vision

Fig. 6-5. The central area gives the most acute vision in light down to the intensity of moonlight. Below this level of illumination, central vision cannot function as well and the central area is nearly blind. Any object that an individual looks at directly is not seen clearly.

Color vision becomes less dependable. Colored lights from beacons, runways, and wing tips are discernible if the light source is strong enough to activate the cone cells. However, other colors outside (and often inside) a dimly lit cockpit will appear gray.

Reaction time of visual accommodation, recognition, and action is also impaired. This time is defined as that necessary to first recognize that an object is present. Additional time is necessary for this signal to get to the brain cells dealing with vision, and stll more time is necessary for

Eccentric fixation

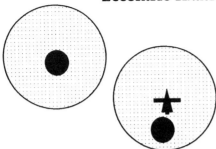

Left—The central blind spot present in very dim light makes it impossible to see the plane if it is looked at directly.

Right—The plane can be seen in the same amount of light by looking below (as is shown here), above, or to one side of it so that it is not obscured by the central blind area.

Dark adaptation

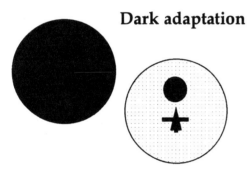

Fig. 6-6. As darkness outside increases, off-center vision must be used.

Left—View seen by a person who is not dark-adapted.

Right—The same view seen by a dark-adapted person who is looking at a point above the plane.

your eye and head to turn toward and focus on the unknown object. Your brain must then determine the importance and significance of the object's presence, and further time is necessary for your body to react, such as moving the muscles necessary to take corrective action at the controls. This whole process can take up to four seconds, depending on the conditions of the environment and your fitness.

SEEING IN THE SUNLIGHT

Whether or not correction is needed for acuity, sunglasses are part of the image of the pilot. Sunglasses are often worn for cosmetic reasons, even when they serve no other purpose. As a result, several considerations must be recognized when discussing the use of sunglasses.

The primary reason to use sunglasses is to reduce the amount of light from every bright source (the sun being the most obvious) to a level that is comfortable that doesn't affect the requirement for adequate visualization. Additionally, there should be no distortion of color. This translates into ensuring that all wavelengths of light rays enter the eye for comprehensive interpretation. At the same time they should filter out harmful ultraviolet and infrared radiation.

Because sunglasses decrease the amount of light entering your eye, the eye reacts by opening the iris (aperture) to allow more light onto the retina. Remembering the analogy to a camera, a larger opening, or aperture, decreases depth of field, which means that objects remain in focus but in a shorter amount of depth. Observe professional tennis players— you rarely see them wearing sunglasses. They do not want to compromise a short depth of field. It allows them to clearly see the tennis ball come from their opponent's racket to their side without having to rely on the focusing mechanism. This same principle holds true in aviation, especially in the traffic pattern.

Some of the specifications for sunglasses include maintaining a reasonable filtering of the amount of light, probably no more than about 15 percent. More than that compromises the light source necessary for safe flight. Wearing sunglasses in low light results in a definite loss of acuity. Some of the glasses that automatically darken in bright light should not be used in the cockpit because of the varying levels of light—from looking outside to reading instruments deep in the cockpit.

Sunglasses should be neutral in color, allowing most wavelengths to pass through. Any colors other than neutral gray could distort the image seen by the eye. For example, green colored sunglasses absorb a high amount of every color except green. The same is true for other colors. With so many controls, CRT characters, and maps in varying colors, it is not safe to wear any glasses that filter out key colors.

A popular color is yellow or amber, which is claimed to make it easier to see through fog or haze. There is a perception of clearer visibility and sharper focus, but it is more subjective than proven. Whatever the color of the lens, that color will be washed out when it reaches the eye. With vision a key source of sensory input, anything that is not a true color can mislead your perception of objects.

Polarizing glasses are also of dubious use in aviation. They are helpful in situations of high glare from reflected sources such as water, snow, and sand, but the trade-off is distortion of light rays passing through the windshields.

A final consideration is filtering out, or absorbing, ultraviolet (UV) and infrared light rays. This is easily accomplished by ensuring that the sunglasses state that they filter out UV light, preferably the full range. The coating is inexpensive.

FACTORS AFFECTING VISUAL ACUITY

In either day or night flight, there are factors, many controllable, that can seriously affect the efficiency of vision. This impairment is more noticeable during night flights. The most important is hypoxia. Because the retina is an actual anatomical extension of the brain, anything that affects your brain immediately affects vision. Lack of oxygen first affects brain tissue. Thus vision is concurrently eroded by reduction of sensitivity of rod cells. Low light conditions add to this erosion. Hypoxia also increases the time necessary for dark adaptation. Such impairment is noticeable starting at about 5,000 feet above the ground level to which you are acclimated.

Carbon monoxide, which builds up in the blood of all smokers, creates hypoxia with the same results. Some have observed that smoking just three cigarettes adds enough carbon monoxide to the blood cells to simulate an additional 5,000 to 8,000 feet of altitude.

Because alcohol can cause hystoxic hypoxia, the same reduction of acuity results even hours after the last drink.

VISUAL ILLUSIONS

Most visual illusions are a result of distortion of light rays as they pass through air containing fog, dust, haze, etc. These components tend to refract the light rays before they reach your eye, causing poorly focused objects, reduced light source, and distorted visual cues. Basic optics states that distant objects appear smaller. The distance of an object from a person is therefore a mental judgment comparing size to already known comparisons or related to nearby known objects. Distortion of these light rays further confuses your brain when it is trying to interpret size and distance.

Space myopia

Space myopia is sometimes also called *empty field myopia*. It means that there are no objects on which to focus beyond 20 feet. Therefore, unless the eye and lens are "stimulated" into focusing, the lens tends to go into a resting state, focusing somewhere between near and far. As a result, outside targets are missed and the reaction time to accommodate to cockpit

Visual cues

Some of the standard monocular (one-eyed) depth cues an individual uses to judge distance are:

- **Linear perspective**—As objects get more distant, they appear smaller.
- **Aerial perspective**—As objects get more distant, they appear hazier.
- **Superposition**—Objects nearer to you obstruct the view of distant ones.
- **Brightness**—Nearer objects are usually brighter than distant ones.
- **Shadows**—With respect to the light source, nearer objects usually cast shorter shadows than distant ones.
- **Texture**—Nearer objects appear "grainier" than distant ones; the level of detail increases in nearer objects.

objects is somewhat impaired. This is easily avoided and corrected by frequently picking out an object beyond 20 feet, such as a wing tip or a cloud edge, and consciously focusing. Staring into space during a boring flight is to be avoided for these reasons.

7

Hearing

Three hours cruising along at 4,500 feet in my homebuilt was exhilarating. This is real flying, I thought. I even opened up the window to smell the fresh air rushing by my face. Because I was flying VFR over the plains, I didn't need to talk to anyone. Then I landed, feeling great. My son came over to me from the hangar. I could see his lips moving as he got closer, but I couldn't hear anything. I also became aware that the ringing in my ears was worse than usual. In the car on the way home, I had to turn up the volume of the radio. Then it dawned on me. I really couldn't hear well. My doctor confirmed this using an audiometer—the first hearing test I've had for years. I not only had a hearing loss but it was significantly worse than before. Now I was wondering if I could pass my FAA medical.

Hearing is second only to vision as an important physiological sense in flight. How well you hear dictates your ability to communicate. It allows you to detect audible changes in engine sounds, the flow of air over the airframe, and subtle changes in the sounds of gyros. Unexpected sounds can alert you to possible problems. The absence of expected sounds during flight operations can also tip you off to potential failure.

Loss of hearing can be disabling, depending on the severity of the loss. The irony is that for most pilots, virtually all high frequency loss of hearing is due to prolonged noise exposure. Because you can easily protect yourself from noise, there is no reason to suffer hearing loss.

ANATOMY AND PHYSIOLOGY OF THE EAR

The anatomy of your ear is divided into the outer, middle, and inner parts. These parts take sound waves (an energy source) from outside your body, concentrate them like a megaphone onto the eardrum, which translates them for your brain to interpret. Hearing is your perception of that sound energy (Fig. 7-1).

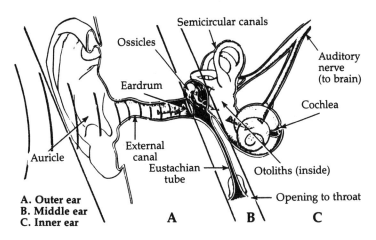

Fig. 7-1. The ear is divided into the inner, middle, and outer parts.

Outer ear

The outer ear includes the auricle, the external canal, and the eardrum. Sound waves are picked up, directed, and focused down the canal to the eardrum by the auricle. The eardrum is set into motion by the force of the sound waves, the drum moving back and forth with each wave.

Anything that obstructs this transmission of wave energy through the air diminishes or distorts the energy necessary to move your eardrum. Earwax, which everyone makes in varying amounts, is the most common obstruction.

The eardrum is also affected by infection, swelling from an ear block, scarring from an old infection, or even perforation, all impairing the transfer of sound energy into mechanical energy.

Middle ear

The middle ear is an air-filled cavity, under equal pressure to the air around you. Within this cavity is a chain of three tiny bones (ossicles) that are set into motion by the vibration of the eardrum. This transforms air wave energy into mechanical energy, which in turn is connected to the cochlea of the inner ear as the signal continues its journey to your brain.

Interference in the motion of the ossicles, especially at their joints, is very common. This interference causes a diminished or distorted signal transmission. Some of the things that can cause interference are fluid within the middle ear, inflammation or stiffening of the joints between the bones, calcification of the joints, and physical dislocation of the three bones. The most common problems occur with a middle ear infection (often with fluid) and an ear block from trapped gas.

Anatomy and physiology of the ear **119**

Inner ear

The inner ear contains the *cochlea* and *semicircular canals*. The cochlea, which resembles a sea shell, is the organ of hearing that converts mechanical energy from the movements of the ossicles into nerve impulses. These nerve impulses are then transmitted to your brain for interpretation.

The ossicles are attached to a flexible window in the cochlea, which moves the fluid behind the window.

The cochlea is filled with this fluid, and the inner walls are lined with thousands of hair-like receptors that move when the fluid moves. This is similar to the movement of tall grass in a field when the wind blows or sea plants moving with the water currents. The movement of the hairs stimulates the nerve ending at the base of each hair cell and produces an electrical impulse. This impulse is then transmitted through the cochlear (also called the acoustic or auditory) nerve to your brain.

Hearing loss due to nerve damage (infection or injury) involves the cochlear nerve. Hearing loss due to noise involves the hairs in the cochlea. It's like walking on wet grass and looking at your footsteps that you left behind. Damage to the hairs is similar, and like the grass, most will repair themselves given enough time. With repeated abuse, however, both the grass and the hairs will be permanently damaged.

Tinnitus, or ringing in the ears, is common and is a result of some degree of insult or damage to the cochlear nerve. Tinnitus is also often associated with noise exposure.

SURROUNDED BY SOUND

Sound is defined in the dictionary as energy that is heard, resulting from stimulation of auditory nerves by vibrations of the ear parts as just described. Sound is a form of wave energy, like electricity, light, and microwaves, and it obeys the same physical laws as any other energy wave.

Physical properties of sound

There are three measurable objective properties with all sound, whether characterized as useful sound or noise. How you perceive and interpret the meaning of these physical signals becomes very subjective and ranges from indifference, through your inability to detect the sound efficiently, to being keenly aware of the cues and their role in flight.

Frequency. Like other wave energy, frequency refers to the number of wave cycles (or oscillations) per second (CPS), also called hertz or Hz.

There is a very large range of frequencies for which mechanical waves can be generated, sound waves being confined to the range that can stimulate your ear and brain to the sensation of hearing. This range is between 20 and 20,000 Hz and is called the audible range. Frequencies below and above this range are called *infrasonic* and *ultrasonic waves* respectively.

Intensity. This measurable property describes the loudness of the sound. Because it defines a physical property of energy, this measurement is directly related to how well you hear or interpret a certain frequency or combination of frequencies. It is this intensity at individual frequencies that is being tested by the audiometer. The unit of measure for intensity is the *decibel (dB)* which is a logarithmic function of pressure (Fig. 7-2).

A whisper generates an energy that corresponds to that reference 10 dB level. A departing jet generates 10 billion times the amount of energy as the whisper does. Therefore, to find the decibel level you would first take the common logarithm of 10 billion, which is 10, then multiply by 10, which yields 100. The departing jet, therefore, generates a 100 dB sound level. You don't have to understand the math, but at least it lets you see where the numbers come from. A general rule of thumb that I once learned was that for your ear to able to detect any increase in intensity the sound level has to increase by 2 dB. Intensities greater than 130 dB are physically painful.

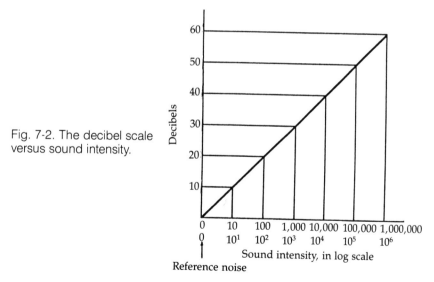

Fig. 7-2. The decibel scale versus sound intensity.

Duration. How long your ear is exposed to a sound determines how well the sound is heard and discriminated or interpreted as being important. Duration also determines the level of potential risk of injury to the ear. Because sound is energy, it follows that short periods of intense sound are potentially physically detrimental to the organs of hearing. Likewise, the same degree of damage can occur with less intense sounds that occur over longer periods of time. Therefore the potential damage is time- as well as intensity-related (Fig. 7-3).

Conversational range. There are two major reasons for your wanting to be able to interpret sounds as they reach your ear. The first is to interpret the sounds of flight—the sound of the engine, the wind over the airframe, and any changes to these sounds that could tip you off as to potential problems. The second, of course, is to communicate. Although your ear can detect a wide range of frequencies (which enhances the first need), the only frequencies necessary for you to hear in order to participate in normal conversation are in the conversational range, or 500 – 3,000 Hz. Above and below this range, the sensitivity of your ear decreases markedly.

Most communication systems in aircraft are not high fidelity because they only operate in the conversational range. Consequently, this is the range most carefully monitored by the FAA in its medical evaluations. Specific intensity levels at 500, 1,000, and 2,000 Hz are one of the few stated specific FAA standards.

Definition of noise

Any sound that you perceive as being too loud, disagreeable, or distracting is considered noise. This is a subjective cue, because what is noise to you might be an important cue to someone else. In any case, noise still implies sounds that need to be filtered out.

There are two types of noise: steady state and impulse. Steady state is what you encounter when you are in or around an operating aircraft, often during flight. Here is where duration of exposure becomes important because there is a direct correlation to intensity, duration, and amount of damage.

Impulse noise is the type that could be produced by a backfiring engine, switching to a radio that is already turned up to full volume, or other short-term (often lasting only a few milliseconds) but loud sounds. Often these sounds come as a surprise and there is no way to anticipate the need for added protection.

At the very least, noise is annoying and distracting in flight and can cause serious interference with your concentration, communication, and performance.

An often overlooked physiological effect of noise on your entire body is fatigue. Noise, as a form of energy acts directly on your body as well as your hearing mechanisms, therefore, it is more than just an annoyance.

Exposure duration per day (hours)	Maximum exposure level (dBA)
8	85
6	87
4	90
3	92
2	95
1 1/2	97
1	100
1/2	105
1/4 (ceiling)	110 or less

Fig. 7-3. Allowable noise exposure.

Other nonauditory effects of noise include interference with sleep and rest, the proprioceptive system and other subjective symptoms such as nausea, disorientation, headaches, and general irritability.

Another result of noise exposure is tinnitus. Each of us has some degree of ringing, and it would be very apparent to us if we were sitting in a super quiet room with no background noise. There are very few places without at least some noise—circulating air, outside noise of traffic, wind, clocks, etc. Even the drone of the cooling fan in the computer I'm using is a constant source of noise. Background noise is something that we all learn to tune out. You normally don't notice how much noise you are exposed to until it stops. Tinnitus is more noticeable after exposure to noise but tends to diminish over time. However, with significant noise induced hearing loss, increased tinnitus is common. There is no cure for tinnitus. Trying to ignore the ringing is the best solution.

The only accurate way of monitoring the effect noise is having on your hearing is through audiometric testing. Only in this way can you be sure of a lack of damage or impairment.

PERCEPTION OF SOUND

The hearing apparatus within your body provides you with a multitude of valuable signals and cues. The properly functioning ear can tell where a sound is coming from.

Your ear is always "on"; that is, loud or abnormal sounds will awake a sleeping person. And most individuals have the ability to filter out the unimportant and tune in the important sounds. You can pick out your call sign amongst many others in conversation with ATC, even if you are concentrating on some other activity.

If your ear can detect its full frequency range of sounds at low levels of intensity, you have access to a vast amount of cues you can use for situation awareness. You could, for example, detect a change in airspeed without looking at the gauges. This type of perception comes only from training, experience, familiarity with the aircraft, and a well-functioning pair of ears.

Even when surrounded by noise, your ear and brain can discriminate important sounds from the unimportant noise, providing the noise isn't overpowering. The healthy ear can detect faint sounds, especially spoken communications, under a variety of interfering conditions—noise, thermal extremes, distractions, and multiple activities occurring at the same time. By the same token, many situations interfere with your ability to interpret the sounds around you, including fatigue, hypoxia, stress, and motivational factors, to name a few.

MEASUREMENT OF HEARING

Because sound is a form of energy, it can be quantified. By sending a pure tone on a specific frequency and at a specific intensity to your ear, the perception of that sound can be identified for all frequencies. This testing is done by an audiometer. The ideal setting is for you to be in a soundproof booth using a headset to listen to each sound. For screening purposes, a good headset in a quiet room will do the job.

All FAA exams require hearing testing to be performed. A common method is the *whispered voice test*, now called a *voice test*. This is a poor substitute for the audiometer because it cannot quantify or identify the frequency at which a hearing loss might be present. Only with an audiometer can reliable results be achieved.

The test results from an audiometer are recorded on an audiogram, which describes a curve for each ear (Fig. 7-4). Normal hearing should be a straight line in the 5 dB range. Some variations from normal are acceptable, but any frequency with a loss of greater than 20 dB is considered significant and needs to be further evaluated.

Over time, by comparing audiograms, you and your FAA examiner can see shifts that are occurring. If high frequencies are being affected, then better hearing protection is necessary. A baseline audiogram is very important so as to compare subsequent changes.

NOISE AND HEARING LOSS

Hearing loss is not inevitable. Several preventive measures can be taken. The first is to recognize that noise is present everywhere and is potentially detrimental, both in performance and in the health of your ear and hearing system. The next is to protect your ears from noise by wearing appropriate hearing protection. The third is to be part of an ongoing hearing conservation program with annual monitoring of hearing abilities and retraining in noise avoidance.

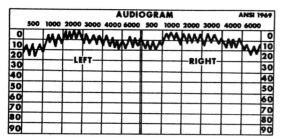

Normal hearing: Has no difficulty with faint speech and little difficulty with speech in a noisy background.

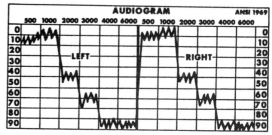

Moderate hearing loss: Has difficulty with normal speech, ringing sensation (tinnitus), many combat sounds not detected, possible hearing aid candidate.

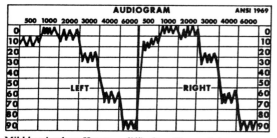

Mild hearing loss: Has some difficulty with speech in a noisy background, ringing sensation (tinnitus) might be present, some combat sounds might not be detected, e.g., clipping barbed wire, dog tags rattling, loose cartridges in pocket, man walking through grass.

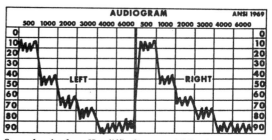

Severe hearing loss: Has difficulty even with loud speech, ringing sensation (tinnitus), needs hearing aid, auditory training, lip reading, speech conservation and speech correction.

Fig. 7-4. Pilots should get regular audiograms.

Hearing loss

Noise is recognized as the most common cause of high-frequency hearing loss. However, other causes of general hearing loss, some of which are not controllable, include:

Alcohol	Allergy	Influenza	Meniere's disease
Aspirin	Burns	Meningitis	Mumps
Cancer	Chickenpox	Mononucleosis	Otosclerosis
Cholesteatoma	Colds	Pneumonia	Quinine
Diabetes	Measles	Arthritis	Ear infection
Head injury	Heredity	Thrombosis	Toxins
Hypertension	Hypothyroidism	Polyps	Tumors

Sources of noise

Airplanes and airport ramps are some of the noisiest environments in which to work. Here you are exposed to sounds, varying from the continuous low-level noise of a cross-country flight, to short periods of engine runups on the ramp. In addition, you encounter noise associated with many activities not related to aviation, such as hobbies, mowing the lawn, downtown traffic, etc.

The Occupational Safety and Health Administration (OSHA) has determined certain levels of noise for many different events and activities (Fig. 7-5). Each is "time weighted," which means that damage is done with lower levels for longer periods of time. For example, eight hours of exposure to noise levels of 90 dB is as harmful as two hours at 100 dB. It's surprising how much energy there is in some sources. Rock concerts reach 120 dB levels, and walking around with headsets at full volume focuses virtually all that energy right into the ear, much like a megaphone.

Decibels	Sounds
(In dB/A)	
0	Threshold of hearing for young ears at 1,000 Hz
20	Whisper at 5 feet
30	Broadcasting studio speech
30–40	Country residence
40–60	Noisy home or typical office
50–70	Normal conversation
60–80	Noisy office, average street noise, average radio
70–80	Automobiles at 20 feet
90	OSHA standard for 8 hours work
80–100	Loud street noise
90–100	Public address system
100	OSHA standard for two hours work
100–110	Power lawn mower
105	OSHA standard for one hour work
100–120	Thunder, snowmobile
110	OSHA standard for one-half hour work
115	Rock concert
130	Pain threshold for humans
140–160	Jet engine
167	Saturn V rocket

Fig. 7-5. OSHA standards for noise exposure.

Airplanes are not quiet. Many small airplanes with reciprocating engines are very noisy. Prop noise ranges from 90 to 115 dB. Even in the passenger cabin of airliners, there are noise levels that are harmful over extended periods of time. As a general rule, any time you must raise your voice to be heard by someone next to you, you are in a noisy area. Furthermore, for every 4–5 dB increase in sound above 85 dB, the safe time limit for exposure is cut in half.

Noise-induced hearing loss

Equally important as the interference of communication, noise also causes permanent high frequency hearing loss. It is an insidious change, taking years to develop significant loss. Hearing aids do not help noise-induced hearing loss. In other words, noise alone can reduce hearing over the years and there is nothing you can do to reverse the process. You won't know there is a change occurring over time unless you check for it. Like so many other issues in medicine, the best and only treatment is recognition and prevention.

Common misconceptions about noise

- Noise-induced hearing loss can be cured.

  Once a hearing loss due to noise becomes permanent, doctors can do very little for you.

- I can tell when my hearing is getting bad.

  Not necessarily. Although some hearing losses occur from a single high noise exposure, most occur so gradually that you can't tell until it's too late.

- Ear defenders (earplugs, headsets) are a safety hazard.

  In a hazardous noise field, you can distinguish a warning shout or other sound better with ear defenders on.

- Headsets provide much better ear protection than earplugs do.

  Each provides approximately the same noise attenuation. Wearing both in very noisy conditions is the best strategy.

- Molded ear pieces offer the best protection and I can hear the radio better.

  You might hear the radio better, but in a noisy cockpit there is very little noise attenuation. Turning the volume up to overcome the background noise could put too much energy against the eardrum.

Many pilots have experienced the temporary loss of hearing after a long trip in a noisy airplane. There are stories about people who start their cars for the ride home and then restart the engine—which is already running. This sort of loss will return in a few days but is an indication that there was a significant noise exposure that could eventually lead to a permanent loss.

Threshold shift

As unprotected exposures to noise persists, there is an increasing risk of hearing being impaired, especially in the higher frequencies. You might not even notice this threshold shift because there is no change in your perception of sound. There is no pain to warn you. There is no way for you to compare your hearing to normal or what is expected from previous perceptions of sounds.

Because this change occurs over several years, it goes unnoticed until there is extensive loss. As the loss becomes even more severe, speech recognition becomes difficult if not impossible, especially when background noise is also present, which is at a dB level equal to the hearing loss.

Threshold shifts can be temporary, as when you are subjected to short periods of sound infrequently. However, with continuous (over months) exposure to even moderate noise, this threshold shift becomes more and more permanent. Only monitoring and comparing results of audiograms will alert you to any shifts.

OTHER TYPES OF HEARING LOSS

Although noise is the greatest and most common cause of hearing loss, especially amongst pilots, there are other causes. Age, health, and individual sensitivity increase loss. In addition, the following are also found when tested with proper equipment and techniques.

Conductive

When there is some defect or impediment of sound transmission from the external ear to the inner ear, conductive loss is identified. Such a loss involves all frequencies, not just high frequencies. Such situations develop from wax build up, fluid in the middle ear from infections, ear block, or allergies and colds. Also, the ossicles can become calcified around their joints similar to what can happen to any joint in the body. Most of these situations are treatable and hearing can be restored.

Sensorineural

Sensorineural loss occurs when the hair cells of the cochlea are damaged or inflamed. This can occur from noise exposure, age, or infection. Tumors have been known to cause hearing loss in this category. Because the lower frequencies are also affected, this is a clue that this form of loss is more than just noise related. This type of loss is generally not curable.

HEARING CONSERVATION

It bears repeating. The only way to cope with noise and hearing loss is through identification, prevention, and conservation of the hearing you already have (or have left after suffering a loss). This program, required in the military of everyone on flying status, should be adopted by the individual pilot. Only you can be responsible for the protection of your hearing, and you are the only one to blame if preventable hearing loss develops.

A successful program consists of three phases. The first is to define a baseline audiogram. If you have never had an audiogram, then that needs to be done as soon as possible. If your AME doesn't do audiograms, seek out one who does or see an audiologist (usually listed in the Yellow Pages of the phone book).

The next phase is to structure a monitoring program. The ideal is to have your FAA exams done by an AME who already does audiograms as part of his FAA medical exam. If this isn't the case, than an annual audiogram from the audiologist is important. You need to keep a copy of the audiogram in your personal file to track any shifts.

The final phase is to wear hearing protection in all noisy areas, especially at work. Noise-induced hearing loss is easy to prevent, if you wear protection. Many of the newer headsets have adequate noise attenuation. Of utmost importance with any headset is the seal between the ear cups and around your ears. If that seal is broken or interrupted, noise can enter your ear. This is especially true with the electronic (active) attenuating headsets.

The simplest and least expensive type of protection is the common moldable foam-type plug. You use this type by rolling it into a tube, inserting it into the ear canal, and holding it there until it expands and stays in place. These plugs are very effective. The more expensive earplugs offer little or no better protection. The inexpensive plugs lend themselves to be purchased by the dozen, so you can always have them available. Keep them in your aircraft, your flight bag, at home, in the passenger section, and in your flight suit or map case. Plain cotton or tissue is useless, as it does not block the sensitive frequencies.

Custom molded earplugs are somewhat controversial. Many pilots swear by them; others find them uncomfortable and ineffective. Be sure to have the manufacturer quantify the amount of attenuation before you purchase them and compare their performance and attenuation standards to a traditional headset.

A common question concerning the wearing of earplugs is their effect on hearing what you want to hear—is there a reduction in communicating? Ear defenders, hearing protection, and earplugs all do the same thing. If the ambient noise level is such that you can't hear or communicate without shouting, then protection is necessary to block out the ambient noise. The intent is to be able to maintain clarity of speech and to detect changes in the sounds of flight. Noise is an interference and can be blocked out with earplugs without sacrificing the ability to hear meaningful sounds.

The other equally important reason is to prevent permanent hearing loss and other associated symptoms such as fatigue. Once you are in the habit of wearing earplugs or attenuating headsets, they represent no compromise to communication.

8

Sleep, jet lag, and fatigue

It was one of those days when nothing went as planned. Clearance for departure was delayed 2 hours. All we could do was sit it out. The poor night's sleep in a noisy motel was catching up with me. Those three cups of coffee helped, but I still wasn't very alert by the time we took off. At cruise, which was boringly uneventful, I found myself missing ATC calls. Maybe it was because of the noise in the cockpit, which seemed to be especially noticeable on this trip. And to add to my misery, I knew I was coming down with the flu, the rest of my family was just getting over it. We were only a couple of hours into the flight and I was beat, already really fatigued, but I couldn't comprehend how impaired I was. understand why.

Probably the most frequently discussed human factor and physiological situation is fatigue. In fact, most physiological events—noise, hypoxia, dehydration, temperature extremes, etc.— include fatigue as a symptom. Lack of sleep is commonly thought of as the most frequent cause of fatigue. There are other causes and I discuss them, but lack of *restful* sleep is a cornerstone and can create a cumulative problem.

Aviation itself is often the source of virtually all causes of fatigue. This mandates that all pilots must be familiar with the various causes of fatigue and the related symptoms. Some causes cannot be controlled (length of flight, circadian changes, illness, climate, etc.), but if you are knowledgeable you can cope with these situations by being better prepared, avoiding controllable causes of fatigue, and maintaining a high index of suspicion of your own performance and that of your other crewmembers.

SLEEP

A basic understanding of the sleep process is important, but even more important is how you deal with variations in your work and rest requirements.

Physiology of sleep

Everyone has the same basic stages of sleep. However, individuals vary in the length and depth of each stage, the number of hours of sleep needed in a 24-hour cycle, and how the benefits of sleep are used.

Stages of sleep. Essentially, four stages of sleep define the depth of consciousness (or sleep) (Fig. 8-1). The deeper you sleep, the more your body and mind are truly at rest. These four stages occur as a series of cycles over the period of sleep, occurring about every 90 to 100 minutes. Associated with these stages is another event, sometimes considered another stage, which is called *REM* (rapid eye movement) sleep. REM often occurs as you return to the first stage of sleep and just before you go back into the next cycle. These four stages of sleep are often called *non-REM sleep*.

Stage 1. This is the time between wakefulness and drowsiness. Your brain waves begin to slow down, your body relaxes, and your body temperature, respiration, and pulse rate decrease. Some people notice (or see in others) a quick jerking movement of muscles, which is an indication of a change in the brain activity. When this happens it might wake you but you quickly return to sleep. This stage lasts only about 1 to 10 minutes, depending on how fast you fall asleep.

Stage 2. During this period your brain activity increases for a time, with many short bursts of thoughts and memories. Your muscles become more relaxed, body functions slow, and breathing becomes steady. If you were to be awakened during this stage, you might deny that you were asleep. This stage lasts about ten minutes.

Stage 3. Continued relaxation occurs, with your respirations and pulse rate becoming even slower. Your body is almost totally at rest, and it would be difficult for someone to wake you during this stage. If awakened, you will not feel rested but might actually feel more tired. It is also sometimes called a *transitional stage* and lasts for about 5 minutes.

Stage 4. Stage 4 is the deepest part of sleep. Your body is completely relaxed and your brain activity is slow. You could be considered unconscious and would be very difficult to arouse. If you did awake, for any reason, you would be very groggy, probably incapacitated for several minutes, and end up with a "disturbed" sleep cycle. This stage lasts for about 30 to 45 minutes and is the longest period of the cycle.

The anatomy of sleep

Sleep consists of four stages, each having its own physical manifestations and each representing a different depth of sleep. Rapid-eye-movement (REM) sleep is superimposed on stage-1 or stage-2 sleep and produces rapid back-and-forth motions of the eyeballs. REM sleep is an important component of nocturnal slumber.

Below is a simplified diagram of the human sleep stages, covering a span of roughly 3½ hours, with characteristics of each described. However, a sleeper passes through the four sleep stages and REM phases many times each night, with the brain's biologic timer dividing the whole term into fairly regular fractions.

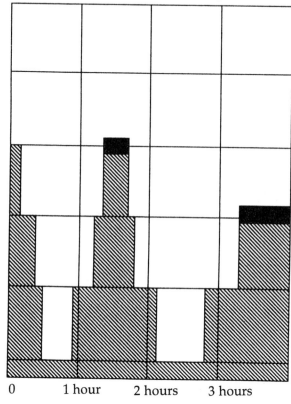

■ Rapid-eye-movement (REM) sleep: rapid eye movements; high-frequency, low-amplitude brain waves; vivid dreams; lack of muscle tone

Wakefulness
High-frequency, low-amplitude brain waves (alpha rhythm); muscle tonus

Stage 1
High-frequency, low-amplitude brain waves, some muscle relaxation; slow eye movement; slowing heart rate

Stage 2
Lower-frequency, higher-amplitude brain waves, with bursts of brain excitation; further muscle relaxation; slow eye movement; slower heart rate; even breathing

Stage 3
Lower-frequency, higher-amplitude brain waves; greater muscle relaxation with few body movements; heart and respiration rates slow and regular

Stage 4
Lower-frequency, higher-amplitude regular brain waves; considerable muscle relaxation with few body movements

Fig. 8-1. Anatomy of sleep.

REM sleep. Concurrent with the four stages of sleep, REM occurs about 90 minutes after you fall asleep. Here your pulse rate and blood pressure fluctuate, larger muscles remain relaxed but smaller muscles (fingers and toes) might twitch, and, of course, your eyes move rapidly. This stage coincides with the cycle returning to stage 1 and can last for 10 minutes before the cycle returns to stage 2. As each cycle repeats (about every 90 minutes), less time is spent in stages three and four and more in REM. Therefore, most of your deep sleep occurs early in the total sleep period, and REM occupies more of the sleep cycle during the end of the session.

Anything that interferes with REM sleep (alcohol, drugs, stress, or being wakened during this stage) results in nonproductive sleep. A good night's sleep implies an uninterrupted series of four non-REM stages and a complete REM stage. In other words, you need to complete at least one full sleep cycle uninterrupted.

As you get older, you tend to awaken more often as you complete the cycle of stage one and enter REM sleep. For a brief moment you are conscious of being awake and possibly feel that you haven't even been asleep, but you return to the next cycle of sleep. This frequent awakening as you become older is not abnormal and is not an indication of true insomnia.

Variations to normal sleep

There are individual variations to a typical sleep cycle. Some people are able to feel rested and function normally with as little as 3 to 5 hours per day. Others require more than 8 hours. The 8-hour norm of sleep is not universal, and you must determine what your optimum amount of restful sleep is.

Some people can fall asleep easily if just given the opportunity, even in noisy uncomfortable locations. They are able to take quick "cat naps" and keep ahead of their sleep needs. Others find it very difficult to get to sleep quickly even in ideal conditions. Again, this can be a normal variation and not something that should be changed. You should avoid quick fixes to try to change a sleep habit that is normal for you.

Everyone's sleep cycle is determined by their own circadian rhythm. In fact, the cycle of sleep is one of the most important rhythms and it can be easily disrupted if your sleep cycle is changed, as in "jet lag." Along with this internal clock, there is also a variation from your rhythm to someone else's. Some people are "larks," or morning people. They awake early, ready to go, alert to the world around them; but they tend to begin to lose that energy about mid afternoon. The "owl," or night person, on the other hand, takes hours to get going after awakening, with their full energy available about mid-afternoon and lasting well into the evening.

Sleep disorders

When your sleep is disrupted or inadequate (not restful), then sleeplessness, or *insomnia*, occurs. There are three different categories of insomnia. The most common and least important is the transient kind, which lasts only a few nights and is a result of excitement (just got a major raise in salary), the "jitters" (anticipating an upgrade checkride you don't feel ready for), and other reasons we have all experienced that keep us from getting to sleep. The mind just won't let you relax or tune out your thoughts. Once the situation causing this form of insomnia is resolved, sleep patterns quickly return to normal.

The next is acute, or short-term, insomnia which results from longer-lasting stress (your company might be sold) or illness (a bad flu). These situations usually resolve themselves in a few days and no longer interfere with sleep. You actually lose very little sleep and can recover after several good nights of restful sleep. However, depending on the amount of sleep lost, your health, age, and other factors, it might take longer to recover.

Chronic insomnia is more serious and comes from continued sources of sleep deprivation. It can last for days, weeks, or even months. The most common source in the general public is serious unresolved stress or illness. For the pilot, it's a combination of several factors, including stress. Some have observed that it's not so much the lack of sleep as much as *when* the sleep is allowed to occur in a 24-hour period. Long-haul trips, day after day of flight instruction, and frequent night flights are all inherent to aviation. Some people can adapt; others can't. If you can't and you feel you are never fully rested, then changes must be made. Insomnia is a symptom; therefore, take care of the cause first without focusing on trying to treat the symptom. Chronic insomnia usually requires the help of your doctor.

Factors affecting sleep

Most pilots are familiar with what interferes with a good sleep. The first factors to be considered are noisy rooms or sleeping quarters, uncomfortable beds, hot or cold temperatures, or too much light. Wearing earplugs can keep out noise, putting a blanket over a window can shut out the light, extra blankets can make the bed more comfortable.

Other controllable factors are self-imposed stresses such as too much caffeine or nicotine. Alcohol is a major disturbance because it interferes with REM sleep, and many believe that if REM sleep is disrupted by alcohol, restful sleep is compromised. This effect can last for several hours after the last drink (and that includes wine and beer if taken to excess). Circadian changes (desynchronosus) can also affect sleep, especially when you are trying to sleep at times your body is not ready to sleep.

Symptoms of insomnia

Insomnia symptoms are similar to those associated with fatigue and are covered in detail later. Generally, there is a pronounced decrease in performance, especially in decision making and fine muscle skills. Motivation to do a good job is diminished, and like with hypoxia, you don't really care. You will have lapses in alertness and a tendency to slip into short periods of sleep (micro sleep) and not even be aware that you were asleep. Small errors and mistakes will be exaggerated. A major problem is the vicious circle of insomnia—stress from not sleeping well and the fear of being an insomniac all lead to poor sleep.

How to sleep

You can take several measures to improve your chances of getting a restful sleep. Try to maintain the same sleep schedule, especially when you are at home. Staying up to watch the late movie and sleeping in late on weekends only confuses your body's rhythms and disrupts sleep cycles. Exercise and keeping in shape is a major factor that allows your body to relax more efficiently and to tolerate those factors that could keep you awake. At home, sleep in sound- and light-proof rooms in comfortable conditions.

Stress often interferes with your sleep. It's difficult to mentally turn off your concerns and avoid lying awake, considering all the bad things that could happen. At night, alone with your thoughts, these stresses often appear out of proportion to reality. Imagination runs rampant. Getting up and writing down your concerns with some ideas on how to resolve them sometimes helps break the thinking cycle and allows you to get to sleep.

Diet plays a role in sleeping. Carbohydrates tend to make you drowsy and therefore can be used before retiring. The old-fashioned remedy of warm milk before bedtime has a physiological basis. Some feel that L-tryptophan, an amino acid found in many carbohydrates, is a sleep inducer. Foods for you to avoid (in addition to caffeine and alcohol) are those high in protein and animal fat, which tend to keep you more alert.

Over-the-counter sleeping pills are almost always antihistamines. Sedation, one of the side effects of antihistamines, might help you get to sleep, but it will not necessarily be a restful sleep. Furthermore, the effects can last for hours after you awake. Also, antihistamines have significant side effects in flight, in addition to sedation, which could still be present if you fly shortly after awakening. Read the label and you'll see that the same kind of chemicals often used in allergy medication are used in sleeping pills.

Staying awake

Using reverse reasoning, the previously mentioned factors can be used to keep from falling asleep. Caffeine is the traditional drug, but timing is important so as not to interfere with sleep when you are ready to sleep. Avoid carbohydrates and sugary foods. In addition to the drowsiness common with carbohydrates, hypoglycemia is a common result. Eat small meals, high in protein; peanuts, for example. Keep active and avoid boring or nonmotivating tasks. Save them for later when you want to sleep. Drink lots of water and change positions frequently, even getting up and walking around.

CIRCADIAN RHYTHMS

It is a recognized fact that your body has biological rhythms, at least 300, that are periodic relative to the revolution of the earth and to the rising of the sun. *Circadian* literally means "about a day" and usually represents a 24-hour day. Another term is *diurnal*, which means that a cycle occurs within a day.

Human rhythms

Studies have shown that if you were to be removed completely from any source of time or outside light, your body's rhythms would settle around a cycle of about 25 to 26 hours. You reset your internal clock (which establishes your rhythms) every day by getting up at the same time, reporting to work at a given time, and, more important, by being exposed to sunlight at these times.

Another term you might have heard is *biorhythms*. It involves an unscientific claim that how you feel and how you should act during a day is based on your biorhythm for that day. This is comparable to astrology. There *are* biological rhythms, which is what we are discussing, but there is no scientific basis for biorhythm predictions.

Circadian rhythms are true rhythms; that is, there are hourly variations for each function, highs and lows, and steady states. A curve can be plotted for each function that has a rhythm.

Common human circadian rhythms

Probably your most important circadian rhythm is your sleep cycle, which I have just discussed. Many people are able to awaken without the help of a clock, and others are able to estimate time without a watch. You feel tired and ready for bed at a specific time, and you tend to follow that urge. If that cycle is not followed, your body responds with the same symptoms recognized for sleep deprivation and for fatigue in general. In aviation, this is a major problem because you might cross several time zones, which means the sun and the people at the destination are several hours off your own established rhythms for sleep.

Weekends at home base can result in a miniature change in sleep circadian rhythm. For example, Friday, Saturday, and possibly Sunday night are usually spent staying up until long after your usual bedtime. You add to this by sleeping in late on Saturday and possibly Sunday. By Monday morning, your body thinks it is on the west coast when you really are getting up at 7 AM on the east coast, relatively speaking—the Monday morning blues, or weekend jet lag.

Fluctuating throughout the day, temperature is another powerful rhythm that affects performance. It reaches its peak about midday and then begins to drop off. Owls, or night people, peak towards the end of the day. Larks peak earlier. Increased circadian temperatures affect your level of activity, feelings, and alertness.

Your appetite is also diurnal. The body expects food at certain times based on how your body is programmed by your eating habits. If you don't eat at expected times, your appetite goes away and you might not have the urge to eat for several hours, especially if you are distracted by other activities. Or you may eat a large meal when your body isn't quite ready, subjecting it to the additional stress of unexpected metabolism energy. Your body also expects to have a bowel movement at a certain time. If it doesn't because you are off schedule, the urge goes away. Over a period of a few days constipation occurs, and you might not be aware that you haven't had a bowel movement. Being dehydrated and failing to eat enough roughage as a result of a long trip complicates this problem.

Symptoms of jet lag

When circadian rhythms are disrupted, desynchronosus (jet lag) occurs. When you travel north and south, there are no time zone changes. Yet you'll experience symptoms similar to those experienced with traditional jet lag. The reason is that a major source of the symptoms is related to the length of the trip, which is fatiguing in itself. The same added problems of dehydration, hypoxia, sitting for long periods of time, and poor nutrition, complicate the symptoms no matter which direction you go.

Jet lag

Physical symptoms
- Fatigue
- Digestive difficulty
- Altered kidney and bowel functioning
- Unusually pronounced reaction to alcohol
- Maladjustment in mood, judgment, and general functional ability

Aviation factors that contribute to physical symptoms
- Oxygen deficiency
- Warm cabin temperature and low humidity
- Long periods of sitting
- Decreased cabin pressure

Preventive measures
- Readjust your sleep schedule.
- Get a good night's rest the night before departure.
- If possible, schedule stopovers instead of straight-through flights when crossing multiple time zones.
- Exercise in your seat and move about the cabin when possible.
- Adjust your meal schedule gradually before departure to the new time zone.
- Try to avoid tension and stress before departure.
- Don't overeat during the flight.
- Avoid alcohol.

Treatments after arrival
- Get plenty of sleep.
- Drink plenty of fluids.
- Eat only food to which you are accustomed at first.

There are, obviously, symptoms that are directly related to traveling across several time zones but only because your circadian changes conflict with the destination's sunlight and activities. These symptoms include headache, poor sleep, constipation, disrupted eating habits, vertigo, poor short-term memory, depression, and others. Note that these are similar to the symptoms associated with fatigue alone.

It is also recognized that for most people, traveling west is easier than traveling east. Part of the reason is that when you are headed west you are traveling with the sun. Since the real "day" for your body is 25 hours, there is less of a disruption. However, you still have to come back east, and it's this continuous changing that is particularly fatiguing.

Coping with jet lag

Studies show that the greatest chance for error occurs between 4 and 6 AM on your current diurnal rhythm (Fig. 8-2). If you travel to a location where you are expected to perform safely, but it is in the middle of the day at your destination and 5 AM your body time, then you are at high risk for making errors. That risk decreases as you begin to adapt to that local time.

Pilots, however, rarely stay for very long in one place during a trip, no matter how far away they fly from their home station. Therefore, in addition to recognizing that you can anticipate that you are going to be affected, there are measures that might help you to cope with this change in body rhythms.

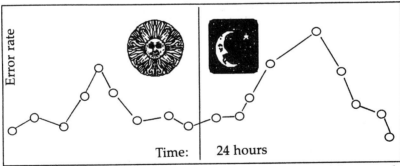

All human functions ebb and flow predictably: the ability to solve math problems, temperature, hormone levels, sensitivity to drugs and pain, oxygen consumption, heart rate and blood pressure and, of course, sleeping and waking. Changing your daily schedule can disrupt this pattern of cycles. Once disrupted, body rhythms readjust at different rates.

At the time of day when your body temperature falls, mental alertness is also depressed. During an all-night trip, your temperature low and mental dip will probably occur between 4 a.m. and 6 a.m.

This graph shows how the likelihood of making an error—from simple lapses of attention to falling asleep—varies through the day. At 4 a.m. the chance of error is 60% higher than average. Between 8 and 11 a.m., people are about 25% less likely to err.

Fig. 8-2. Jet lag has an adverse effect on performance.

A suggestion is to get into the sun as soon as possible relative to your destination's time zone. Become active and involved with your destination's time zone activities. You need to be familiar with the effects of caffeine and alcohol and to use them in such a way so as not to interfere with alertness and sleep at your destination. For example, alcohol on arrival will interrupt your sleep when you want to sleep, and so will caffeine. Eat lightly, keeping in mind the sedative effects of carbohydrates. "Jet lag diets" are of questionable value according to most circadian experts, but some of their basics are helpful, such as the type of foods to eat and the other suggestions already mentioned.

The better your health and fitness, the better you can tolerate the change and the quicker you can adapt. Increase your fluids—especially water—and minimize the diuretic effects of alcohol and caffeine. Eat plenty of high-fiber foods, such as raw vegetables and bran.

Try to rest before the trip; otherwise, you are fatigued even before you get there. Wise long-haul pilots watch with knowing glances as their younger crewmates enjoy the night life in an exotic new city, only to suffer the fatigue of the next day on the leg back. It's tempting to enjoy the layover, but the price you'll pay the next day might be too expensive.

FATIGUE

As I have stated throughout this chapter, fatigue is the common denominator of virtually all symptoms related to deprived sleep and desynchronosus, as well as many other physiological stresses unique to flying. You must recognize that many of the causes are occurring at the same time that the symptoms are present. A quick accumulation of causes and effects often creep up on the unsuspecting pilot. Like hypoxia and alcohol, fatigue is an insidious deterrent to safety, because one of its main symptoms is a lack of awareness and a feeling of indifference to its effects.

The two general kinds of fatigue are acute and chronic. Like sleep, the acute kind is related to current events and activities and you will recover when the situation is resolved. The chronic kind is more serious in that there is a cumulative effect over several months, creating more fatigue without the benefit of adequate recovery. Such fatigue makes your body vulnerable to illness, increased stress and is generally unhealthy.

Causes of fatigue

The following are specific causes of fatigue that you must be aware of. You can then monitor your performance when these conditions are present and be suspicious of deteriorating performance.

Lack of restful sleep. The key word is *restful*. It doesn't matter how long or where the sleep is achieved. If it is not restful, fatigue is the result. It often becomes a vicious circle. You are so fatigued that you cannot relax because you are still mentally rehashing the day's activities and anticipating the next leg or trip. You are unable to allow sleep to take over and you become more fatigued.

Dehydration. Often overlooked as a cause of fatigue, dehydration is a common occurrence on the flight deck. Being dehydrated results in fatigue that might not be noticed. The solution is simple—drink lots of water. By the time you feel thirsty, dehydration is already present.

Caffeine. Although considered a stimulant and often used to stay awake (an acceptable practice under the right conditions), drinking too much caffeine keeps your body in a high degree of alertness, even to the point of being tense. That, coupled with any trip that might require a lot of mental and physical energy (and adrenaline flow), leaves you fatigued when the destination is reached. This is a form of withdrawal and is a significant factor if you are not rested enough for the next flight, whether in a few hours or the next day. The letdown of not having the stimulation of caffeine leads to fatigue.

Noise and vibration. Most prop-driven aircraft and all helicopters are noisy. Noise is a form of energy that is not well tolerated by your body for long periods of time. This is frequently proven when pilots begin to wear earplugs and noise attenuating headsets and realize that they are not as tired after the trip. Since you can't avoid noise in most aviation situations, fatigue is a factor unless adequate protection is worn. Vibration is similar (except the frequencies are lower) and still causes fatigue. Little can be done to prevent the vibration, but the combination of earplugs and noise attenuating headsets, along with adequate padding in the aircraft seats, will help.

Illness. Your body fights illness through its own metabolism. Colds and flus are common, and some pilots tend to go ahead and fly while they are ill. These situations are fatiguing because of the increased energy needed by your body and the fatiguing effects of the illness itself. Recall how tired and miserable you felt the last time you had the flu or a cold.

Over-the-counter medications. Many medications have antihistamines, which have sedation as a side effect. The combination with caffeine (often used in these medications to overcome the effects of drowsiness) is fatiguing. Now you are battling not only the illness but also the effects of the treatment used to fight the illness.

Hypoglycemia. Fatigue is the most serious effect of this common self-imposed stress. Proper nutrition and prevention is the best way to deal with hypoglycemia. If you are prone to these symptoms, carrying some quick energy in the form of snacks, peanuts, or candy will help. Fatigue from hypoglycemia is slow to develop, and you probably will not relate how you are feeling to being hypoglycemic.

Hypoxia. To many, fatigue is the first sign of being hypoxic. This is a very subjective sign, and you might think that your feeling of fatigue is the result of something else. Working at altitude, whether in the plane or on the ground, will cause fatigue.

Impaired vision. Pilots in general do not like wearing glasses, especially as they get older. Not wearing glasses (and hoping the eyes and brain will sort the out-of-focus images) is fatiguing. Most have heard of eye strain and that is what the eyes are doing; they are being strained. The obvious solution is to wear glasses all the time, even for reading, and with adequate lighting.

Thermal. Excessive heat and cold is a common source of fatigue. Your body is working to maintain its core temperature and requires calories and energy to accomplish this task. The result is fatigue, even after temperature control is reached.

Boredom. You have to be physically and mentally active to keep from being bored. Although not directly fatiguing, the feeling is perceived as fatiguing and many of the same symptoms are present.

Circadian change. Fatigue is the most common complaint with long haul trips across time zones. It's the combination of the length of the trip and the desynchronosus.

Skill fatigue. This little recognized source of fatigue is a result of demands of persistent concentration with high demands for skill. This is an operational problem related to your motivation to continue pushing yourself beyond your capabilities. There is a conflict between your ego and your good judgment. The result is fatigue, which is not noticed until after the trip and is especially dangerous if there is another trip (or leg) soon after. This is common in emergency medical evacuation where the mission becomes all-important, or when practicing for a checkride.

Unresolved stress. Unresolved stress is common for everyone. It's been said that nothing is more fatiguing than the eternal hanging on of an uncompleted task. Personal stress that is not resolved drains your body of energy and is often associated with depression, which is also fatiguing or gives the perception of fatigue.

Symptoms of fatigue

A variety of symptoms are directly related to fatigue. Others are also associated with other situations. Hypoxia, for example, has several symptoms similar to those of fatigue. Therefore, there is a cumulative effect of various causes resulting in a more pronounced and significant symptom.

Symptoms of acute fatigue

- Need for larger stimulus

- Errors in timing

- Loss of accuracy and control smoothness

- Unaware of error accumulation

- Ease of distraction

- Neglect of secondary tasks

- Inattention

Probably the most important symptom of fatigue, as with hypoxia and lack of sleep, is the feeling of indifference, of "settling for less" in performance. You are unaware that you are fatigued and allow your personal acceptable tolerances and limits for performance to expand, which allows for mistakes or substandard skills.

Other specific fatigue symptoms unique to a pilot in flight include the following:

Increased reaction time. You take longer to react to a change or emergency. Automatic response to any abnormal flight is slowed, such as recovery from a tight turn that is losing altitude or recognizing a stall. It has the potential to turn minor problems into major accidents—both in the air and on the ground.

Channelized thought processes. As a fatigued pilot, you tend to concentrate on one thought or activity at a time, rather than several, which is essential in flying. Concentration is also narrowed, as you focus only on what the weather is ahead and not plan your approach. You might be focused on issues outside the cockpit, such as an argument at home or the unknown results of your medical evaluation. Flying requires a multitude of thoughts, all processed by the brain in a sequence or sometimes at the same time. The number of separate thoughts that can be processed decreases as fatigue gets worse.

Fixation. Here is when you fixate on a single instrument, staring at a blinking warning light on the panel, or listening intently to a strange sound that is not a factor of the flight. The instrument scan becomes less efficient and traffic is missed because you are concentrating on some object below.

Short-term memory loss. You might quickly forget what ATC's last clearance was and you didn't think to write it down. Or you forgot to change the radio and are calling departure on tower's frequency. You hear a crewmate call for flaps during other activities, and being fatigued, you forget, especially if you are distracted.

Impaired judgment and decision making. Stupid mistakes are made, and while they might be insignificant, they can become another link in a growing chain of events leading to an accident. You take chances and shortcuts rather than following acceptable procedures—and you really know better but just don't realize you're messing up.

Easily distracted. When fatigued, you will be easily distracted, such as when you notice a map falling from the panel and quickly reach for it rather than holding back. A sound or other visual cue away from the scan becomes more important than the scan for a brief moment. You will miss an item on the checklist because you are distracted by conversation that is irrelevant to the flight. (The sterile cockpit policy helps prevent this.)

Sloppy flying. Your fine motor skills are compromised, and you find yourself holding onto the yoke with your hand rather than your fingers. You lose the fine tuning of your turns and climbs and change of power settings. More important, you have to think about what to do rather than flying using well-learned skills. You have to think too long about which direction to turn to change heading, or in what order controls are changed to begin a descent. Much of flying is automatic, habitual. Anything that interferes with these skills impairs you and you might not notice the problem.

Decreased visual perception. It takes longer to focus (accommodate) from a distant object to a near object. This becomes especially critical while flying an instrument approach to landing. The scan takes longer because you can't focus well or you might just skip a part of the scan.

Loss of initiative. You don't really care anymore when you are fatigued, and you are unwilling to maintain a high level of skill or accuracy. You become passive about your own high standards of flying. You let someone else make an error and won't say anything.

Personality change. You become more irritable and are easily depressed with minor problems. There is a decreased tolerance to minor irritants.

Attitude. It bears repeating that you are willing to settle for less and are not even aware of your change in attitude and performance.

Depression. Even though you might normally have a positive outlook on life, fatigue can generate a rich imagination of things that could go wrong. Depression, although short-term, can result in a gloomy perception of life. Fatigue and Depression are a poor combination of feelings to be used in flight.

To put the topic of fatigue in perspective, the following is a possible scenario of what could happen to you on a typical flight. The obvious continuous thread of concern is your fatigue. I wrote the following excerpt for *Business & Commercial Aviation* magazine in 1991.

Let's begin the scenario. It's already been a long day with several stops and waiting for several hours at two of the stopovers. This is now your last leg and you're flying.

You are cleared to taxi and, enroute to the active, you go through the rest of your "before take off" checklist. You are transfixed by an emergency vehicle heading across the tarmac to the terminal and as a result of this minor *distraction* you miss the command to set flaps. Your copilot has to remind you later on into the list.

At the last minute, tower tells you to "hold your position for landing traffic" which seems a long way off on final. You let tower know about your dissatisfaction of having to wait for traffic that, in your opinion, is a safe distance. You are usually patient in these conditions, but right now you are *more irritable and easily annoyed*.

You are now cleared for takeoff on 23 Right and to fly a heading of 210. You forget the clearance and maintain runway heading until ATC reminds you of the 210 heading. Then you call departure on the tower frequency, another lapse in *short term memory*.

You climb out into the clouds as you *fixate your concentration* on a flashing yellow light on the annunciator panel, nothing significant, but you also are sliding into a turn as you stare at the light. Your copilot gets you back on your scan after tactfully saying "heading 210."

You finally reach cruising altitude when ATC requests you to turn 30 degrees to the right for traffic, your copilot is asking where the approach plates are, you are trying to trim the altitude hold, and the waypoint light is flashing. Your mental focus is really on the radar which is showing thunderstorms on the flight path. Only after ATC has to remind you of your heading change do you realize your *thoughts were channelized* on only one situation—the radar—when you should have been alert to everything.

The rest of the cruise was uneventful—boring. Your mind is wandering as you go through your scan. You begin to think about the unopened letter from the IRS sitting on your desk, your FAA medical is due next week and your blood pressure is borderline. Your teenage son got his first speeding ticket yesterday. You imagine many undesirable scenarios for each of these situations and you are beginning to scare yourself—you fear you are *becoming depressed* even though nothing serious has actually happened.

Finally, you're "cleared to descend to 4000 at pilot's discretion" while still 75 miles out. You begin an immediate descent. Your copilot questions your *judgment* and wonders that your *decision* to go down so soon is premature, knowing it's bumpy lower and your passengers are busy working on reports. "What difference does it make? Besides, who is in charge anyway!" you snap back.

ATIS reports 1,000 and 1. You choose to fly the ILS by hand. You find yourself chasing the needle, driving with a firm grip on the yoke instead of flying the airplane with a gentle touch. Then your first bounce is hard and your second floats to a mushy touchdown. You think to yourself that you haven't had this *sloppy flying* since you were a student. Your final act of frustration is to yell at your copilot for not alerting you to your altitude.

Most of us have been in one or more of these situations. Fatigue is insidious, and there often is no way to avoid its symptoms. The degree of impairment, however, is going to be a result of your awareness of and insight into the whole subject of fatigue.

Coping with fatigue

Unfortunately, there is often a fine line between acceptable fatigue and fatigue that could seriously impair your abilities. It is ultimately up to you to make the final decision to fly based on your perception of your tolerance to fatigue. Being healthy and physically fit and avoiding the causes that were mentioned earlier are the only practical means of assisting yourself in determining if you are safe.

9

Stress management, CRM, and the safe pilot

I was preflighting the aircraft for the third and final leg of the trip. I had brought some personal problems onboard the aircraft at the start of the day and it seemed as if the stress had been piling up all day long. Bad weather, diversions, sick passengers . . . you name it, I had experienced it on this trip. The stress was manifesting itself in the form of headaches, irritability, and worst of all—poor judgment. I hate to give up control of the aircraft, but it was obvious to myself and crewmates, that we would all be better off if I let the copilot fly the last leg.

STRESS

If you have been piloting aircraft for any length of time, whether for pleasure or career interests, chances are you have experienced some stress as an occupational hazard. In fact, if from no other source, time is often the culprit. In an aviation environment, time drives most of us. Multiple tasks must be performed simultaneously to get them all completed. Remaining fuel is directly related to time. Demands often exceed the time available. This is of crucial concern in general aviation, where one person must often make all of the decisions and perform all of the tasks alone.

Everyone experiences stress to varying degrees throughout their lives. Some more than others. In fact, stress is essential to keep us from becoming complacent. Someone once said that stress is the price paid to be a race horse instead of a plow horse.

Stress, therefore, by itself, is not the problem. How you cope with stress can become the problem.

As I mentioned, flying airplanes can be a stressful activity. There is much to learn and much to remember. You learn something new every time you fly. You are being continually monitored and checked. You might have high expectations for yourself, often leading to becoming a perfectionist. These often unrealistic expectations increase the amount of stress with which you must deal.

Stress can be defined as any activity—either self-imposed or imposed by situations beyond your control—that you are subjected to and that you have to cope with. How you cope determines how you are affected and what degree of impairment is noticed. If stress becomes unmanageable, then a variety of symptoms develop, such as anxiety and unhappiness and sometimes panic—distress. No one can be free of stress. If you can learn to cope with stress effectively, you will become a better pilot.

Stress that is not dealt with effectively leads to distress. When you are able to cope, the stress becomes eustress. If you are unable to cope, you become distressed. Your distressed body will respond with a variety of symptoms, such as an upset stomach, headaches, muscle cramps, and diarrhea. The most common symptom is a feeling of fatigue. Therefore, the variety of symptoms, especially fatigue, are cumulative with those from other sources described in the other chapters.

Some situations that are commonly seen with pilots under stress are distraction from tasks, inattention to flight activities, preoccupation with insignificant problems, judgment errors, a mind set on only one way to do something, and technical errors. The responsible pilot who begins to notice these changes in himself now adds these deficiencies to the underlying stress causing the changes. Your high expectations as a pilot become eroded, which is stressful in itself. Thus there develops a circle of stressful and often unrealistic perceptions that lead you to be an impaired pilot.

If you tend to become stressed, you probably have a rich imagination of how badly things can turn out, even though nothing serious has actually happened. Stress causes you to continually ruminate about your situation, and you become mentally obsessed with your status. You go to bed thinking about your problems and wake up where you left off—thinking about your problems.

The only way to deal with stress is to first recognize that stress is present, which is sometimes difficult if you have an independent personality. Even after sensing there might be too much unresolved stress, you will often feel that you can and must deal with it yourself. This situation has been proven many times to be a great deterrent to resolving a stressful life—trying to work out the problem without the help of others.

Only through talking out the problems with someone who can be unbiased will these stresses be identified and dealt with. Sometimes professional help is necessary to break through the denial that there is stress affecting your performance and that help is needed.

Checklist for stress

Stress is inherent in aviation, but as they say, too much of anything is not good for you. Be aware of and alert for indications of stress in your life including:

- ☐ Anxiety
- ☐ Irritability
- ☐ Insomnia
- ☐ Depression
- ☐ Trembling, weakness
- ☐ Fixated attention
- ☐ Speech difficulties
- ☐ Forgetfulness
- ☐ Nightmares
- ☐ Impulsive behavior
- ☐ Increased smoking or overeating

- ☐ Inability to concentrate
- ☐ Indigestion
- ☐ Loss of appetite
- ☐ Sweating
- ☐ Emotional tension
- ☐ Headaches
- ☐ Confusion
- ☐ Neck pain
- ☐ Chronically tense muscles
- ☐ Increased self-doubt
- ☐ Proneness to accidents
- ☐ Alcohol abuse

Current FAA rules require pilots to disclose any treatment by a medical professional on the FAA medical application form. This includes therapists counseling someone with stress. This is not a cause for concern and certainly not a reason to avoid help. The FAA, indeed everyone, would prefer you to seek help, resolve the stress, and press on. The FAA will not question or deny your seeking help—unless the stress has been allowed to get so severe that it compromises safety.

CRM

History has shown that human nature is imperfect and unpredictable. Aviation is a good example. People who choose to fly, whether for fun or profit, are aware of the hazards associated with taking a highly technical machine into the air. Yet, as past (and probably future) accident reports attest to, we tend to let human shortcomings interfere with the safety of our endeavors. Just as aircraft have operating limitations, so do pilots. And individual personalities, egos, and attitudes determine the parameters of each pilot's effective operating range. *Pilot error* are two words that have been creeping into more and more accident reports in recent years.

And while all accidents are tragic, it is difficult to accept the fact that there are those accidents in which the information needed to prevent the catastrophe was available but unused. To combat this problem, a new concept has emerged that is steadily becoming a cornerstone of every training environment—CRM.

Cockpit Resource Management, or *CRM* (more commonly called *Crew Resource Management*), is a term now common in aviation, especially commercial aviation. This concept of improving the safety of flight through viewing the crew as a management team just like any business is only a few years old. CRM considers all resources—pilots and flight attendants, even those on the ground (mechanics, dispatchers, and ATC). Therefore, even single-pilot operations need to consider the techniques of CRM.

The intent of this chapter is not to give comprehensive insight into how to accomplish the goal of improving the management of cockpit and crew resources. New information is coming out all the time from the experiences of companies who are generating their own CRM programs, often under different titles. Articles and books and seminars are becoming more evident as more is learned about the optimum way to develop, teach, and reinforce the principles of good CRM.

Most pilots give their aircraft a thorough preflight, yet many forget to preflight themselves. The "I'm Safe" checklist should be part of every pilot's flight preparation.

I—Illness. Do I have any symptoms?

M—Medication. Have I been taking prescription or over-the-counter drugs?

S—Stress. Am I under psychological pressure from the job? Do I have money, health, or family problems?

A—Alcohol. Have I had anything to drink in the last 24 hours? Do I have a hangover?

F—Fatigue. How much time since my last flight? Did I sleep well last night and am I adequately rested?

E—Eating. Have I eaten enough of the proper foods to keep me adequately nourished during the entire flight?

Equally important is the impact of your medical airworthiness—your health and well being—on how you practice management techniques.

You can be legal and well trained in CRM, as well as experienced and proficient. However, if you are not medically airworthy and do not respect the issues discussed in this manual, then you are not safe simply because you will be unable to function in an acceptable manner.

A long-term NASA research program has identified and shown that nearly 80 percent of air carrier (and other flying) accidents and incidents are related to some form of human factors. A common characteristic is that the problems encountered by aircrew are often associated with poor group decision-making, inadequate leadership, ineffective communications, and poor management of available resources. It was also noted that training programs place strong emphasis on the technical aspects of flying, often at the expense or even lack of training in the various types of crew management strategies and techniques that have been found to be increasingly essential to safe flight operations.

WHAT IS CRM?

The basic meaning of CRM is crew utilization of all resources available in all phases of flight. This needs to be further defined, using traditional terminology common in any situation dealing with people, personalities, and tasks.

The cockpit crew was once considered the sole source of skills and expertise concerning flight and management performance. However, it is now recognized that the cabin crew (flight attendants and available trained passengers) is also essential in a total team, as well as ATC and company personnel on the ground.

The term *resources* pertains to any kind of resource that can be used to safely fly an aircraft, especially under less than ideal or expected circumstances. The crew, meaning all usable people on board, is the first to be considered. Ground crew, such as dispatchers, meteorologists, mechanics, doctors, Air Traffic Control, company operations, and other associated personnel are also available resources.

The foundation of any successful business is the management of available resources. The best resources, in abundant supply, are worthless if not managed properly. Companies often fail because of poor management of the resources of people, equipment, and facilities made available to their managers. The same is true on an aircraft. CRM is now recognized in aviation as the way to improve this situation.

Another way of considering the definition of management is that it represents the clear understanding of "who's in charge," "who's responsible," and "who's available" to manage and use the resources to perform essential tasks plus a mutual respect for each of these entities.

WHAT'S LEARNED IN CRM?

This list can be long when considering specific components of CRM skills. The following are the key elements of any CRM program.

Decision-making skills

Decision-making skills are necessary for all crewmembers, in all situations. This means taking into account the information from the various resources and making an intelligent and professional decision at that moment. Such decisions cannot be effective if poor CRM skills are practiced. You must be confident of the choices and be able to competently communicate your decisions.

Decisions, decisions, decisions

Cockpit Resource Management training puts a great deal of emphasis on improving the decision-making process. In addition to organizing and fully utilizing the resources around him, a pilot must be able to fully utilize his personal resources. A model widely used in the aviation industry that provides a means of making orderly decisions is the DECIDE model. It works as follows:

D—Detect: The pilot detects the fact that a change has occurred that requires attention.

E—Estimate: The pilot estimates the significance of the change to the flight.

C—Choose: The pilot chooses a safe outcome for the flight.

I—Identify: The pilot identifies plausible actions to control change.

D—Do: The pilot acts on the best options.

E—Evaluate: The pilot evaluates the effect of the action on the progress of the flight.

Leadership skills

Leadership techniques are very individualized, but everyone can be taught basic qualities of being a leader as well as being a follower or team player. Such insight is not just for leading others but to also understand

and respect the challenges to any and all leaders during all phases of flight. Part of the team is a mutual respect for the leader and a clear understanding of who is ultimately responsible. Additionally, the leader must respect the opinions and observations of the rest of the team.

Communication skills

Communication is probably the most important factor in any relationship, whether in a marriage, with friends, in clubs, organizations, companies, or flying airplanes. Without knowing and comprehending what the other is telling you, there is chaos. Failing to communicate is the age-old problem for everyone. Many studies have shown that most people are poor communicators and even worse listeners. If a situation is not clearly understood or heard by all parties resulting in a common interpretation, then this is a setup for an accident.

Judgment skills

The use of good judgment is difficult to teach, but it can be done. It must be associated with real world situations and real world practice. Attitude, personality, intelligence, and knowledge are key elements, much of which is learned only from experience and maturity along with continued reinforcement of the skills that can be taught. Judgment also comes from applying lessons learned in situations that went wrong. That means keeping an open mind and being willing to change old habits.

Crew coordination skills

Crew coordination comes from applying all these skills and working as an effective team to accomplish a common objective—getting the aircraft off the ground, to its destination, and back on the ground with the passengers thinking your job is simple. This becomes extremely crucial in an emergency situation, where everyone must depend on the resources and skills of each other.

There are other skills that accompany those just defined, and they are learned in most CRM courses. These include stress management, respecting situation awareness, problem solving, team management, and other interpersonal skills.

CRM TRAINING PROGRAM

A good training program in CRM should include at least three distinct phases: an awareness of the many CRM issues, a practice and feedback of lessons learned using CRM techniques, and continual reinforcement of CRM principles. CRM, therefore, is defined in a variety of ways. The FAA has a good example:

- It is a comprehensive system for improving crew performance.
- It is designed for the entire crew population.
- It can be extended to all forms of aircrew training.
- It concentrates on crewmember attitudes and behaviors and their impact on safety.
- It provides an opportunity for individuals to examine their own behavior and make individual decisions on how to improve cockpit teamwork.
- It uses the crew as the unit of training.
- It is a training program that requires the active participation of all cockpit crewmembers.

CRM is here to stay, even if it evolves into other programs with different names. The traditional CRM techniques and skills will be used and reinforced long into the future. The sooner you and your crewmates begin to incorporate this attitude into flying, the quicker our flying environment will become even safer.

10

Inflight
medical emergencies

You're cruising along in the company jet. Your copilot is finished with her duties and the passengers are engrossed in conversation. Someone knocks on the cockpit door: "Hey Bill, Frank just banged his head on the cabinet over the sink. He might have knocked himself out, but he's okay now. The bad news is he's bleeding like a stuck pig. Can you come back and help us? We don't even know where the bandages are." Your copilot offers to help, but you are fast approaching a weather system and ATC is beginning to vector aircraft ahead of you. Both of you need to be in the cockpit for the next 30 minutes. You reply: "We've got our hands full up here for awhile. The first aid kit is below the sink. Do what you can and keep me informed, especially if you think Frank is getting worse."

There is only a minimal chance that you will experience a passenger having a medical problem in flight. Hopefully, you are following good health maintenance program and are sure that you are medically airworthy before you begin your flight. This is not true, however, with passengers and crewmembers who are not following good health maintenance. Medical emergencies do occur in flight and, although uncommon, can be more than just distracting. If someone becomes ill or injured, you can do little in the confines of an aircraft with limited medical aids. There are, however, some basic techniques that can help you deal with the problem and still fly the airplane.

The greatest challenge to you is determining what the medical problem is and how serious it is. Then it becomes necessary to decide what to do and how quickly you must do it. No matter what medical problem others in your plane are experiencing, one activity that takes precedence over all others—fly the plane. It sounds simplistic, but your urge to deal with the sick or injured is at best distracting, and it is easy to get caught up in the situation and become removed from the responsibility of flying.

Most medical emergencies can wait until you get the plane on the ground. Declaring an emergency to ATC might require some paperwork afterwards, but the controllers are trained to get you to the airport with the appropriate facilities. They will want to know the extent of the problem, which means you will have to decide based on your observations and insight and then tell them. They are able to help you from there, even getting in touch with a doctor or emergency personnel. It is better to err on the side of assuming the problem is potentially severe and letting the doctor decide if you overreacted.

Often the medical emergency affects someone who can tell you what's going on. They can often take their own actions along with your advice and reassurance. If the emergency involves someone unconscious, then basic CPR, if indicated, is about all that can be done, if even that. Remember, your role as the pilot is to first fly the plane. If possible, ask someone else on board to help the ill person, and then decide the next step—either press on or head for an emergency airport.

Short of using basic first aid, most medical emergencies ultimately have to be seen by medical professionals. Therefore, insight into basic first aid and what you realistically can do in flight is essential. In larger commercial aircraft, more extensive care can be given, depending on the resources available—medical personnel, equipment, space, and a medical kit.

FIRST AID

Most injuries requiring first aid include lacerations, bumps (contusions), sprains, and broken bones (fractures), suspected or real. Most bleeding can be controlled with pressure over the laceration. Don't waste too much time looking for "pressure points" unless you know exactly where they are and there is extensive or uncontrollable bleeding. Pressure must be maintained for a minimum of five minutes for minor cuts, longer for extensive lacerations.

A bloody nose can be controlled by simply holding your nose as if you were going to jump into a swimming pool. This pressure must be also held for at least five minutes. Techniques such as a cold compress behind the neck or holding a tissue under the nose has little, if any, effect. The bleeding is usually from small vessels in the front of the nose, and the objective is to put pressure on these bleeding vessel(s).

Sprains, contusions (hard bumps), and suspected fractures are treated the same way initially. Immobilize the injured part, put ice (if available) over the injury, and wrap it with some protective material. This will be all that is necessary until medical assistance is available.

Burns require only protection until seen by a doctor. Ice or cold water might help. Do not put on any ointments or creams.

First-aid kits are easy to find in drug stores and usually contain all that is needed. It's easy to make your own kit, with bandages, tape, gauze, scissors, elastic bandages, safety pins, cotton swabs, tweezers, and a basic first aid manual. Put everything into an easily accessible plastic bag or small container.

Contents in your personal first aid kit
(For use by passengers, not pilots)

- Aspirin, acetaminophen, ibuprofen
- Cold and cough remedies
- Mild laxative
- Antacid
- Sunscreen
- Ice bag (chemically activated)
- Antifungal and itch agents
- Antibacterial cream
- Elastic bandages
- Adhesive bandages, cotton swabs, tape
- Large compress
- Tweezers
- Scissors
- Antidiarrhea/antinausea medication
- Basic First Aid Manual (Red Cross)

Remember, all you need to do during this period before you can land is to keep things stable and the patient relatively comfortable until you get to the airport.

Fainting is a common occurrence and is often self-limiting; that is, once the person is prone or lying down and blood can get to the brain, recovery often takes place quickly. Try to determine why the person fainted. Was he scared, hypoglycemic, hyperventilating, or did something more serious take place (heart attack, stroke, diabetic collapse)? If the person does not recover in a few minutes and is not able to tell you what is happening, consider it to be a more serious problem and seek advice.

If the passenger is able to talk, he might be able to help you help him. Sometimes, like with diabetics, providing some candy or juice helps. If there is no improvement no matter what you try, tell ATC that you have an unconscious or seriously ill passenger that needs immediate medical attention. They will direct you while you fly the plane.

Some true medical emergencies do require immediate attention, such as a stroke, heart attack, or diabetic collapse. There is, however, little you can do, especially if the person is unconscious and you are in a small airplane. If oxygen is on board, try to get the mask over the mouth and nose. This might help. If there still is a problem, then CPR should be considered, but only after you get clearance for an emergency landing at an airport with medical support. Again, fly the airplane and let someone else work on the passenger. If there is no one else, just fly.

It is even difficult to do CPR in a larger aircraft. It's possible, however, and hopefully you will have someone aboard to provide assistance. You might be able to or have to guide another passenger by explaining what to do.

Choking often occurs with food. The person tries to swallow a large firm piece of food, such as meat, and it gets stuck in the pharynx. It's fairly obvious what is happening, as it often happens during a meal and the person is having trouble breathing and is usually holding his neck or pointing to his throat. He is unable to speak and explain. If you can get the obstruction out by removing it from the open mouth, then try. However, the best procedure is the Heimlich Maneuver.

TRANSPORTING ILL PASSENGERS

The military has transported sick and injured people for years. They have specially equipped aircraft with adequate medical supplies and equipment. Medical personnel are on board, often including doctors. Civilian air ambulances are now very common and are also often well-equipped and -staffed. These services are professional and competent because they are trained and experienced and have access to adequate resources.

The flight environment and restrictions within an airplane can make an existing medical condition worse and even trigger other problems. Therefore, it is usually unwise for you to transport people known to be ill in your aircraft if it is not medically equipped or staffed. Unless the passenger is accompanied by medical personnel with adequate resources and expertise and you have a release from the company doctor, it would be prudent to defer the trip until you are fully informed of your responsibilities and liabilities if something goes wrong with the passenger.

Several situations unique to flight make most aircraft ill-suited to transport of the ill or injured. These include lack of adequate space to

When passengers (including pilots) should not fly (unless in a medically equipped "air ambulance")

- Recent heart attack
- Uncontrolled hypertension
- Severe heart failure
- Symptomatic cardiac valvular disease
- Uncontrolled cardiac arrhythmia
- Angina
- Severe lung disease
- Recent stroke

- Uncontrolled epilepsy
- Recent skull fracture
- Recent eye surgery
- Sinus or ear congestion
- Late pregnancy
- Uncontrolled diabetes
- Diverticulitis or ulcer
- Brain tumor
- Acute gastroenteritis

work on a patient, vibration, hypoxia, hyperventilation, inability to perform basic tasks such as blood pressure reading, listening to the heart and lungs in noisy conditions, inadequate intravenous fluid and medicine control, and lack of other medical resources. If the patient becomes unexpectedly critical during the trip, you have no means available to assist him.

The liability of transporting passengers who are already ill or injured in a poorly equipped or staffed airplane also becomes a major factor. The best solution would be to check with a doctor, as well as an attorney familiar with aviation law and medical liability, before allowing any sick passenger on board.

BASIC SURVIVAL TECHNIQUES

The military requires survival training for all flight crews. However, this topic is rarely discussed in the civilian aviation community because the chances are slim of not being found within a few hours after a crash landing. Yet those who fly in and over remote locations, such as mountains and wilderness areas, are wise to consider the real possibility of having to survive for several days before search and rescue can get there. Filing flight plans is an obvious means of protection, but many fail to take this simple step.

Many good manuals and pamphlets can tell you how to "live off the land" and cope with weather extremes. A scout manual also serves the same purpose. All such manuals are available in most book stores. Such a resource is a necessary item in your survival kit.

Several priorities must be dealt with in any survival situation. The first is to tend to injuries, if any, and to ensure that all persons on board are accounted for. The next step is probably the hardest—stop and think.

The following high-priority steps can be assigned to each person. Find shelter, especially if the weather is bad or threatening. Get all your supplies in that shelter. Then, look for water. Food is not important at this stage because the human body can go for days without food.

Here are a few suggestions for the basic essentials to include to your survival kit: matches that have been sealed with candle wax, a small candle, safety pins, a knife, some thin pliable wire (for snares), aluminum foil, a small thin plastic tarp, some fish hooks, nylon line, a plastic whistle, a small compass, a strong balloon (to use as a water container), salt, bouillon cubes, a small flashlight (with batteries covered to prevent contact), a signal mirror, and water purification tablets. This kit, plus your first aid kit, can provide the tools necessary to cope with just about any environmental situation.

Keep in mind the word STOP. It stands for Stop, Think, Observe, and Plan. With some minimal preparation, and the self-confidence that survival in extreme environments is possible, your chances for getting out are greatly improved.

11

Pilot
health maintenance

"If it ain't broke, don't fix it." Or, "I feel fine, why worry?" That's what Captain Dave's philosophy was until, at age 51, he had his first heart attack. Even though he was back flying two years later, he looks back and realizes that he should have known better. His father died at 55 of heart disease, and his brother had by-pass surgery when he was 48. But Dave liked the good life, enjoyed steak and potatoes with all the fixings, a few cocktails before dinner, and a cigarette with his coffee throughout the day. In fact, he was so busy enjoying life that he couldn't find time to exercise. And like he said after the heart attack, "I felt fine. I figured that if something happened or I got sick, then I'd deal with it after it broke. The problem was I didn't know I was broke already! I sure didn't need some doc poking around looking for something wrong or his nurse preaching about getting in shape." Two years off the line, scared silly that he wouldn't ever get back flying, got his attention.

Protecting your FAA medical certificate is not the only reason you must be more aware of your health than other people. Furthermore, health is not just a matter of being productive in your job. Safety is an important objective in any flying activity, and your health and that of your crew and support personnel must be considered in any safety program. The unhealthy pilot is a potential safety risk. Plenty of health educational resources, ranging from newspapers and magazines to a wide variety of good (and not so good) books and manuals, are available in drug stores, supermarkets, and bookstores.

It is a topic, more often than not, that is taken for granted. Those who do not make a conscious effort to maintain good health are at greater risk of developing a medical problem in the future. Even more significant, your poor health could make you less than safe—incapacitated or distracted—leading to events that show up in accident statistics.

No one can force you to be healthy, except maybe the FAA when it identifies an unhealthy and unsafe medical condition and holds up your certification until the problem is resolved. Wouldn't it be a better long-term goal to keep ahead of your health rather than waiting for someone else to challenge your medical certificate or for you to experience a "boy, that was close!" in flight? Here are some suggestions to assist you in your health maintenance.

NUTRITION AND DIET

Before considering what you should do to maintain health, it's important to review some basics of nutrition. Granted, a lot of information is currently in the press about what you should and shouldn't eat. However, little has changed in nutritional insight over the past several decades. Whenever looking over the variety of diets, food products, and supplements with which you are surrounded, always keep in mind the basics that you were taught in school.

Basic food components

All foods are made up of three basic substances: protein, carbohydrates, and fat. Other components are vitamins and minerals, but they are present in adequate amounts in any balanced diet.

Protein is the basic substance of all cells in your body and is required by all living things. Approximately 20 percent of your diet should come from protein. It is a major player in your body's metabolic processes and tissue growth. During digestion and metabolism, ingested protein changes into peptides and amino acids, basic chemicals that are the building blocks of all proteins. Proteins are commonly found in animal products—meat, fish, poultry, and dairy products. Fruits, vegetables, and grains are other sources but to a lesser degree. Ingested proteins cannot be stored and must be replaced every day.

It is a misunderstanding that ingested protein directly replaces protein lost from the body, such as from muscles. All foods are broken down during digestion to simpler components, and then the body forms its own protein in appropriate locations in your body; therefore, it is not true that eating more proteins builds muscle mass. Proteins in your diet provide the elements for your body to enhance muscle tissue. Calories from proteins are also necessary, and protein already in your body mass is sometimes used as a source of calories. The body's proteins, however, can be spared by ingesting more fats and carbohydrates. In other words, if sufficient nonprotein calories are not available, then your body's proteins become part of the metabolic process, to generate calories.

Fats are a very concentrated (and the primary) source of energy. Only ethanol (the alcohol in beverages) is close. Because your body needs this energy at various times during any day, unused sources are stored in your body in fat cells and tissue. Approximately 25 percent of diet should be fat. Each person has his or her own rate of use of this energy and ability to store energy in fat. Just controlling caloric intake is not going to be successful in all people. Therein lies the challenge and dilemma of weight control. As with the other food components, ingested fat does not go directly into body fat. It reaches the fat stores via the metabolic route and any unused calories are stored for future use.

Dietary fats are often classified into three different categories: saturated, monounsaturated, and polyunsaturated. Most saturated fats are solid at room temperature and are found in animal products, especially beef and pork.

The majority of diet should be carbohydrates, approximately 55 percent. Carbohydrates are all broken down and metabolized to glucose in your body (also called blood sugar). The function of glucose is to provide immediate sources of energy and is, therefore, an important body "fuel" to be used by muscles and especially the brain.

In addition to these calories being stored in your body's fat tissue, some are stored in the liver as a backup if adequate blood sugar is not available. Carbohydrates are no more fattening than fat or proteins. This misconception is common even though fat has more calories per weight. Granted, the body metabolizes each component in a different way and at a variable rate, but you cannot maintain an ideal weight solely by avoiding carbohydrates. In fact, that would be unhealthy.

Carbohydrates are found in grains, potatoes, beans, and peas. Other vegetables and fruits have smaller amounts of carbohydrates in the form of starches and sugars. Plain sugar, by the way, is an "empty calorie" because it does not have other nutrients, vitamins, or minerals associated with those calories.

An important carbohydrate is fiber. Fiber is essentially carbohydrates that your body cannot digest or break down into usable materials. Fiber is important in a balanced diet because it assists in helping move ingested foods and byproducts through your gastrointestinal system. Lack of fiber leads to constipation.

Vitamins and minerals

Vitamins and minerals are adequately supplied to your body with a basic balanced diet. Vitamins, by the way, provide no nutritional or caloric value. They act like catalysts, assisting in the biochemical metabolism of the body. Vitamins are excreted in the urine and therefore need to be replaced. Taking supplemental vitamins does no harm and in fact might help in working conditions that do not always provide the best in food. However, all vitamins are the same, no matter who manufactures, markets, or sells them.

Calories

Calories are a part of every food that you eat. Calories that are not used are either stored in fat tissues or excreted. But this varies with individuals because some have a metabolic system that easily gets rid of excess calories. Others have a difficult time losing weight because their metabolism is such that it is very efficient in using available calories and stores the rest. Nevertheless, your caloric input is still what decides your weight. Most overweight people are simply taking in more calories than the body needs to function.

Diets often fail over time because there is the lack of a maintenance program that keeps caloric intake under control after the initial loss. Counting calories, like basic fuel management principles with your airplane, is the best way to keep your weight under control. Furthermore, rather than being nutritious over the long run, many diets are quick fixes at the expense of your body's metabolic process and generally fail after a few months.

Calories burned per minute
(for a 170-pound person)

Golf	4.4
Walking (3 mph)	5.3
Swimming	5.3
Calisthenics	7.3
Biking (10 mph)	7.3
Tennis (doubles)	7.5
Aerobics	7.8
Stair climbing	7.9
Handball	10.5
Jogging (5.5 mph)	11.5
Skiing (cross-country)	12.3

Your body, with usual levels of activities, needs less than 2,000 calories to function, often less than 1,500. Therefore, by counting calories, keeping track of your intake in a diary, and staying around 1,000 to 1,200 calories per day, you will usually accomplish weight loss. As you approach your optimum weight, more calories can be added. This is very simple and it works, but most people need more motivation to stick to calorie counting. That's one reason there are so many different and creative methods to losing weight.

KEEPING IN SHAPE

Exercise is as important as diet in a health maintenance program. Exercise means different things to different people. The main objectives are to increase the efficiency of your heart and lungs (aerobic), to keep your body's muscles, tendons, and bones in tone, to assist in a weight-control program, and to maintain an increased sense of well being.

The basis of any aerobic exercise is to gradually bring your pulse rate up to a target rate, often defined as 220 minus your age for a maximum heart rate. (Actually, getting up to 85 percent of the level is still beneficial.) Then, the object is to maintain that rate for no less than 20 minutes, after which you slowly return to your resting pulse. Aerobic exercise is accomplished by several methods—jogging, fast walking, biking, cross-country skiing, swimming, etc. While jogging might be the most productive in a shorter period of time, it is not enjoyed by everyone. It is also very hard on hips and knees over a long period of time. What is important is to start some form of exercise program and stick with it.

Try for three times a week, or no more than 3 days between exercise. For aerobic conditioning, working out to achieve more than your maximum heart rate is not safe nor will it gain any more than reaching the 85 percent level. Furthermore, the more you exercise and the more competitive you get, the greater the chance of injury. That injury could keep you from flying during healing.

FLIGHT PHYSICALS

Aircraft performance and standards can be measured in absolutes, and if you fly the aircraft "by the numbers," it should perform as stated. On the other hand, the measurements of your body's physiological status is expressed in ranges, not absolutes. However, for either mechanical or human machines, there are only two ways to determine if something is going wrong or about to fail or fall apart. Either you wait for something to happen (or change) and then take corrective action (crisis management), or you test the machine periodically to deliberately try to identify a problem, hopefully in the early stages of failing, and treat the problem before it gets out of hand. For mechanical machines, this strategy of early testing is called a *preventive maintenance program*. For the human machine, it's the medical evaluation or physical examination in a health maintenance program.

The FAA requires all pilots to have a periodic medical exam—the flight physical. Without this requirement, it is doubtful that many pilots would seek out an exam on their own. The reason, of course, is the potential threat that something will be found that could ground you. And it happens. Many pilots reason that as long as they feel good, there is no need to have further tests to see if anything is wrong. This is not the way they would view keeping ahead of their airplane's airworthy status. The difference is the perceived lack of control that you have over the results of your medical evaluation as opposed to the maintenance check of your aircraft.

It is important to recognize what happens in a typical exam. By being aware of this, the threat of losing control should be minimized. It still is a trade-off—looking for something wrong and then unexpectedly finding something wrong—or finding something wrong in time to be corrected before the problem becomes unacceptable. The other choice, of course, is waiting for something to go wrong and then hopefully being able to correct the problem. Therefore, the key to health maintenance is a combination of what was explained earlier—common sense life styles—and the preventative medical evaluation.

There are varying levels of medical exams, ranging from a simple overview, such as an FAA or insurance physical, to a comprehensive medical evaluation that includes several tests and evaluations. While even a basic exam is important, only a comprehensive physical will really tell you and your doctor very much that can help you. Here is a description of the typical medical exams available to you as a pilot. All medical evaluations consist of obtaining a medical history, doing a physical exam and a series of tests, and then reviewing the results.

The medical history

Your medical history is the most important part of any medical evaluation, especially for your doctor. How you feel, what has changed in your life, your habits, your family's medical status—all are important clues to your health. But to you as a pilot, this is also the one area where there is a reluctance to be completely candid and thorough. It's that threat thing again—and your denial that a simple symptom could be meaningful or helpful to the doctor. Many of these simple symptoms are valuable in a doctor's overall opinion of your health. Your understandable rationale, however, is to not mention anything unless you think it's significant.

The items of a good history should always be the same. You need to be familiar with the usually asked questions in order to have consistent answers and explanations. It's especially important if there is a problem in the future. Although some medical evaluations have only a brief review of your medical history, you need to know everything that has happened to you medically, and you should keep this information in your personal file. There will be a time in your flying days that you will need to share that information with someone, even if but to compare data over a period of time to detect changes or trends.

Frequently the question states, "have you *ever* had a history of . . .?" That means have you ever had "X" disease, injury, surgery at *any* time in your life. Even if it was decades ago that you had the problem, broken bone, surgery, or hospitalization, it's important to you and your doctor.

It would be wise to have a copy of a typical history form that you have filled out completely, checking with family members to confirm dates, ages, and events. Check with your personal doctor to make sure that everything is adequately evaluated and explained. Keep all this in your personal files for future use.

Another part of the medical history is called "Review of Systems." This is a review of how you feel, what symptoms you have, and how you perceive your body is functioning or not functioning. The doctor is interested in any significant pain, discomforts, congestions, aches, dizziness, and any other symptom that is not normal for you. Equally important is a change in any of these feelings—is it better or worse, occurring more often or less, etc. It's important to realize that what you think is insignificant might in fact be important to the doctor as he considers all the data from the rest of the evaluation. Let the doctor decide what to do and let him elaborate if he thinks it's important.

You should have your shot records (immunizations) in your file and bring the dates to your doctor. You will also be asked about your habits— smoking, drinking, coffee, exercise, diet, etc. He is, by the way, not just interested in what you have been doing the last week; he also wants to know what you have done in the past, even years ago.

The physical examination

Once again, like the history, the physical will be as extensive as the doctor feels it ought to be, depending on why you are having a physical. For example, a doctor could spend 15 minutes listening to your heart but often, only a few minutes is necessary if there are no abnormal findings. Basically, the doctor is looking, feeling, listening, and smelling for anything that isn't normal or expected.

Usually the doctor will start from the head and work down in his physical exam. Head, neck, chest, abdomen, genitourinary, and extremities will all be examined, in addition to most or all of your orifices. Somewhere in his routine or during the evaluation, he or someone else will check your blood pressure and pulse.

A discussion about high blood pressure is in order here because this part of the exam causes the most concern to the greatest number of pilots. Blood pressure is the hydraulic pressure within the arterial system. Normal blood pressure is about 120/80 (remember, there are no absolutes in medicine). The top number (systolic) of this reading is the highest pressure exerted by the heart during a contraction. The bottom number (diastolic) is the resting pressure, or the lowest pressure reached in the artery before the next contraction and during the relaxed phase of the heart's muscular activity. For obvious reasons, blood pressure does not go to zero between contractions.

Blood pressure is supposed to be high under conditions of extra work, illness, stress, and, of course, poor health. Blood pressure that remains elevated despite control of these factors is called *hypertension*. Hypertension usually needs treatment or certainly a change in your habits. Usually, a doctor will consider starting medication if your blood pressure consistently stays above 140/90.

A pilot should take every measure to keep blood pressure under 140/90 by controlling known causes of the elevation. These measures include weight reduction if you are overweight, reduction in salt and sodium intake, an exercise program, and control of stress. Some people's blood pressure goes up as soon as they have someone check their blood pressure (white-coat hypertension). If you are one of these hyper-reactors, it would be wise to purchase your own blood-pressure measuring equipment and keep a written record of your readings. Bring this record with you to your doctor to show that is is normal under usual conditions.

Blood and urine tests

Medical technology has advanced to the point where a multitude of test results can be achieved from a few tubes of your blood and a small sample of urine. The cost is reasonable enough to warrant full blood profiles (a series of 25 or more blood test results). The other side of that benefit is that many test results are of little value in a screening situation (as opposed to diagnostic). At times, these results of minimal worth are not within acceptable, or normal, limits. The doctor is now faced with the dilemma of what to do next. More tests could be considered even though, realistically, there is little clinical significance to a profile's single test result. Or he can choose to minimize the medical significance of the result because the rest of the medical evaluation is normal. In any case, to the pilot, test results in the not normal range could be considered by the flight surgeon and the FAA as being abnormal or unacceptable until proven otherwise—another reason to be sure your medical and certification needs are met by competent aeromedical physicians.

Be that as it may, results from blood tests do tell your doctor a great deal of information and provide insight about how well your body is functioning. Key blood test results include thyroid, liver and kidney function, cholesterol, HDL, LDL, triglycerides, blood count, and blood sugar as well as others relative to metabolic and heart functions.

When you look at the computer print-out of your blood test results, you will notice that absolute single number normals are nonexistent. Normal ranges are stated. These ranges, by the way, will change as the medical profession gains more knowledge as to the significance of the results relative to your health. A good example is that the upper limits for acceptable total cholesterol in 1987 was considered to be 275. Now that level has been reduced to 240 or even 200 in some situations.

Normal, abnormal, not normal

It's difficult to convey the significance of a medical evaluation result—is it normal or abnormal? These terms are used commonly in any medical discussion, yet they frequently have a different meaning to a doctor and a pilot.

There is little doubt about the meaning of *normal. Normal* is not only an acceptable result; it also implies that the result is perfect, or at least near perfect for that person. But what do you commonly call something that isn't normal? Abnormal? But that could be misleading to the pilot and to the doctor.

Abnormal has a varying definition. *Abnormal*, especially to a doctor, is something that is not only less than normal, but unacceptable, a result or finding that requires further evaluation or treatment. Yet, it is impossible to be normal in every parameter that is used to define good health. Something that is abnormal is not necessarily unacceptable to people not in the medical profession.

For example, using total cholesterol again, a value of 200 would be considered normal (as is a blood pressure of 120/80 or vision of 20/20). That doesn't mean that any value above those just stated (or outside the "normal" range) is abnormal or unacceptable, although your doctor might put that value in an abnormal category until it is proven to be acceptable.

Cholesterol and saturated fat content of common foods

	Portion Size	Chol (mg)	Sat Fat (g)	Sat Fat Calories
Butter	1 Tbsp	31	7	63
Margarine	1 Tbsp	0	2	18
Coconut oil	1 Tbsp	0	12	108
Milk, whole	1 C	33	5	45
Milk, 2%	1 C	18	3	27
Milk, skim	1 C	9	1	9
Ice cream	1 C	59	9	81
Yogurt	1 C	11	2	18
Ribeye steak	3 oz	70	5	45
Ground beef	3 oz	74	7	63
Poultry (no skin)	3 oz	72	1	9
Fish (sole)	3 oz	59	0.3	3
Shrimp	3 oz	134	0.2	2
Frankfurter	1	27	7	63
Egg	1	274	2	18
Peanut butter	1 Tbsp	0	2.8	18

In other words, when talking to your doctor, in their minds something abnormal is already unacceptable. To a nonmedical person, abnormal might be okay once additional tests are done to prove that the result is safe. So maybe another term should be used by pilots when discussing the results of their exams—*not normal*.

Not normal should mean that although the value is not perfect, it is not really abnormal or unacceptable either. Knowing that the rest of your medical evaluation is within normal limits now places the less than normal value in the acceptable range.

Yes, this is making an issue of a minor point. But note how some people react when they say their cholesterol is 242, their vision 20/30, or their blood pressure is 135/85. Some get very excited and concerned. Pilots are used to relating to absolute terms. If a test result is above (or below) that value that is perceived as being normal, then they reason that it is unacceptable. Not true. This is all the more reason to have periodic exams to rule out anything that really is acceptable but might not be normal. You will find this attitude in virtually all aspects of medical tests—weight, sugar in the urine, pulse rate, EKG rhythm, murmurs, etc. It is important, therefore, to fully understand the significance of all medical test results relative to your health and not be hung up on absolute values.

The electrocardiogram (EKG)

The *electrocardiogram (EKG)* is a test that measures the internal conduction of an electrical current through your heart muscle. The EKG does not put any current into your body; it measures the current that is made by the cells in your body. The readings come from 12 leads (connections) attached by suction cups or patches to the chest wall and to your arms and legs. The machine then measures the current and reports the results as tracings on a piece of paper. From this, the doctor can recognize rhythm disturbances, poor oxygen supply to heart muscle, conduction defects (like heart blocks), heart size, and other results about the heart muscle and its conduction system.

The EKG is a valuable screening aid, but like many medical tests, it is not a completely accurate, definitive, or reliable diagnostic tool. In other words, the tracings can be interpreted by different doctors as being normal or abnormal. At times, it's a judgment call, subject to interpretation, and necessitating other opinions. If the reading is considered abnormal, other tests can be done (exercise EKG, or "stress test," Thallium scans, etc.) to rule out any pathology that could be the source of the abnormal results. This added data now makes the abnormal result acceptable. It's not normal, but it's okay.

The spirometry test

Spirometry, or *pulmonary function test*, is a measurement of your lung's ability to function—and what its air capacity is and how fast you can exhale. This is tested by blowing into the machine as quickly and forcefully as you can and then for as long as you can. Some people cannot do this test well because they don't understand how to blow into the machine. Here's a tip: Practice blowing out a match that is held in front of your wide-open mouth (do not purse your lips). Continue to try blowing out the match as you increase its distance from your mouth. The intent is to empty the lungs as quickly as possible and for as long as possible.

Vision and hearing tests

Vision and hearing tests are tests common to all pilots, and the significance of these results is explained in their respective chapters. It is worth repeating that because these test results are vital to your safe flight and medical certification, it is imperative that you not take short cuts. A good eye exam by an ophthalmologist (an M.D.) should be done early in your flying, followed with periodic exams as you get older. This is in addition to those screening tests with your AME. Hearing is equally important, but the short cut of using the whispered voice test or conversation test tells you very little in terms of a quantitative evaluation of your hearing. Audiograms using an audiometer are preferred, at least once every one or two years.

Drug testing

Urine and blood can be tested for just about any chemical or substance known to man. High tech equipment can detect minute amounts; therefore, a company or government agency can check for anything it wants to check for and even determine the level or amount that is considered significant. This includes medication, nicotine, carbon monoxide, chemicals, alcohol, and drugs.

DOT and FAA, in 1989, mandated that certain professional pilots be tested for drugs (cocaine, marijuana, amphetamines, PCP, and opiates). Alcohol was not initially included in this list, although it is recognized that, in aviation, alcohol is a far greater problem than hard drugs. Nevertheless, the urine is tested for the presence of these drugs as well as the level or amount in the urine.

This is a two-step process. The first test is for screening the urine for the presence of drugs. Several materials and even foods can result in a "false positive" for a specific drug. In addition, however, the amount of that drug is also measured and must be at a certain level before being noted as positive. If that level is reached, then a confirmatory test is done—gas chromatography/mass spectrography—which is virtually 100 percent accurate. These tests define a footprint for every known chemical in a series of curves. No other chemical matches that curve, which means that if the test is positive, the chemical is present.

Then the level or amount present is once again determined. That level must be reached before a positive result is reported. That level is often fairly high, which means that once a test result is reported, not only is the drug present in the urine, but it is there at a level that confirms usage.

12

Protecting your FAA medical certificate

Fran knew she had reason to be scared when her doctor told her she had a murmur during a routine insurance exam. "Now what I am going to tell my AME? He's sure to ground me! Maybe I shouldn't say anything," she thought to herself. Then she recalled a recent story of how another pilot lost his medical because of a murmur and it took the FAA 6 months to recertify him. But how could she be grounded when she felt so good? She asked her CFI, who wasn't sure what to do, and her AME wasn't someone she was willing to ask for advice. Now what? In desperation, she called the FAA, not using her real name, and got the advice she was looking for: Get a medical evaluation from a heart specialist and then find an AME who has a reputation for working with the FAA. They even gave her some names to call. She felt better already, knowing she could do something about it.

Only a few decades ago, the standards for flying as a transport pilot were good past medical history, freedom from material structural defects, normal judgment of distance, freedom from disease of the ductless glands, and sound pulmonary and cardiovascular systems. These standards were part of the old Air Commerce Regulations for certification. Times have changed.

The fear of losing your medical because of the AME and FAA denying you is often more intense than the fear of busting a checkride. There is nothing more threatening to you than the required FAA flight physical—not even a checkride. The main reason for this perception is the fact that denials do happen and you feel out of control.

However, this fear is fueled by many embellished, misleading, and erroneous war stories of pilots being denied their medical certification either for a minor reason or because the FAA took months and/or years to reach a conclusion. It's no wonder that pilots dread this annual ordeal and seek out the most lenient AME so as not to "rock the boat."

Much of the threat comes from a poor understanding of how the certification process works, relying more on crew lounge counsel than on facts. In your defense, however, there is little accessible credible information that explains how the process is supposed to work. There is plenty of misinformation and poor counsel that tends to lead you into traps, delays, and unnecessary red tape.

FAA medical certification is a good example of crisis management by the pilot. As long as you can get by your flight physical, there is little incentive to learn how the FAA medical certification process works—until a problem is picked up during an exam. This attitude is a source of great stress to you. Knowing how the certification process works is essential to remove one more source of distraction in the cockpit—worrying about the FAA medical exam due next week!

WHO'S WHO?

Here are the key players in the FAA medical certification process.

Aviation Medical Examiner (AME)

Aviation Medical Examiners (AMEs) are doctors who are designated by the FAA to examine pilots. They are not employed by the FAA. They can have any medical specialty, probably are not pilots, and often fit you into their schedule with the rest of their patients. An AME has no authority to certify you unless everything is normal in the examiner's eyes. Anything suspected as being abnormal or unacceptable has to be reviewed by FAA doctors before you can be certified. AMEs now have more authority, providing they strictly follow FAA guidelines for evaluations.

Flight surgeon

All aeromedical doctors in the military are called flight surgeons—they have earned their professional wings by being trained in an extensive aviation medicine course. Many AMEs have only minimal knowledge and interest in aviation medicine and certification although they have been trained in a short FAA course. Civilian "flight surgeon" equivalents are AMEs who tend to be the more knowledgeable and effective and have the reputation of knowing FAA procedures. An AME/flight surgeon is someone who specializes in working with pilots and the aviation community, in addition to their usual medical practice. They are not designated as such in directories, but their reputation with the pilot group and even the FAA defines them as a "flight surgeon/AME" and not just another FAA medical examiner. The only way you can determine what role an AME chooses to play is by talking to other pilots or even the FAA. They know from experience which AMEs are willing to work with the pilot in complicated cases.

Oklahoma City (Oke City)

The FAA's office in Oke City is where all applications for certification (Form 8500-8) go for review by FAA-employed aeromedical doctors. They receive in excess of 2,000 forms per day, and all the results are fed into a computer. If anything is abnormal, left blank, or incorrectly filled out, the computer rejects the form, which means it must now be reviewed by a medical person (not necessarily a doctor). If there is doubt as to the significance of the results of the exam, one of the doctors gets involved.

The Oke City level has much more authority to certify and deny than in years past. It is also this office that will direct the pilot (not the AME) to complete further tests, if indicated, to determine certifiability.

Regional Flight Surgeon

The FAA has several regions around the country. Within each region is a flight surgeon who has more authority than the AME and can often guide you and/or your AME in problem cases, especially if clarification is needed about the significance of a problem and what additional tests are expected. These doctors still are responsible to Oke City but can sometimes provide an okay to fly while other medical tests are being done.

Federal Air Surgeon

The Federal Air Surgeon is the chief flight surgeon responsible for all civilian aviation medicine issues, including medical certification. Although most of the evaluations and decisions come out of Oke City, the Federal Air Surgeon has the final say in very complex files.

The Federal Air Surgeon and his staff are those who are responsible for ensuring that the public is protected from unsafe pilots. With adequate documentation of what your true health is, the FAA will try to certify all pilots if they meet specified standards. In fact, it creates much more work for the FAA to deny you, so there is added incentive to avoid frivolous denials.

WHAT'S WHAT?

Here are some other terms commonly used in the certification process.

FAR Part 67

FAR Part 67 outlines the medical regulations that specify aeromedical standards for certification. These standards are usually quite general as compared to military medical standards, which are comprehensively spelled out. This FAR has stayed pretty much the same for many years, although there is still the intent by the FAA to revise their standards. The current FARs are adequate for now because there is plenty of room for interpretation, allowing for exceptions, or waivers, based on thorough medical evaluations.

FAR 61.53

FAR 61.53 is a specific regulation within Part 61 (which refers to all pilots—commercial and general). It is noted on the back of your medical certificate as a medical requirement by which you are governed. Specifically, it states: "OPERATIONS DURING A MEDICAL DEFICIENCY. No person may act as pilot in command, or in any other capacity as a required pilot flight crewmember while he has a known medical deficiency, or increase of a known medical deficiency that would make him unable to meet the requirements for his current medical certificate."

In other words, you are not legal if you have any problem that would make you unsafe and unable to pass an FAA flight physical just before your next flight. This places the burden on you to determine if you are legal and safe each time you fly.

Form 8500

All FAA forms dealing with the application and evaluation for medical certification are labeled as 8500s, or FAA Form 8500. The next number refers to the specific form, whether it's the medical certificate (8500-9), the waiver (8500-15), the eye evaluation form (8500-7), or the application for medical certification (8500-8). It's this form number—8500-8— that is usually being referred to when someone states simply "8500." By the way, FAA Form 8500-8 is a legal document and you are responsible for its accuracy.

Limitations

This is a requirement stated on the medical certificate that you must follow to be legal. For example, the most common limitation is the need to

You cannot fly if you have:

- Had a heart attack
- Passed a kidney stone
- Been unconscious
- Asthma
- An ulcer
- Been diagnosed as chemically dependent
- Been put on long-term prescribed medications
- Diabetes
- Migraine headaches
- A mental disorder requiring medication
- Recently had major surgery or injury
- An abnormal EKG
- Had a stroke
- A heart murmur

Until:

The FAA has reviewed your medical file

and

authorized you to return to flying.

wear or possess glasses for correction of vision. The certificate is "limited" by the requirement to wear glasses. If you are not wearing glasses during flight and you have the limitation that you must wear glasses, then you are in violation of the regulations.

Waiver

The term *waiver* has a double meaning. One is a "Statement of Demonstrated Ability," which means that you have demonstrated your ability to fly safely despite the fact that you don't meet absolute standards, such as single eye vision, deficient color vision, missing limbs, hearing loss, etc. Such a waiver is granted after special practical evaluations or a "medical" checkride and then becomes a separate document that supplements your medical certificate.

The other meaning is the usual terminology expressed when discussing medical problems (illnesses and diseases and their treatments) and whether or not they are certifiable. If a disease initially considered to be unsafe can be proven to be safe inflight, then the standards are waived. It's like an exception to the rule because it can be proven that the rule doesn't apply to that particular pilot. This waiver is not a separate written document but a letter stating that after review of the medical file, you meet the intent of federal regulations. This is one reason medical FARs should not be too specific because it allows the FAA to use their professional discretion as to whether or not you are safe, or, at least, an acceptable risk. This letter is not something that you carry with you, but you should have a copy in your personal file. The actual waiver of demonstrated ability does have to be carried with you and shown to any examiner who asks to see it.

TYPICAL CERTIFICATION SCENARIO

The intent of the FAA medical certification process is to identify any medical, mental, physical, or psychological condition that would make you unsafe and to anticipate any abnormal or unsafe conditions that might develop between the time of the current exam and the next required medical evaluation. Problems with this process occur when unexpected abnormals are found during the physical. If the AME doesn't know how to deal with the new finding or doesn't want to become involved, he will have the entire application sent to the FAA for their review.

During this review, which could take a minimum of six weeks just for the FAA to get to your file, you are grounded. It's the lack of control you have during this delay that is the most threatening to you. You perceive your certificate and your livelihood as being judged by some bureaucratic doctors who are making their decision based on an impersonal file of medical reports, and you have nothing to say about it.

As stated previously, what often happens is that some pilots will seek the most lenient AME, one who is also less knowledgeable about the certification process and is unwilling to do more than fill in the squares, certify only those he feels are legal, and send the rest to the FAA to decide. Some AMEs tend to discourage pilots who have a medical problem that the AME feels won't be certified, often stating that the pilot will never fly again. The fact is that the FAA certifies many conditions often thought by some of the pilot community to be a permanent grounding. These conditions include hypertension using medication, by-pass heart surgery, heart attacks, kidney stones, history of alcoholism, and many more.

Two of the most common controllable problems leading to delays or even denials are failing to answer all questions ("filling in all the squares") on the front of the application form (FAA Form 8500-8) and not explaining all new affirmative answers or changes from previous exams. The new 8500-8 (revised in 1991) has some different questions and a revised format. Your AME should be able to explain what is required of you. On the back of the form, the AME is supposed to clarify all of your affirmative responses, fill in his portion dealing with his findings during the examination (including test results), and then state his action—certify, deny, or defer.

Here is where some AMEs will not take the time or effort to further evaluate and explain to the FAA a medical situation that could be questioned later. The AME has the opportunity in his section to satisfy the FAA's expectations. However, to some AMEs, it's simpler (especially when he is busy and doesn't want to get involved), to deny you and let the FAA take over the recertification process.

This is why the FAA will correspond with you (not your AME) when there is a problem noted or there is an incomplete file. The FAA expects you to initiate and coordinate the requests necessary to complete the process. This "passing the buck" to the FAA becomes a very time-consuming process and certainly not in your best interest. It need not happen that way (Fig. 12-1).

IDEAL CERTIFICATION SCENARIO

The key to an efficient certification process, whether you are healthy or not, is to work with a knowledgeable AME—a flight surgeon. Unnecessary delays and red tape do not have to occur. As noted before, these AMEs anticipate what the FAA requires for further testing, arrange for the evaluations, work up a completed file, may discuss your case with one of the FAA doctors, and then, and only then, submit the file for FAA review. A major cause of unnecessary delays is having reports from several different doctors arriving in Oke City at different times. It's best that a complete file be prepared before submission so that everything is together when it reaches an FAA doctor's desk.

In less complex situations, a flight surgeon can often be authorized by the FAA, by phone, to certify you based on the results of his evaluation. The FAA also respects these AMEs, knows they have a reputation of being thorough and professional, and often relies on their judgment in coming to a final decision. Even the FAA in Oke City or the regional flight surgeon can help or give you guidance. Call them—anonymously if you like. Despite what their image is made out to be, they are paid to help the pilot (Fig. 12-2).

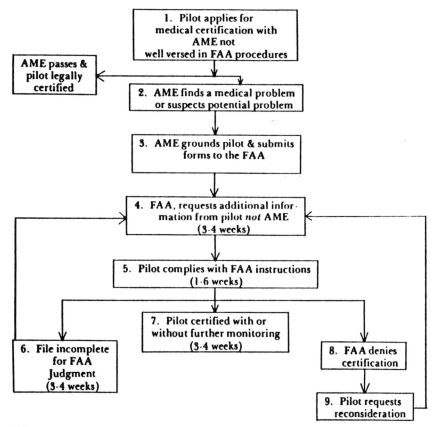

COMMENTS:

#1. The typical AME is not highly knowledgable regarding expeditious handling of problem certifications.
#2. Often AME does not tell pilot significance of findings - allows FAA to be "bad guy" & inform pilot he is grounded.
#3. Often prematurely submits report to FAA.
#4. FAA requires additional medical information to reconsider a pilot's fitness.
#5. Pilot sometimes left on his own to work with specialists & handle additional paperwork required by FAA.
#6. Because of misunderstanding concerning intent of further evaluation & requirements, FAA requests further data, pilot is back at box 4.
#8, 9. By this point pilot often finds himself trying to coordinate & achieve cooperation from 3 entities - the original AME, any specialists who have entered the picture, & the FAA.

Key to improperly handled sequence is not knowing & properly *anticipating* the FAA needs *in advance* of their requests. Tremendous amounts of time can be lost waiting for the FAA to respond to previous paperwork submission - only to learn more paperwork is necessary.

Fig. 12-1. Improperly managed certification sequence. Reprinted with the author's permission from *FAA Medical Certification: Guidelines for Pilots* (c) 1992 Iowa State University.

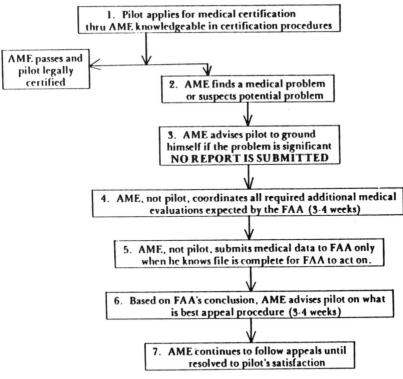

1. Pilot applies for medical certification
   thru AME knowledgeable in certification procedures

AME passes and
pilot legally
certified

2. AME finds a medical problem
   or suspects potential problem

3. AME advises pilot to ground
   himself if the problem is significant
   NO REPORT IS SUBMITTED

4. AME, not pilot, coordinates all required additional medical
   evaluations expected by the FAA (3-4 weeks)

5. AME, not pilot, submits medical data to FAA only
   when he knows file is complete for FAA to act on.

6. Based on FAA's conclusion, AME advises pilot on what
   is best appeal procedure (3-4 weeks)

7. AME continues to follow appeals until
   resolved to pilot's satisfaction

COMMENTS:

#1: This is the key to success of control: that the AME is knowledgeable in the certification process and aviation medicine, and is experienced in working with the FAA in protecting the healthy pilot's medical certificate.

#2: AME will try to anticipate potential problems which ban be resolved without compromising your responsibilities as a pilot.

#3: This is the second key to success: no report is made to the FAA until both the AME and pilot are satisfied with the file. If pilot's condition is not significant, pilot continues to fly.

#4: AME can make appointments with other specialists and already knows what the FAA will require for further evaluation. There is no need to wait for FAA's direction.

#5: AME submits entire file to FAA, with cover letter, rather than making the FAA the coordinator of the varied medical reports. AME may also alert FAA about coming file.

#6: AME can then determine what courses of action to follow once everyone knows what is necessary to satisfy FAA requirements.

#7: The AME should commit himself to the pilot to assist him thru the entire appeals process and explain why such actions are necessary.

Fig. 12-2. Properly managed certification sequence. Reprinted with the author's permission from *FAA Medical Certification: Guidelines for Pilots* (c) 1992 Iowa State University.

GROUNDED

The most feared word in aviation is *grounded*, meaning the same as *denial*. It's the word used when the FAA feels you have a medical condition that isn't safe.

There are some conditions that will ground you for a few days or weeks (a bad flu, a broken bone or sprain, appendicitis, etc.), and you resume flying when you and your doctor agree that you have no restrictions to any activities. There are other conditions, more serious, that require approval from the FAA before you can return to the flight deck. Such conditions include the passing of a kidney stone, a stomach ulcer, a bleeding ulcer, a concussion, and major surgery. Still other medical problems (i.e., the nine mandatory denials) usually begin as a denial but often can be reconsidered.

A denial, contrary to what many think, is never final. In other words, the FAA will always consider additional information from additional tests and medical opinions. The passage of time without progression of the medical problem is also taken into consideration. Therefore, if you want to return to flying, you should continue to gather additional data with the help of an AME/flight surgeon to prove you are safe. If you have a condition that is controllable or curable, it is up to you to work at your health.

Medical certification

Key points:

- A denial is never final unless you accept it as final.
- If you are fit to fly, the FAA should certify you.
- If you don't fly, no report need be sent to the FAA.
- Seek competent advice before requesting recertification.

There are several medical conditions that require mandatory denial at the time they are discovered. These are: a character or behavior disorder severe enough to be unsafe, a psychosis, alcoholism, drug addiction, epilepsy, disturbance of consciousness without satisfactory explanation, heart attack, significant coronary heart disease, and diabetes requiring any medication. It's also important to recognize that this refers to a "history of," which means that if at any time in your life you have had any of these conditions, denial is mandatory.

That's the bad news. The good news is that the Federal Air Surgeon, through the medical regulation FAR 67.19, can "special issue" a certificate, even for the mandatory denials, if it can be proven that the condition, treated or untreated, will not be a safety issue.

GETTING YOUR MEDICAL BACK

If you are denied for any reason, from failing to submit a completed application to having a serious medical condition, the process is the same. In the hands of a competent and helpful AME, additional tests are accomplished, a file is compiled, and discussions are held with the FAA doctors.

The FAA expects certain minimum tests to be done. Some personal doctors will say that such tests are not necessary. However, in most cases, the FAA will still require these evaluations and will not consider certification until they are done. The FAA will not accept the doctor's unproven opinion that what you have is not significant. Unless there is objective evidence to back up that opinion, the FAA cannot act favorably. It might take several attempts with new information to convince the FAA that you are safe.

As mentioned earlier, FAR 61.53 (which deals with your responsibility to be medically qualified every time you fly) is in effect only when you fly. This is a simplistic statement, but it is the key to you keeping control during the re-certification process. Providing you are working with an AME and everyone is in the process of evaluating your condition, then nothing has to be reported to the FAA as long as you don't fly—you ground yourself. This allows you the time to complete your evaluations and precludes premature submission of incomplete files to the FAA. The sense of urgency, which inevitably results in very lengthy and often unsatisfactory delays, is relieved because nothing needs to be submitted until you are ready. You remain in control.

A responsible pilot's fear is not just that something will be found during a medical exam; it's the feeling that the condition must be reported to the FAA immediately, leading to the familiar "war stories" of prolonged and unfair results. If you don't fly, and the AME respects you and your commitment, then you and the AME have "breathing room" to work out the problem before anything is reported.

In summary, if you are willing to accept the responsibility of being familiar with the FAA certification process and work with an AME while you are healthy and before any problem unexpectedly develops (avoiding crisis management), there is less of a threatening situation whenever the time comes for the FAA or company physical. Waiting for something to happen, going to an AME who gives a "pink and breathing" physical, and being informed only through crew lounge counsel will lead to your own bona fide "war story" of losing your medical for unexpected reasons. Look for the competent AME now by checking around. Don't wait until a problem develops. Then practice good health maintenance.

Appendix

The ideal pilot's medical evaluation

As described in chapters 11 and 12, one of the greatest fears to you as a pilot is losing your FAA medical. It's often a "catch-22"—the more extensive the medical evaluation to determine your health, the greater the likelihood of finding something abnormal and unacceptable to the FAA. Not a very comforting situation!

However, any preventative maintenance program, whether for your aircraft or your body, must be comprehensive enough to tell you what to expect. Feeling fine and having a current medical is not an assurance that you are healthy. The following is a more structured description of what you should expect from an "ideal medical evaluation." Such an exam is often referred to as an *executive-type physical*, implying that executives need more tests and an extensive examination. I call it a *Health Maintenance Exam*, or *HME*.

Several tests are not necessary at every exam but should be taken initially to establish a baseline. As you get older or risk factors that need to be monitored are identified, your doctor can advise you what tests need to be repeated in future exams. For example, a chest X-ray is important for your file, but if you are not a smoker or no pathology is found in the initial X-ray, then chest X-rays are not necessary every time you have a complete medical evaluation. Your doctor can advise you on the frequency.

Once you have made an appointment with your doctor for an HME, you can expect to fill out a comprehensive history form, either sent to you prior to your appointment or filled out in the waiting room. Your medical history, past and present, is the most important part of any medical evaluation. Be prepared for this form each time by having an already-completed copy to which you can refer, especially if you'll be filling it out while sitting in a noisy and distracting waiting room. Your own filed history form can also ensure consistency in your responses.

Although sharing your medical history with a doctor can be scary, don't hold back on symptoms or problems that you feel aren't important, or worse still, symptoms or problems that you feel are important to which you don't want to attract attention. If you are not emotionally ready to tell everything, then there is no sense in going on with the exam. Quite often, HMEs are sought by the pilot who wants to confirm that everything is fine (he or she already feels great) and avoided by the pilot who is truly at risk for a medical problem and probably suspects it but doesn't want to know.

Because your personal and family histories are important, be sure that section is complete. Check with your family to be sure your information is accurate and complete. All surgery, injuries, visits to any health professionals (doctor, therapist, counselor, etc.), use of medication, visits to emergency rooms or treatment centers, hospitalizations, and any other related medical or psychological evaluations need to be listed. The form is confidential, and confidentiality is a key part of any doctor-patient relationship. If you have questions about any items on the form, ask a nurse or the doctor. If you have a sensitive subject that you want to discuss only with the doctor, then leave that space blank on the form and wait until you see the doctor. You should not be pressured into completing the form by anyone, but be sure the doctor is aware of and understands your concern.

You probably will go through a battery of tests before you see the doctor. Some doctors have blood tests done before your appointment so that they have the results available when they see you. Either way, you should expect the usual tests done for any FAA exam—vision, hearing, height, and weight. Checking for glaucoma is very important if you are over 35 and a must if anyone in your family has glaucoma. In addition, a chest X-ray, resting EKG, and breathing test (spirometry) should be done, especially during your initial HME.

The results from these tests are subject to interpretation by the doctor. For example, a squiggle on the EKG might be insignificant to one doctor and significant to another. That's okay as long as any "significant" results are further explained. That's the biggest reason for an HME—being prepared to explain "not normals." Your personal medical file, which explains the problem from previous evaluations, expedites resolving any question your AME or the FAA might have.

A complete urinalysis should also be done, not just a dip stick. A microscopic evaluation is important. Here the doctor is looking for something in your urine that shouldn't be there, such as blood, sugar, protein, some products of metabolism, pH, and specific gravity. You probably recall that the doctor wants you to fast—nothing to eat for 12 to 14 hours before your appointment. But don't avoid water. In fact, you should drink plenty of water; otherwise your urine will be too concentrated.

Probably the most important part of testing is looking at what's in your blood. As I stated in chapter 11, a few tubes of blood can tell the doctor a lot, oftentimes more than he wants or needs to know. If you are a pilot, most abnormals have to be explained further in anticipation of the FAA perceiving you as a risk. Therefore, whenever a blood test result isn't in the normal range, ask your doctor to do whatever tests are necessary (even repeating the test) to rule out any significant problem.

Blood tests are important in evaluating your liver, thyroid, kidneys, heart, and blood cells, as well as other metabolic functions. It is these tests that are affected by not fasting. Other things that can affect results are alcohol, caffeine, too much exercise, smoking, fatty foods, and stress. Because diabetes can be such a major problem in maintaining your medical, testing your blood and urine sugar two hours after you ingest food (two-hour postprandial blood sugar) is important, especially if anyone in your family is diabetic or if at any time you have had sugar in your urine (as tested at every FAA exam).

Acceptable results are identified by most laboratories with the use of a computer. A printout tells you what the lab's "normal" range is and where your results are in relation to that range. However, as with the EKG, all results are subject to interpretation by your doctor. All the information is considered, along with the other data from your history and physical exam, and compared. Therefore, a single test result is not significant until it is considered along with the rest of your HME results.

The final step is the actual physical exam. Often the doctor asks additional questions, kind of a system review—how do you feel, is your appetite okay, any trouble with bowel movements or urination, any aches or pains, etc. Then the doctor examines you, checking every orifice, pushing and prodding various sections of your body, listening for sounds, checking pulses, looking for anything that is not normal or that has changed from previous exams.

Some specific examinations include looking into your eye (the only place where blood vessels and nerves are not covered with skin), feeling for lumps in your neck and armpits, having you swallow while checking your thyroid (your thyroid rises when you swallow so it can be felt), and listening to your chest. Breath sounds vary, and deep breathing accentuates any abnormal sounds. The heart is evaluated by listening at various locations of your chest and with you in various positions.

When the doctor pokes around in your abdominal area, he or she is looking for enlarged organs (the liver is below your right rib cage, your spleen on the left), feeling for masses or tumors within your abdomen that shouldn't be there, and listening for sounds that shouldn't be there.

The rectal exam is important, especially as you get older (40 and over). Many things can be discovered during this humbling exam—hemorrhoids, tumors, fissures, and prostate problems, to name a few. The same is true for females with the pelvic exam and pap smear. Checking a stool specimen for blood is also important over age 40.

The extremities are last, checking for range of motion, strength, and swelling. The back and spine are in this category, and a common problem with pilots is sitting for long periods of time in less-than-comfortable seats.

The final phase is putting all this information together and coming up with a diagnosis—are you healthy, do some problems need monitoring or additional evaluation, and does something need treatment now or in the future? The doctor can only advise you; it is up to you to decide to follow that advice. If you question the findings, get another opinion, especially if you feel it could affect your FAA medical certificate. Of course, if you are not sure, contact an AME and find out what effect your problem has, if any, on certification.

Rationalizing that "if it ain't broke, don't fix it" is tempting. But how do you know you it "ain't broke?" All things considered, finding out early that something is wrong and fixing it is better than waiting and finding out that something could have been corrected or resolved had you intervened in time. If you do have a problem that prevents you from flying, the sooner you find out, the sooner you can pursue other career options.

Index

A

alcohol, 93-102
  Alcoholics Anonymous
    (AA), 101
  effects on liver, 14
  hangover, 97-98
  histotoxic hypoxia, 29, 95
  OTC medication, 87
  performance effects, 96-
    97
  physiological effects, 94-
    97
  recognizing a problem
    drinker, 99-101
  tolerance, 98-99
  treatment for depen-
    dency, 101-102
anatomy, human body, 9-21
anoxia, 23
atmosphere
  effects of, 8-9
  barometric pressure, 4
  carbon dioxide, 3
  carbon monoxide, 29-30,
    34-35
  composition of, 1-3
  nitrogen, 3
  oxygen, 3, 23-34
  ozone, 4
  physics of gases, 4-8
  poisons in the air, 34-35
  water vapor, 3-4

Aviation Medical Examiner
  (AME), 175

B

barometric pressure, 4
biorhythms, 137-138
Boyle's law, 5, 7

C

cabin decompression, 36
caffeine, 88-91, 137
  causing fatigue, 142
  OTC medication, 87
  side effects, 90
  sources, 88-89
  tolerance, 90-91
carbon dioxide, 3
carbon monoxide, 34-35
  effects of exposure to, 35
  hypoxia and, 29-30
  symptoms, 35
  treatment, 35
circadian rhythms, 137-138
  causing fatigue, 143
colds, 80
concussion, 10
conduction, 66
convection, 66-67
  communication skills, 154
  coordination skills, 154
  decision-making skills,
    153
  definition, 152

  judgment skills, 154
  leadership skills, 153-154
  training program, 154-155

D

decompression, 36
  altitude chamber ride, 44-
    45
  rapid (R/D), 44-45
decompression sickness
  (DCS), 40
  factors affecting, 42-43
  prevention, 42
  scuba diving/flying and,
    43
  symptoms, 41
dehydration, 77
  causing fatigue, 142
depression, 146-147
diabetes, 15
disorientation, 46-64
  coping with, 62-63
  illusions (see illusions)
  motion sickness, 63-64
  positional, 49-50
  postural, 48-49
  spatial, 59-60
  temporal, 50-51
  types of, 47-62
  vertigo (see vertigo)
  vestibular, 51-58
Divers Alert Network
  (DAN), 43

drugs, 93
  illegal, 102-103
  testing, 102-103, 173
  types of, 102
dysbarism, 36

E

ear (see hearing)
effective performance time
  (see time of useful consciousness)
electromagnetic spectrum,
  105
evaporation, 67
eye (see vision)

F

FAA medical certificate
  AME, 175
  certification office, 176
  certification process, 175-
    176, 179-182
  denials, 182-183
  Federal flight surgeon,
    176
  flight surgeon, 175-176
  Form 8500, 177
  limitations, 177-178
  protecting, 174-184
  reapplying, 184
  regional flight surgeon,
    176
  regulations and forms,
    177-179
fatigue, 28, 131, 141-147
  causes, 141-143
  coping with, 147
  symptoms, 143-147
Federal Aviation Regula-
  tions (FAR)
  Part 61.53, 177
  Part 67, 177
first aid, 157-159
  contents of kit, 158
flicker vertigo, 63
flight physiology, x

determining ability to fly,
  xi-xii
incapacitating symptoms,
  xi
flight surgeon, 175-176
  Federal, 176
  regional, 176
flying
  above 5,000 feet AGL, 22-
    45
  affects of smoking and,
    29-30
  atmospheric challenges
    during, 1-9
  disorientation, 46-64
  fundamentals of, viii
  health maintenance, 162-
    184
  hearing, 118-130
  human body challenges
    during, 9-21
  inflight medical emergen-
    cies, 156-161
  temperature extremes,
    65-78
  transporting ill passen-
    gers, 159-160
  vision, 104-117
fog, visual illusions, 61-62,
  116
frostbite, 76

G

Graham's law, 7-8

H

hayfever, 80-81
haze, visual illusions, 61-
  62, 116
headaches, causes of, 98
health, 162-184
  blood and urine tests,
    169-170
  calories, 165-166
  cholesterol and saturated
    fats, 171
  drug testing, 173

electrocardiogram (EKG),
  172
examination, 168-169
exercising, 166
flight physicals, 166-173
food components, 163-
  164
hearing tests, 173
medical evaluation, 170-
  172, 185-188
medical history, 167-168
nutrition and diet, 163-
  166
obtaining a FAA medical
  certificate, 174-184
pulmonary function test,
  172
spirometry test, 172
vision tests, 173
vitamins and minerals,
  164-165
hearing, 118-130
  anatomy of the ear, 118-
    120
  conductive loss, 128
  conserving/protecting,
    129-130
  loss, 124-125, 128-129
  measurement tests, 124
  noise, 122-123
  noise-induced loss, 127-
    128
  noise sources, 126-127
  sensorineural loss, 129
  sound, 120-123
  sound perception, 123-
    124
  tests, 173
heat stress, 71-73
heat stroke, 72, 74
Henry's law, 7, 40
histotoxic hypoxia, 25, 29,
  95
human body
  anatomy and structure, 9-
    21

biorhythms, 137-138
blood vessels, 18-20
central nervous system, 10
controlling temperature of, 68-69
decompression sickness (DCS), 40-43
ear, 36-39, 118-120
eye, 106-108
gastrointestinal system, 13, 40-43
health maintenance, 162-173
heart, 16-17
kidneys, 14-15
liver, 14
lungs, 17-18
metabolic system, 13-15
musculoskeletal system, 12-13
pancreas, 15
self-imposed medical problems, 79-103
senses, 11, 104
sinus problems, 39
spinal cord, 10-11
teeth problems, 39
thyroid, 15
hyperventilation, 33-34
causes, 33
symptoms, 34
hypoglycemia, 91
causing fatigue, 142-143
hypothermia, 74-75
hypoxia, 20, 22-34, 143
absolute attitude, 30
acclimatization, 30
alcohol induced, 29, 95
ambient temperature, 30
carbon monoxide induced, 29-30
classification of, 23-25
compensatory stage, 27
critical stage, 27-28
disturbance stage, 27

duration of exposure, 30
factors influencing tolerance to, 29-31
histotoxic, 25, 29, 95
hypemic (anemic), 24-25
hyperventilation, 33-34
hypoxic (altitude), 23-24
indifferent state, 26-27
prevention, 33
rate of ascent, 30
stages, 25-28
stagnant, 25
symptoms, 28-29
time of useful consciousness (TUC), 31-32
treatment, 33

I
illusions
angular motion, 57-58
autokinesis, 60
coriolus, 54-55
elevator, 61
landing visual, 62
leans, 55-56
oculogravic, 56, 61
oculogyral, 60
rotational, 57-58
somatogravic, 61
vection, 59-60
vestibular disorientation, 54-58
visual, 60-62, 116-117
visual cues, 61-62
water refraction, 62
injuries, 81-82
insomnia, 136-137

J
jet lag, 138-141
coping with, 140-141
symptoms, 139

L
light, 105-106
electromagnetic spectrum, 105

optics and physics of, 108-109
red, 112
loss of consciousness (LOC), 10

M
medical emergencies
first aid, 157-159
inflight, 156-161
survival techniques, 160-161
transporting ill passengers, 159-160
medication
OTC, 80-88
prescription, 92-93

N
night vision, 111-114
dark adaptation, 112
improving, 113-114
preserving, 112
types of, 111
nitrogen, 3
noise
causing fatigue, 142
definition of, 122-123
losing hearing from, 127-128
misconceptions, 127
sources, 126-127
threshold shift, 128

O
over-the-counter (OTC)
medications, 80-88
acetaminophen, 87
alcohol, 87
analgesics, 86-87
antihistamines, 83-85
aspirin, 86-87
caffeine, 87
causing fatigue, 142
cough suppressants, 87
decongestants, 85-86
ibuprofen, 87

over-the-counter (OTC) *cont.*

    ingredients contained in, 84

    nose sprays, 86

    phenylpropanolamine (PPA), 87-88

    sleeping pills, 85

oxygen, 3, 23-34

    lack of (*see* hypoxia)

oxygen dissocation curve, 20

ozone, 4

P

peripheral vision, 59-60, 113

physicals (*see* health)

Physiological Deficient Zone, 9

Physiological Efficient Zone, 8

positional disorientation, 49-50

postural disorientation, 48-49

R

radiation, 67, 77-78

rapid decompression (R/D), 44-45

S

situation awareness, indications of loss, 48

sleep, 132-137

    anatomy, 133

    disorders, 135

    factors affecting, 135-136

    fatigue (*see* fatigue)

    improving, 136-137

    insomnia, 136-137

    physiology, 132-134

    stages, 132-134

    variations to normal, 134-135

smoking, 91-92

sound, 120-123

conversational range, 122

definition of noise, 122-123

duration, 121-122

frequency, 120-121

intensity, 121

measurement tests, 124

noise sources, 126-127

perception, 123-124

physical properties, 120-123

spatial disorientation, 59-60

    treatment, 59

stress, 148-150

    checklist, 150

    Crew Resource Management, 150-155

survival techniques, 160-161

T

temperature

    basics of heat exchange, 66-68

    causing fatigue, 143

    cold stress, 75-77

    conduction, 66, 75

    controlling body, 68-69

    convection, 66-67, 75

    evaporation, 67

    flying when cold, 73-77

    flying when hot, 70-73

    heat stress, 71-73

    hypothermia, 74-75

    hypoxia and, 30

    radiation, 67, 77-78

temporal disorientation, 50-51

time of useful consciousness (TUC), 31-32

U

ultraviolet (UV) light, 77

V

vertigo, 51 (*see also* vestibular disorientation)

flicker, 63

vestibular disorientation, 51-58

    illusions, 54-58

    motion sickness, 63-64

    otolith organs, 51-58

    semicircular canal, 51-53

viruses, 80

vision, 104-117

    acuity (20/20), 109-111

    anatomy of the eye, 106-108

    astigmatism, 110

    color, 109, 113

    corrective lenses, 110-111

    empty-field myopia, 116-117

    factors affecting, 116

    illusions, 116-117

    impaired, 143

    light and lenses, 105-109

    myopia, 110

    night, 111-114

    optics, 108-109

    peripheral, 59-60, 113

    photopic, 111

    presbyopia, 110

    refraction, 108

    refractive error, 110

    scotopic, 111

    seeing in the sunlight, 114-116

    space myopia, 116-117

    sunglasses, 114-116

    tests, 173

    visual cues, 117

W

water vapor, 3-4

weather

    atmospheric conditions, 1-9

    fog, 61-62, 116

    haze, 61-62, 116

    temperature extremes (*see* temperature)

    wind chill factor, 75

Other Bestsellers of Related Interest

The classic you've been searching for . . .

STICK AND RUDDER: An Explanation of the Art of Flying—Wolfgang Langewiesche

Students, certificated pilots, and instructors alike have praised this book as *"the most useful guide to flying ever written."* The book explains the important phases of the art of flying, in a way the learner can use. It shows precisely what the pilot does when he flies, just how he does it, and why. 400 pages, 88 illustrations. Book No. 3820, $19.95 hardcover only

FLIGHT SAFETY: A Primer for General Aviation Pilots—Alexander T. Wells, Ed.D.

To learn to fly as safely as you can, turn to this book. With it, you'll understand all the factors that can affect flight safety, including pilot health, experience, and skill; flight planning; weather; takeoffs and landings; midair collisions; in-flight hazards; and ground operations. Plus, you get over 400 objective questions you can use to review the material. 256 pages, 43 illustrations. Book No. 4169, $29.95 hardcover only

BASIC FLIGHT PHYSIOLOGY
—Richard O. Reinhart, M.D.

With this book, you'll see how poor nutrition, circulatory and respiratory ailments, atmospheric conditions, fatigue and jet lag, drugs and alcohol, and many other components of your health affect "medical airworthiness." Plus, you'll learn how to deal with in-flight medical emergencies, meet and maintain FAA medical standards, and develop cockpit resource management skills. 248 pages, 75 illustrations. Book No. 4141, $34.95 hardcover only

MAKE YOUR AIRPLANE LAST FOREVER
—Nicholas E. Silitch

Even if you're not an experienced mechanic, you can extend the operating life of your airplane, increase its safety and dependability, and keep high-priced emergency repairs to a minimum. This book will show you how. It covers the aircraft engine as well as techniques for testing avionics and related equipment. 160 pages, 83 illustrations. Book No. 2328, $12.95 paperback only

NIGHT FLYING
—Richard F. Haines & Courtney Flatau

This book addresses the potential risks of flying at night and offers you methods of reducing those risks by presenting solutions to night flight's unique problems. The first part of the book deals with human factors. The second part of the book covers aids, equipment, and procedures. And the final section covers ground instruction, flight simulators, and practice maneuvers. 288 pages, 140 illustrations. Book No. 4098, $16.95 paperback, $29.95 hardcover

THE PILOT'S AIR TRAFFIC CONTROL HANDBOOK—Paul E. Illman

Told from the VFR pilot's point of view, this in-depth look at airspace system operations focuses on the human elements of pilot and controller. An understanding of what one expects of the other and the responsibilities that belong to each are examined—answering important questions often asked by VFR pilots. Direct quotes and suggestions from ATC personnel are highlighted. 240 pages, 88 illustrations. Book No. 2435, $16.95 paperback only

GENERAL AVIATION LAW
—Jerry A. Eichenberger

Although the regulatory burden that is part of flying sometimes seems overwhelming, it need not take the pleasure out of your flight time. This survey of aviation regulations gives you a solid understanding of FAA procedures and functions, airman ratings and maintenance certificates, the implications of aircraft ownership, and more. It allows you to recognize legal problems before they result in FAA investigations and potentially serious consequences. 240 pages. Book No. 3431, $16.95 paperback, $25.95 hardcover

UNDERSTANDING AERONAUTICAL CHARTS—Terry T. Lankford

Filled with practical applications for beginning and veteran pilots, this book will show you how to plan your flights quickly, easily, and accurately. It covers all the charts you'll need for flight planning, including those for VFR, IFR, SID, STAR, Loran, and helicopter flights. As you examine the criteria, purpose, and limitations of each chart, you'll learn the author's proven system for interpreting and using charts. 320 pages. 183 illustrations. Book No. 3844, $17.95 paperback, $27.95 hardcover

THE PILOT'S GUIDE TO WEATHER REPORTS, FORECASTS & FLIGHT PLANNING
—Terry T. Lankford

Don't get caught in weather you're not prepared to handle. Learn how to use today's weather information services with this comprehensive guide. It shows you how to access weather services efficiently, translate briefings correctly, and apply reports and forecasts to specific preflight and in-flight situations to expand your margin of safety. 397 pages, 123 illustrations. Book No. 3582, $19.95 paperback only

AVOIDING COMMON PILOT ERRORS:
An Air Traffic Controller's View—John Stewart

This essential reference—written from the controller's perspective—interprets the mistakes pilots often make when operating in controlled airspace. It cites situations frequently encountered by controllers that show how improper training, lack of preflight preparation, poor communication skills, and confusing regulations can lead to pilot mistakes. 240 pages, 32 illustrations. Book No. 2434, $16.95 paperback only

BE A BETTER PILOT: Making the Right Decisions—Paul A. Craig

Why do good pilots sometimes make bad decisions? This book takes an in-depth look at the ways pilots make important preflight and in-flight decisions. It dispels the myths surrounding the pilot personality, provides straightforward solutions to poor decision-making, and determines traits that pilots appear to share—traits that affect the way they approach situations. 240 pages, 76 illustrations. Book No. 3675, $15.95 paperback, $24.95 hardcover

CROSS-COUNTRY FLYING—3rd Edition
—Paul Garrison, Norval Kennedy, and R. Randall Padfield

Establish and maintain sound flying habits with this classic cockpit reference. It includes revised information on Mode-C requirements, direct user access terminal usage (DUAT), LORAN-C navigation, hand-held transceivers, affordable moving maps, and over-water flying techniques. Plus, you'll find expanded coverage of survival equipment, TCAs, fuel management and conservation, mountain flying techniques, and off-airport landings. 328 pages, 148 illustrations. Book No. 3640, $18.95 paperback, $29.95 hardcover

ABCs OF SAFE FLYING—3rd Edition
—David Frazier

This book gives you a wealth of flight safety information in a fun-to-read format. The author's anecdotal episodes as well as NTSB accident reports lend both humor and sobering reality to the text. Detailed photographs, maps, and illustrations ensure that you understand key concepts and techniques. If you want to make sure you have the right skills each time you fly, this book is your one-stop source. 192 pages, illustrated. Book No. 3757, $14.95 paperback only

Prices Subject to Change Without Notice.

Look for These and Other TAB Books at Your Local Bookstore

To Order Call Toll Free 1-800-822-8158
(24-hour telephone service available.)

or write to TAB Books, Blue Ridge Summit, PA 17294-0840.

Title	Product No.	Quantity	Price

☐ Check or money order made payable to TAB Books

Charge my ☐ VISA   ☐ MasterCard   ☐ American Express

Acct. No. _____ Exp. _____

Signature: _____

Name: _____

Address: _____

City: _____

State: _____ Zip: _____

Subtotal $ _____

Postage and Handling
($3.00 in U.S., $5.00 outside U.S.) $ _____

Add applicable state and local
sales tax $ _____

TOTAL $ _____

TAB Books catalog free with purchase; otherwise send $1.00 in check or money order and receive $1.00 credit on your next purchase.

Orders outside U.S. must pay with international money order in U.S. dollars drawn on a U.S. bank.

TAB Guarantee: If for any reason you are not satisfied with the book(s) you order, simply return it (them) within 15 days and receive a full refund.   **BC**